THE MORAL DEFENSE OF
HOMOSEXUALITY

THE MORAL DEFENSE OF HOMOSEXUALITY

Why Every Argument against Gay Rights Fails

Chris Meyers

ROWMAN & LITTLEFIELD
Lanham • Boulder • New York • London

Published by Rowman & Littlefield
A wholly owned subsidiary of The Rowman & Littlefield Publishing Group,
Inc.
4501 Forbes Boulevard, Suite 200, Lanham, Maryland 20706
www.rowman.com

Unit A, Whitacre Mews, 26-34 Stannary Street, London SE11 4AB

British Library Cataloguing in Publication Information Available

Library of Congress Cataloging-in-Publication Data Available

Meyers, Chris, 1968–
The moral defense of homosexuality : why every argument against gay rights fails / Chris Meyers.
pages cm
Includes bibliographical references and index.
ISBN 978-1-4422-4931-8 (cloth : alk. paper) — ISBN 978-1-4422-4932-5 (electronic)
1. Gay rights—Philosophy. 2. Gay rights—United States. 3. Homosexuality—Moral and ethical
aspects. I. Title.
HQ76.5.M49 2015
323.3'2640973—dc23
2014050081

∞ ™ The paper used in this publication meets the minimum requirements of
American National Standard for Information Sciences Permanence of Paper
for Printed Library Materials, ANSI/NISO Z39.48-1992.

Printed in the United States of America

CONTENTS

PREFACE

It is common practice in a preface for the author to tell some story about how he or she came to write the book. In a book like this one—defending the morality of homosexuality and arguing for gay rights—one might expect that story to involve personal struggles of discrimination or sentimental descriptions of loved ones who are gay. But the motivation for the writing of this book is not like that. I am not a homosexual, nor do I have any close friends or relatives who are homosexuals.

One might be suspicious of a book on the morality of homosexuality and gay rights that is written by a straight man with very little acquaintance with gay people. I would share that suspicion were the author to argue that homosexuality is a sin or that same-sex marriage should be against the law. It would be easy to dismiss that author as arguing on the basis of ignorance. Of course, I too might be ignorant about the lives of gay people, but my arguments are not *based on* that ignorance. Rather, I assume that most gay people are not so different from me and most of my heterosexual friends and relatives. This is not to deny that gay people might be different from me in their beliefs, values, and dispositions. But I am sure that they also differ from each other in their beliefs, values, and dispositions. The differences matter much less than the similarities. Most people, gay or straight, share similar desires for opportunity, equality, companionship, dignity, and the liberty to live their lives according to their own goals and values.

I should confess that I have not always had the most tolerant or enlightened attitude toward gay people. In my youth I adopted the same mildly homophobic attitudes of the culture around me. But even then I never understood why anyone would think of homosexuality as a *moral* issue. We might not like the way certain people live, but if they are not hurting anyone then why should we care? It seems very strange to me that anyone could think of sexual preference as a moral issue at all. It is puzzling why we are even having this debate.

Having said that, opponents of gay rights might be tempted to accuse me of being ignorant about the anti-gay position. Not so. I have acquainted myself with all the arguments against homosexuality and gay rights. When I say that I do not understand them, I do not mean that I am unfamiliar with them. The reason that I do not understand the anti-gay position is that their arguments do not make any sense. This is not something that I will merely assume from the start. On the contrary, in this book I try to make as much sense as I can of the arguments against homosexuality and gay rights and then show that even the best versions of these arguments fail.

So why did I write this book? And why should I care so much about gay rights? I came to write this book rather by accident. It all started with a psychology professor in Kentucky named "Bob"—a man I've never met—who happens to be gay. He wrote the following e-mail message to a friend of mine, a fellow philosopher named "Sara," with whom he had been collaborating on an unrelated project.

> We have a LUNATIC on campus who is writing crazy things, and claims that gay sex is "morally disordered," and wants the university to rescind the domestic partner benefits. He's speaking today on "What is marriage?" Apparently it [marriage] is not what you think. I've attached an article he's using. I've already got many things down about how stupid it is, particularly its use of medieval notions of biology. Anyway, I was wondering if you wanted to collaborate on a rebuttal?

The attachment was an article entitled "What Is Marriage?" written by conservative law professor Robert George and a couple of graduate students, Sherif Girgis and Ryan Anderson. (The article was published in the *Harvard Journal of Law and Public Policy*.) Sara agreed to co-write the rebuttal. But her specialization is in epistemology and philosophy of mind, not ethics. So she thought it would be useful to bring a moral philosopher (me) on board. She forwarded her colleague's e-mail to me, with this message of her own.

> Chris—I know you are busy, but if you have time would you look at this CRAZY attached article? The dude is speaking on my friend's campus in Kentucky, and I am about 1/3 of the way through and the arguments are so insane I would really like to bring a real ethicist in on this.

I agreed to help. I read the "What Is Marriage?" article, wrote a rather long rough draft of a paper criticizing it, and sent it to my co-collaborators.

Unfortunately, Sara and Bob dropped the ball and that rough draft figuratively sat on a shelf figuratively collecting dust for over a year. Not wanting my efforts to count for naught, I eventually decided to revise the paper myself and send it off for publication. I was, however, unable to fit all of the arguments and criticisms into an article-length manuscript. So I decided I would make a book out of it. And voilà!

Now for the second question. It is obvious why Bob the psychologist should care about the issue. The authors of the anti-gay article are accusing him of moral depravity because of his sexual orientation and are lobbying to deny him important benefits. But why should *I* care about the issue? They are not denouncing *me* or trying to deprive *me* of any rights.

There are two reasons why I care. First, it is a matter of justice. I am opposed to injustice of any kind, even injustice that does not affect me personally. I don't care about *gay* rights, I care about *human* rights (and since gay people are human, that happens to include gay rights). I am not pretending to be some kind of heroic champion of justice. Opposing injustice, when doing so involves no risk or sacrifice, is something any minimally decent person should be willing to do. This might not be a book I would have otherwise wanted to write, but it did not require any significant sacrifice to produce it. Much to my surprise, writing the book turned out to be rather easy and quite enjoyable.

My other motivation is a little more personal. As a professional philosopher, I cannot bear to see bad arguments go unchallenged. Unfortunately, all too much of what passes for debate on moral or political issues in our society today consists of rhetoric, slogans, name calling, appeal to emotions, and downright fabrication. Even when good arguments are presented on one side of the debate, they are typically distorted or ignored by the other side. The purpose of philosophy, as least in part, is critical thinking. That means questioning things that we tend to take for granted, assessing and critiquing arguments on both sides of a debate, and basing our beliefs on arguments and evidence, rather than on wishful thinking, habit, conformity, blind obedience to authority, or irrational emotions. I am not an activist for gay rights; I am an activist for rational thinking, at least when it comes to moral issues and public policies. And it just so happens that the gay-tolerant view—that there is nothing morally wrong with homosexuality and that gay people deserve the same rights and liberties as straight people—is better supported by the arguments than the alternative anti-gay view. The ultimate purpose of this book is to promote critical thinking on moral and political issues generally.

Part of this book was completed during a sabbatical from the University of Southern Mississippi during the fall semester of 2013. I would like to thank my colleagues at the Department of Philosophy and Religion for their collegiality and their willingness to accommodate my unusual needs, which result from living almost a thousand miles from where I work. I would also like to thank Bob and Sara for getting me started on this project. I also want to thank them for leaving me to work on it alone. I am sure their contributions would have improved on the final product, but it might have lacked the unity and cohesion that comes from having a single voice. I would also like to thank Eileen Papazian. Her immense capacity to sympathize with others inspired me, many years ago, to cultivate a more tolerant disposition. And her unparalleled proofreading skills uncovered typos and errors that escaped the eyes of several other careful readers.

Most of all I would like to thank my wife, Natacha Vacroux, for her help and encouragement. She patiently proofread every word of this book and made numerous helpful suggestions and criticisms. I am not sure I could have finished the book without her. Or if I could have, it would have been rather half-baked and sloppy. More importantly, I would also like to thank her for being my wife. When writing about marriage, I found myself praising the institution and advocating the many benefits of married life. This is largely because my own marriage is such a happy one. Nothing in this world is perfect, but I could not hope for a better partner.

I

INTRODUCTION

WHY GAY RIGHTS IS REALLY A MORAL ISSUE

The issue of equal legal rights for homosexuals has focused on different specific issues at different times over the past twenty to thirty years.
Lately the focus has been on the full recognition of same-sex marriages
and, to a lesser extent, the rights of same-sex couples to adopt children.
Ten or fifteen years ago there was more focus on allowing gay people to
serve in the U.S. military. If we go back even further in time, the focus
was on anti-sodomy laws and protection from harassment. Another issue that is just starting to get proper attention is job discrimination. In
most states in the United States, an employee can be fired on the basis
of his or her sexual orientation.[1]

Few people in the United States today would accept laws banning
people from serving in the military due to their race, religion, or political affiliation. Nor would they accept the idea that couples belonging to
a certain race, religion, or political affiliation should not have their
marriages recognized or should be legally prevented from adopting
children. And we do not allow job discrimination on the basis of race,
religion, or political affiliation. So why should sexual orientation be any
different?

Same-sex marriage is the hot issue today, and so this book will focus
more on marriage equality than on the other gay rights issues. Nevertheless, most of the arguments in this book will apply to gay rights issues
generally. That is because this book is not primarily about political
equality and legal rights. It is about the deeper moral views that motivate opposition to equality for gay people and legal recognition of same-
sex relations. The reason for this approach is simple. If there is nothing

morally wrong with homosexuality, then there is no reasonable basis on which to deny homosexual individuals and same-sex couples the same rights and privileges enjoyed by heterosexual individuals and opposite-sex couples.

These days, those who oppose equal rights and liberties for homosexuals rarely state outright that homosexuality is morally wrong. They are usually rather coy about their moral disapproval. Instead, they claim to oppose openly gay military service because it will "undermine unit cohesion." They say they are opposed to gay marriage because it would involve "redefining what 'marriage' means." They try to ban adoption of children by same-sex couples because they say that allowing gay couples to be parents would be "bad for the children." But no one would take these arguments seriously if they did not think that there was something morally wrong with homosexuality.

For example, suppose someone were to argue that we should not allow non-Christians to serve in the U.S. military because doing so would "undermine unit cohesion." I think most reasonable people would find such an argument ludicrous. We would dismiss such a claim *not* because we think there is no truth to it. Maybe it would be easier to get soldiers to work together if they all belonged to the same faith. Maybe not, but it is at least conceivable. Nevertheless, even if it were shown to be true that having a one-faith military would improve cohesion, no reasonable person would think that we should make adherence to a specific religious faith a necessary condition for military service. The reason why we would not seriously consider banning non-Christians from military service is because it would be unfair to non-Christians. And this is in part because there is nothing morally wrong with being a non-Christian. On the other hand, a law banning convicted burglars from military service would not be unfair. That is because there *is* something morally objectionable about being a burglar.

The same goes for same-sex marriage and the objection that it would constitute "redefining what marriage means." Normally we do not automatically think that redefining a practice or an institution is necessarily something to be avoided. It depends on whether the practice or institution is redefined for the better or for the worse (or neither better nor worse). Sometimes we even use this very language of "redefining" to praise people for their innovation. For example, if I were to say that "Johnny Unitas forever *redefined* the position of quarterback," or that "Marcel Duchamp's 'Fountain' *changed the meaning* of fine art," no one would think that I was condemning these men for what they did. So the redefining-of-marriage argument by itself is not convincing. There is a crucial assumption in this argument, and that is that homosexuality is morally wrong and so allowing same-sex couples to marry would redefine marriage in ways that would make it morally inferior to our current conception of marriage.

Thus, the real question is whether there is anything morally wrong with homosexuality. Of course, even if there is something morally wrong with homosexuality, that would not necessarily mean we should deprive homosexuals of all the rights, liberties, and privileges that we grant to heterosexuals. After all, we allow even convicted rapists and murderers to get married. And there are some forms of morally bad behavior, like adultery, that we do not take as justification for curtailing an individual's civil rights or liberties. Thus, even if there were something morally objectionable to homosexuality, the argument would still have to be made for why we should not legally recognize gay marriage, why openly gay people should not be allowed to serve in the armed forces, why gay couples should not be allowed to adopt, and so on. If there is nothing morally wrong with homosexuality, however, then that pretty much ends the discussion. If homosexuality is not morally wrong, then we should not even ask whether we should deny gay people those same rights and liberties that we grant to everyone else. For this reason, I will be focusing on the question of whether there is any reason to think that homosexuality is morally wrong.

PHILOSOPHY AND MORAL ARGUMENT

When we make a genuine inquiry about the morality of some practice, we are asking a *philosophical* question. For that reason, this book is a book on philosophy (specifically moral philosophy). To fully understand the nature of our question, and the topic of this book, it might be helpful to give at least a sketch of what we mean by philosophy (in general, and moral philosophy in particular).

Philosophy is, of course, not the only domain in which morality is studied. Cultural anthropologists, for example, study the moral beliefs and practices of different human societies. Psychologists examine cognitive processes involved in making moral judgments and study the factors that can shape or influence these judgments. But when anthropologists, psychologists, and other social scientists study morality, they study the moral judgments that people actually make. They do not try to determine whether these moral judgments are true or false. They are not concerned with whether certain actions really are right or wrong, only whether certain people happen to think they are right or wrong (and why).

Thus the social scientific study of morality is *descriptive*. It is a study of facts about how the world actually is, not how it should be. We, on the other hand, are concerned not so much with whether people in fact approve or disapprove of homosexuality but whether they *should* approve or disapprove. We are concerned not with whether people think homosexuality is morally wrong, but whether it *really is* morally wrong. In other words, our inquiry is a *normative* one. That means that we are concerned not only with how the world is, but also how it should (or should not) be.

Of course, philosophy is not the only domain that is concerned with morality in the normative sense. There are, for example, some people who are concerned with whether certain practices are morally right or wrong and seek guidance from their pastors or from their sacred texts. When your priest or reverend says that some action, usury, let's say, is morally wrong, this should probably be interpreted as a normative claim. It means, roughly, that you *should not* lend money for profit. But this differs from philosophy in an important way. Although it is a matter of genuinely normative ethics, is not a *genuine inquiry* into questions of normative ethics. The pronouncements of holy scriptures and the advice of religious ministers are based on authority and accepted on faith. They are not arrived at through critical thinking. Critical thinking about normative questions of right and wrong is the purview of moral philosophy. (Of course, it is possible that your pastor might carefully weigh the pros and cons, consider each side of a moral issue, and give you good reasons why a certain practice is morally right or wrong. In that case, however, your minister would be doing moral philosophy.)

The next question then is, What is philosophy? If you ask a dozen philosophers this question, you might get a dozen different answers. So I will not try to give a definition of philosophy that all philosophers would accept. For our purposes, all that is required is an explanation of how the term "philosophy" will be used in this book. Philosophy, in the sense that we are concerned with, involves the formulation and assessment of *arguments*. When philosophers talk about arguments, they do not mean disputes, disagreements, or even debates. An argument, in the philosophical sense, involves giving reasons supporting the truth of a statement or a belief. It is an attempt to justify what we believe or to defend our beliefs from criticism.

Argument in this sense must be contrasted with *rhetoric*, the art of persuasion. Debates can involve arguments, but more often they rely on rhetoric. The goal of rhetoric is to get others to agree with your claims; it does not matter whether those claims are true. Examples of rhetoric include all of the tricks used in political speeches, especially language that triggers emotional responses in the audience. For example, whenever liberals talk about income inequality, conservatives immediately shout "class warfare!" Merely evoking this phrase does not provide us with any *reason* why we should not be worried about income inequality or try to do something about it. Instead, the use of this phrase is intended to end the discussion before it even begins. Rhetoric is also used heavily in propaganda and advertising. Arguments, on the other hand, aim at discovering the truth through rational consideration of the evidence.

Since the goal of philosophy is truth, it involves more than just argument. With many claims—whether they be moral, political, historical, or scientific—arguments can be found on *both* sides. The job of a philosopher is not to pick a side and then find all the arguments in favor of it. Instead, a good philosopher examines the arguments on both sides and only then agrees with whichever side has the best evidential support overall. In this way, a philosopher is more like a judge, who impartially weighs the evidence, than a lawyer, who chooses only the arguments that favor her client. A useful way of putting this is that philosophy involves *critical thinking*: questioning one's beliefs. This might not be how all philosophers would describe their practice, but it is a conception of philosophy with a rich history that goes back to Socrates, who claimed that his wisdom consisted in knowing that he was ignorant, unlike most other people who are equally ignorant but falsely believe that they know. The primary goal of Socrates's interrogations (known today, appropriately, as the "Socratic method") was to expose the ignorance of his interlocutors. It is only when we realize that we do not already have the truth that we make a serious effort to find it.

CHANGES IN PUBLIC OPINION

Public opinion about the morality of homosexuality and gay rights has changed quite rapidly over the past ten or fifteen years. A notable illustration of the growing tolerance is the increasing number of gay characters on television sitcoms like *Will and Grace*, *Glee*, and *Modern Family*. There are also sympathetic portrayals of homosexual relations in big-budget Hollywood movies like *Brokeback Mountain* as well as openly gay television hosts like Ellen DeGeneres and Rachel Maddow. There was even a very popular TV show called *Queer Eye for the Straight Guy*.[2] And this phenomenon of acceptance is not limited to some suburban, liberal youth subculture. In April of 2013 a current NBA player came out of the closet. More recently, a college football All-American came out as he announced eligibility for the NFL draft and was drafted by the St. Louis Rams in the seventh round. An ESPN poll of current NFL players found 86 percent were okay with having a gay teammate.[3] You could hardly find a venue as mainstream and macho as professional basketball or NFL football.

Of course, that is all just anecdotal. But there is also quantifiable evidence for this trend. Opinion polls demonstrate a dramatic shift in American attitudes about homosexuality in recent years. For example, *New York Times* opinion polls showed that support for gay marriage rose from 27 percent in 1996 to 39 percent in August of 2008 and to 49 percent by August of 2012.[4] Similarly, polls conducted by CBS News in September 2012 showed that 51 percent of Americans support the legalization of gay marriage, compared to only 42 percent just four months earlier.[5] No doubt, there are many reasons for this rapid shift in attitudes. But part of the explanation might be the fact that it is *true* that there is nothing morally wrong with homosexuality and that it is *true* that justice demands full legal recognition of same-sex unions. The recent shift in attitudes would thus be a case of genuine moral progress. In this way, the sudden shift toward approval, or at least tolerance, of homosexual relations would be similar to changing attitudes in the past about slavery or women's rights. Few people in our society today think that it is okay to own slaves or that women should be denied the right to vote or own property. It seems quite likely that these racist and sexist views have changed because they were mistaken or based on other beliefs that are false. The same might very well be true of the disapproval of homosexuality. As the general population becomes more educated about gay people, attitudes toward homosexuality become more tolerant and accepting.

So why write a book trying to show why homosexuality is not morally wrong? Doesn't it seem that most people have already been, or are soon going to be, convinced? Those are fair questions—the sort of questions that any author of a book like this one should be able to answer. Why is this book worth reading? Though there are several good reasons why such a book is important and necessary, they all revolve around one central idea, and that is that it matters not just *what* we believe, but also *why* we believe it.

WHY HAS PUBLIC OPINION CHANGED? (AND HAS IT REALLY CHANGED?)

It is true that public opinion *polls* about the morality of homosexuality have changed rapidly over the past ten or twenty years, but that does not mean that individual Americans are changing their minds about homosexuality. Though the polls report an increased approval of 20 percent in the past fifteen years or so, this changing in the polls does not mean that one out of four people in America has had a change of heart about this issue. For one thing, recent studies have indicated that the slightly more than 50 percent approval rate of gay marriage that consistently appears in surveys today might be overstated by 5 to 7 percent, due to the *social desirability bias*. A certain portion of those polled disapprove of same-sex marriage but still *say* they approve because they do not want to appear to be bigoted.[6]

More importantly, much of the change in opinion polls can be attributed to young adults who were not polled when they were children. They approve of gay marriage by almost 70 percent. These young adults (or two-thirds of them) have *always* approved of homosexuality, since they first formed a stance on the issue. Thus, the best explanation for the change in public opinion is the change in the set of individuals who constitute "the public." To put it simply, young gay-tolerant individuals are being added to the adult population while older homophobes are dying off.

Changing demographics, however, do not account for all of the change found in public support for gay marriage and other gay rights. A recent Pew Research poll found that 14 percent of the respondents reported that they had changed their minds in favor of gay marriage (while only 2 percent have changed their minds in the opposite direction and now oppose it).[7] Even when people do change their minds about homosexuality, however, it is usually not because they have been convinced by good arguments or because they were swayed by considerations of impartial justice or that their decision is based on a rational weighing of the evidence. The biggest factor in determining whether a heterosexual approves of homosexuality is whether that person has any friends, relatives, or coworkers whom they know to be gay. (Of those in the Pew poll who reported changing their minds, 32 percent said it is because they know someone who is gay, while another 18 percent said it was simply because same-sex marriage is inevitable.)

An illustration of this can be seen in the case of Rob Portman, Republican senator from Ohio. In March of 2013 he changed his official stance on gay marriage. This was quite a surprise since, prior to this sudden 180-degree change, Portman had voted repeatedly to deny gay rights, voting in favor of laws banning gay marriage and laws forbidding gay couples to adopt. But Senator Portman's more enlightened view was not due to some realization on his part that there is nothing morally wrong with homosexuality or that justice demands equal rights for gay people. What changed his mind was that, two years earlier, his son had announced to the family that he was gay. This means that if Portman had *not* had a gay son (or if his son had remained in the closet), he would probably continue to strongly oppose gay rights.

As a professional philosopher, I am disappointed to find that many people who change their minds about important social issues do so for reasons other than being convinced by reasons, arguments, or evidence. That means that the issue might be more intractable than it seems. In a hundred years, gay marriage might come to be as accepted as interracial marriage is now, if current trends continue. But it is only because all the homophobes will eventually die off and be replaced by more tolerant generations. It disturbs me partly because it indicates that human beings for the most part do not listen to reason. But it disturbs me for a deeper reason. If the change in attitudes about homosexuality is not progress that comes from increased knowledge and understanding, then it is progress that is insecure. Attitudes could change back again. It is not really progress at all but merely a change that just so happens to be in the direction of progress.

I am not saying that life experiences should have no influence on our moral judgments. When people undergo a radical change in attitude about homosexuality because a loved one is gay, it is generally because they had false beliefs that gay people are different from straight people in important ways—that they are irresponsible, dishonest, or perverse or that gay couples do not genuinely love each other. (This is probably true of most prejudices, whether racial, cultural, or gender based.) Acquaintance with gay people humanizes them. I do not deny that this can be a legitimate factor in shaping our moral judgments. But it should not be necessary. For one thing, I might not know any gay people. Not knowing any gay people should not excuse homophobic bigotry. Also, there may be certain people whose values and practices I find so distasteful that I could never be comfortable with them—soccer fans, for example. That should not prevent me from recognizing their rights and tolerating their practices (as long as those practices are not harmful and do not violate the rights of others).

J. S. MILL AND THE IMPORTANCE OF CONSIDERING FALSE OPINIONS

Thus, one important reason to consider the arguments underlying the gay rights issue is that if we do not have good reasons for our tolerance for homosexuality, support for gay rights might wane. Attitudes and beliefs that are unsupported by reasons and evidence tend to be fickle.

Instead of moral progress we would have only changing attitudes and alternating opinions. Another reason why it is important to consider the arguments for and against homosexuality and gay marriage is found by reflecting on the purpose and value of philosophy.

Examining arguments and rationally critiquing opinions on important issues help us in at least three important ways. 1) Doing so allows us to find the truth. 2) Doing so helps us to better understand and appreciate that truth, once we find it. And, 3) doing so allows us to know not just whether something is true or false but *what makes it* true or false. These three reasons were offered as arguments against censorship by John Stuart Mill in *On Liberty*, one of the most widely read books in political philosophy. Though Mill used these three points to argue for free speech and freedom of the press, they also provide a powerful argument for the value of philosophy and the importance of rational, critical thinking.

Mill was especially worried about the silencing of unpopular opinions. He first pointed out that an unpopular opinion—no matter how widely it is rejected or how obviously false it seems—could turn out to be true. If we censor some position—or dismiss some opinion without serious consideration—just because we assume it to be false, then we might miss out on the opportunity to correct our beliefs. We will go on persisting in our false opinions because we have not considered alternative views and have not allowed our own beliefs to be challenged. We human beings are fallible; we sometimes believe things that turn out not to be true. Sometimes this is not our fault. We might be subject to intentional deception of others. Other times it is no one's fault at all. We seem to have good evidence for a belief, and we believe on the basis of that evidence, yet it turns out to be false despite the evidence.

More often, we persist in our false beliefs because we are lazy or biased or gullible or stubborn. We see and hear what we want to; and we ignore counter-evidence. This is not entirely due to moral failing. As humans, we are hardwired with certain psychological tendencies toward self-deception. At any rate, knowing that we are fallible and prone to error, and assuming that we ought to prefer truth and knowledge over false belief and ignorance, we should be eager to give a hearing to dissenting views. It might require a fair degree of humility to admit one could be wrong, but there is more dignity to admitting error than stubbornly persisting in false opinion.

But what if our beliefs are not just true but also quite certain? Why should we bother putting them to the test if they are true *and* we know they are true? Mill answers that challenge by arguing that it is only through actively defending our beliefs from criticisms and contrary views that we come to have a greater understanding of the truth. For example, we all know that the earth is not stationary. It spins on its axis and orbits the sun. We are quite certain about that, so why bother trying to prove it to those who disagree? The reason is this: virtually everyone living in an industrialized society today knows that the earth rotates on its axis and orbits the sun, but how many people can explain *how* we know that? We can look up at the same night sky that Galileo and Copernicus observed. How did they, based on those observations alone, come to conclude that the geocentric view of the universe is false? Learning the answer to that question will help you gain a better understanding of the movements of planets. It will also provide you with an illustration of good scientific method.

Mill worried that if we never have to defend our true beliefs from challenges, then we will have only a shallow understanding of them. With only a vague and dim understanding of the truth, we will be vulnerable to deception. I suspect that this is part of the reason why there is still debate over teaching evolution in schools. Since most people know only the basic framework of the theory of evolution and natural selection, they are easily confused and deceived by creationists into thinking that the theory is still controversial among scientists and not well established. They fail to appreciate the enormous explanatory power of natural selection. If Mill's view is right, then maybe intelligent design should be taught in schools. But it should not be taught *alongside* evolution, as if they were two equally plausible scientific theories. Instead, students should study and compare the evidence for each theory. They should be taught the criticisms of evolution and also, most importantly, how evolutionary biologists answer those criticisms. Once they gain a richer understanding of evolution, from studying the arguments for natural selection and the replies that biologists give to creationists, they will realize that creationism and intelligent design are not viable options.

Mill also worried that without having to argue for our beliefs, even if they happen to be true, we will lack conviction in them. They will become "dead dogma." We will affirm them in words but not in deeds. It is only by defending our beliefs against criticisms and dissenting opinion that those beliefs come to be internalized. For example, many people in the United States will say that they believe that democracy is the best form of government. And yet many of those same people will support attempts to disenfranchise some of their fellow citizens with "voter ID laws." Part of the reason for support of such laws, no doubt, is that people have been deceived into thinking that voter fraud is a real problem. In fact, the most careful and comprehensive study of voter fraud, conducted by the Brennen Center for Justice at New York University's Law School, found that voter fraud is extremely rare. Virtually all allegations of voter fraud have been wildly exaggerated or, even worse, completely fabricated.[8] And of course some of the support for voter ID is nothing more than a cynical attempt to deny the vote to a certain class of people. For example, the voter ID law passed in Texas does not allow voters to use university ID cards as identification but does allow gun ownership licenses. Could there be any justification for that other than the fact that gun owners are much more likely than college students to vote conservatively?

Much of the support for voter ID laws, however, is based on a lack of understanding of why voting is important in a democracy. If people had to defend their belief in democracy from criticism—for example, from the arguments of staunch antidemocrats such as Plato or Thomas Hobbes—they might come to have a better appreciation of the importance of equal representation and universal enfranchisement. Instead of simply *saying* that they believe in democracy in the abstract, they might gain a better understanding of what democracy is and might be more likely to support laws that strengthen and extend democracy, instead of laws that weaken and curtail democracy. They might try to make voting *easier* for the citizens of their country, not harder. They might even try to make voting mandatory, as it is in Australia.

Mill used these arguments to advocate for freedom of the press and open public discourse of controversial topics. His arguments have a strong inspirational power. However, he might have been overly optimistic about the degree to which reason and good arguments would prevail, in the public mind, over slogans and rhetoric. He also could not have anticipated the corporate control of media and information and how this threatens democracy and distorts public discourse in our age. Still, Mill's arguments continue to be relevant and persuasive today, even if somewhat naïve. But whether or not Mill was exactly right about public policy and the power of free speech, his arguments make a convincing case for the need of philosophy and critical thinking for us as individuals. It also provides a powerful statement of what constitutes good philosophy. For, if nothing else, philosophy is critical thinking in its purest form. It involves, above all, questioning those things we take for granted.

As Mill's arguments show, those who support gay rights and already believe that there is nothing morally wrong with homosexuality can still benefit from analyzing the best arguments on the other side. For one thing, it is not enough to know that homosexuality is not morally wrong; it is also important to understand why, to understand exactly what is not wrong about it. Not only will this lead to a greater understanding of the issue, but it will also help us to gain a greater understanding of the nature of morality. In other words, it will help us to understand which features of actions make them morally right or wrong, which features of practices or institutions make them just or unjust. And it is equally important to understand which features of actions, practices, and institutions are not morally relevant. This will help us to make better judgments about the morality of other issues.

Another benefit from analyzing the arguments for and against gay rights is that it strengthens our conviction in the truth. This is especially important because the gay rights issue is a political issue. If one's belief in the heliocentric theory of the solar system lacks strong conviction, there might be no harm in that. But those who lack conviction in their moral and political beliefs will be less motivated to act on them. If those who are gay tolerant do not understand the reasons why they should support gay rights, they might be less willing or less able to confront conservatives who want to deny gay rights. This sort of wishy-washiness serves only to enable perpetuation of injustice.

There is one more important reason why we must carefully consider opinions and views that we disagree with. It turns out that ignoring dissenting opinion can lead us into error for reasons that Mill, who was writing in the 1860s, was unaware of. Research in social psychology has discovered that when likeminded people discuss an issue, their views tend to move toward the extreme. For example, if moderately pro-life people discuss the abortion issue together, with no representatives from the pro-choice side, they will eventually come to accept a radical pro-life position. And likewise, if moderately pro-choice people discuss the abortion issue, they will end up accepting a radical pro-choice view. This is referred to as "group polarization"—the tendency of homogenous groups to form beliefs or make decisions that are more extreme than the beliefs or decisions that any of the individual members would come to on their own.[9]

Why is the phenomenon of group polarization likely to cause us to have false beliefs? It is because the change in one's beliefs, from more moderate to more extreme, is not due to the quality of the arguments but only due to the partisan, one-sided representation of the arguments, as well as various social pressures such as the need to conform. If your original moderate view is correct, then the more radical view you come to hold as the result of group polarization will be incorrect. (And if your view starts out already on the wrong side, then the more radical version of that view will be even further from the truth.) Of course, it could be that the more radical view is the correct view. But that is unlikely. If the more radical view were correct, then why wouldn't you have come to that view on your own? It is unlikely that group polarization will lead to a more correct view since the shift in opinion that it causes has nothing to do with the quality of the arguments but only with the fact that they are all on the same side that you already happen to be on. Remember that the same phenomenon will make those on the other side move in the opposite direction, further in opposition to your view.

To avoid group polarization and its irrational influence on our beliefs, we should always try to consider, as seriously as possible, views that are in opposition to ours, and especially the *arguments* given in support of those opposing views. The views may be false, but even false beliefs sometimes contain a kernel of truth.

AVOIDING STRAW MAN ARGUMENTS

The importance of critical thinking and the philosophical analysis of ideas that we disagree with is especially important for controversial moral issues, such as gay rights. On the one hand, I am quite confident that those who oppose gay rights are mistaken. But we cannot just *assume* they are mistaken and thereby dismiss their views without a fair hearing. Furthermore, when we do analyze the arguments on the opposing side, it is especially important to be as fair to those arguments as possible. We must defend our moral views from the best arguments on the other side. Otherwise our opponents could declare a mistrial. It would be easy to convince a gay rights–friendly audience that the opponents of gay rights are wrong by presenting a caricature of the anti–gay rights position and then refuting that caricature. Or we could select only the weakest anti-gay arguments and show that they are false. But then we will not have really proven much of anything. This strategy of making it seem as if you have refuted an opposing view, when really you have only refuted a caricature of the view, is what philosophers call a *straw man fallacy*.

The straw man fallacy is so common in debates on social and political issues that it might be worth taking a moment to examine it more carefully. Here is an example. Climate change deniers often point to unusually cold weather as evidence against global warming. Washington, D.C., had a freakish snowstorm in early February of 2010, and Fox News commentators used that as evidence to conclude that global warming is not happening. (They conveniently ignored the fact that at the same time that D.C. was experiencing "Snowmageddon," there was no snow at the Winter Olympics in Vancouver.) The assumption seems to be that if global warming were true, then we would never observe unseasonably cold temperatures anywhere. But that is not what the global warming theory claims. The claim is that *average* temperatures are increasing—that means averaged for the entire year and averaged across the entire planet. Climate change deniers misrepresent the global warming claim and then refute the misrepresentation. But obviously their criticism—that it is unusually cold somewhere, at some time—is irrelevant to the real global warming issue.

One straw man argument that we see frequently made, or at least implied, by opponents of gay rights is the characterization of gay rights as "special rights." This argument is rarely spelled out explicitly (probably because spelling it out makes it obvious how weak it is). But the idea is something like this:

1. Gay rights would give "special rights" or "special protections" to gay people (i.e., rights and protections that straight people do not have).
2. We should not give more rights or more liberties to gay people or gay couples than we do to straight people or straight couples.
3. Therefore, we should not grant any gay rights.

This is a straw man because it mischaracterizes both the rights that homosexuals are demanding and also the arguments in support of these rights. When someone argues, for example, that homosexuals should be protected from discrimination in the workplace, they are not arguing that *only* homosexuals should be protected from job discrimination. They are not even arguing that only homosexuals should be protected from the sort of job discrimination that is based on sexual orientation. Instead, what they argue for is the right of every person, gay or straight (or bisexual or transgender), to be free from workplace discrimination on the basis of sexual orientation. It would be *just as wrong*, in this view, to fire someone for being straight as it would be to fire someone for being gay. It only seems like it is a specifically gay right—and we refer to it under the heading of "gay rights"—because straight people are virtually never fired for being straight. The same can be said for gay marriage or military service. The position of the gay rights advocate is that it would be just as wrong to refuse to recognize straight marriages as it would be to recognize gay marriages; it would be just as wrong to ban people from military service because they are straight as it would be to ban them because they are gay. The gay rights position is thus based on equality, not a plea for special treatment.

So although gay rights supporters will benefit from analyzing the arguments in defense of gay rights, this book is not intended to preach to the choir. This book is primarily designed for those who are undecided on the issue as well as for those who oppose gay rights but are willing to reconsider their views if those views can be shown to be false. This is another reason why it is so important that we find the best arguments against gay rights and present them in the most convincing way possible. Otherwise, opponents of gay rights can always say "I oppose gay rights for better reasons than that. You have not shown that *my* reasons for opposition to gay marriage (or gay adoption or gay military service) are not good reasons."

Of course, no argument will convince a fanatic. I do not expect to convert members of the Westboro Baptist Church, even if they were to read this book (which they probably won't). But I believe that at least some people who might oppose gay rights are not crazy fanatics. And I hope that at least some of those people can be convinced by evidence and good argument. It is important for people to listen to reason and think critically about their moral views. After all, we cannot all have gay sons.

THE SIMPLE MORAL ARGUMENT FOR WHY HOMOSEXUALITY IS NOT MORALLY WRONG

Sometimes people oppose granting rights, opportunities, equalities, or liberties to members of certain groups for self-interested reasons. For example, many people who oppose relaxing restrictions on immigration are motivated by a fear of losing their job to a lower waged immigrant worker. It is unlikely, however, that this sort of self-interest could explain opposition to gay rights. Although there are some anti-gay activists who argue that granting gay people equal rights will somehow harm straight people, I suspect most of them do not really believe this. (Nevertheless, we will explore this argument in chapter 8. And in doing so, I will assume that those who make this argument do so in good faith.)

Others oppose immigration because they oppose a certain group of people whom they identify with immigrants. In other words, it is because they are prejudiced against Latinos (or Asians or Muslims or other minority groups). Likewise, there may be some people who oppose gay rights just because they are prejudiced against gay people. No doubt this explains some of the opposition to gay rights, but we must not dismiss the arguments against gay rights just because some of those who make such arguments are motivated by disdain or homophobia. Bad people can still make good arguments. And this does not make the argument itself bad. And anyway, though some opponents of gay rights might simply be bigots, I doubt that this could explain why almost 50 percent of Americans continue to oppose same-sex marriage.

When someone is prejudiced against members of a certain group, the prejudice is usually connected to false beliefs about that group, such as beliefs that that group is inferior or morally depraved. It is clear that most people who are anti-gay think that there is something morally objectionable to homosexuality, either as an orientation, a practice, or a lifestyle. Thus the bulk of this book is aimed at analyzing this claim. We will consider carefully the question of whether there is anything morally wrong with homosexuality and whether there is any legitimate reason not to grant full rights to homosexuals and same-sex couples.

I believe that there is nothing morally wrong with homosexual relations between two consenting adults. Yet, instead of starting with that belief as an assumption in this book, I offer it as a hypothesis to be tested. In science, we test hypotheses by assuming that they might be incorrect and trying to show that they are false. I will take a similar approach here by shouldering the burden of proof and formulating the strongest arguments that homosexuality is morally wrong and that the various gay rights claims (same-sex marriage, openly gay military service, etc.) should not be recognized.

The bulk of this book will consist of careful consideration of those arguments that aim to show that homosexuality is morally wrong. At this point, however, let me present one reason for thinking that homosexuality is not morally wrong. Not all untested hypotheses are equal. Scientists do not simply test every conceivable hypothesis or pick some randomly for testing. Instead, they focus on hypotheses that have the greatest initial plausibility, ones for which there already are reasons to think they are probably true. Similarly, I think a preliminary argument can be made for the hypothesis that there is nothing morally wrong with homosexuality (either as an internal disposition or as an outward practice). I will call this the "Simple Argument" in defense of homosexuality. It goes like this:

1. For an action or practice to be morally wrong, it must have some wrong-making feature.

In other words, if an action is morally wrong, there must be something about the action that makes it wrong.

2. Wrong-making features include the following: the action or practice i) causes harm or ii) violates some competent person's autonomy or iii) is unfair or iv) violates someone's individual rights or v), etc.

This second premise can be extended. It should include an exhaustive list of features that make an action or practice morally wrong.

3. Homosexual relations between two consenting adults do not have any of these features. In other words, i) it is not harmful, ii) it does not violate anyone's autonomy, iii) it is not unfair, iv) it does not violate anyone's individual rights, v), etc.

This, of course, is not to say that homosexual relations can *never* be morally wrong. For example, if a man is married to a woman and has secret homosexual liaisons on the side, that would be morally wrong. But it is not the homosexuality per se that makes such behavior morally wrong. What makes it wrong is that it involves betrayal and the violation of one's marriage vows. It is wrong because it is *adultery*, not because it is *gay* adultery. The argument is intended to show only that there is nothing wrong with homosexual activity per se. Homosexual relations can be morally wrong for reasons other than that they are homosexual; but heterosexual relations can also be wrong for those same sorts of reasons.

4. Therefore, homosexual relations between mutually consenting adults are not morally wrong.

This argument is obviously valid. To say that an argument is valid means that if the premises 1–3 are true, then the conclusion (4) must be true. The conclusion might still be false but only if at least one of the premises (1, 2, or 3) is false.

Some readers who have been morally opposed to homosexuality up to this point might find this argument convincing. This argument will be a revelation. But there will probably not be very many of these people. Most people who think homosexuality is morally wrong are unlikely to be so easily convinced that it is not wrong. There are two possible reasons for why someone might maintain moral opposition to homosexuality despite this argument: a bad reason and a good reason—or more accurately, a bad reason and a less bad reason. The bad reason why some people might maintain moral disapproval of homosexuality, despite the Simple Argument that it is not wrong, is that homosexuality just *seems* wrong to them, even though they have no reason for thinking it is wrong. The less bad reason why some will continue to oppose homosexuality and gay rights is that they think there is something about homosexuality that makes it morally wrong. These people have some reason for being opposed to gay rights besides just a gut feeling or intuition. To this extent, their opposition to homosexuality is more legitimate, or less illegitimate, than those who have no reason at all. But whether their opposition is truly legitimate depends on how good those reasons are. Let us look at these two reactions to the Simple Argument in a little more detail.

MORAL SEEMINGS—THE VERY BAD REASON TO THINK HOMOSEXUALITY IS WRONG

The very bad reason why someone might remain unconvinced by my Simple Argument is that homosexuality just *seems* wrong (to that person), though he is unable to offer any reasons why. Sometimes this happens because, although there are good reasons to support one's moral belief, they are difficult to articulate. But often when people find themselves at a loss to give justification for their moral views, it is because they simply don't have any justification. This is a phenomenon that social psychologist Jonathan Haidt refers to as "moral dumbfounding."[10] For example, most of us have a deeply ingrained aversion to incest. (This is probably at least partly the result of evolution.) An innate disapproval of incest is generally a good thing because, in most normal cases, incest *is* morally wrong. Incest is usually wrong for a number of reasons: it involves exploitation of children (especially when it is incest between parents and their children, or aunts/uncles and their nephews/nieces), or it is psychologically harmful to one or both of the parties involved, or there is a threat of producing children with birth defects, or it sets a bad example to others (and it would be wrong for these others to engage in incest).

But now consider a case where none of these factors apply. A young man and a young woman meet in college and fall in love. After dating for four years they decide to get married. When contacting family in preparation for their wedding, they discover that, by a remarkable coincidence, they are half-siblings. (They share the same biological father.) Though this revelation is disturbing, they do not *feel* like brother and sister, since they never met until they were adults, and they are very much in love. They decide not to cancel their marriage plans. However, they do decide that the man should have a vasectomy to ensure that they do not bear any children. (If they decide they want to have kids, they will adopt.)[11]

Many people still feel that this relationship is morally wrong. When asked to explain why, however, those who disapprove typically find themselves at a loss. None of the usual reasons apply. There is no reason to think that there is any exploitation involved since they met as adults. Since they dated for several years before discovering that they were related, there is no reason to think that their relationship will be psychologically harmful to either of them (or at least not more likely so than any other romantic relationship). They will not have any biological children, so there is no reason to worry about genetically defective offspring. And their circumstances are too unusual to set a bad example.

(It would be virtually impossible for you to follow their example and try to fall in love with someone that you are *unknowingly* related to.)

Nevertheless, many people persist in claiming that this incestuous relationship is morally wrong. When pressed to explain why, these people will often respond by saying something like this: "I don't know *why* it is wrong, it just *is*." This is moral dumbfounding. These people have strong moral attitudes about some issue but cannot give any legitimate reasons for why that attitude is appropriate. Of course, we often make moral judgments for reasons that we are not able to explain. This does not necessarily mean that we do not have, or could not find, good reasons for them. Sometimes we are simply unable to formulate or articulate those reasons. But most often in such cases we can eventually pin down our moral objections, with some effort or with help from the prompting of others. For example, if someone were to challenge my belief that torture is morally wrong, I might be at a loss to explain—at least initially. It seems so obviously wrong that I never bothered to question it seriously. But with some careful reflection, I could come up with several reasons why torture is wrong.

Dumbfounding is different. When people are morally dumbfounded they have no justification for their moral judgments. The only reason for their moral judgment is a gut feeling or visceral emotional reaction. It just *seems* wrong. But *seeming* wrong is a terrible reason for a moral belief, at least when it is the only reason for that belief. Consider someone who makes an absurd moral claim. For example, Joe says that it is morally wrong for men to wear white socks. This is a sincere moral claim on Joe's part. Joe disapproves of men who wear white socks and tries to prevent them from doing so. He tries to avoid wearing white socks and feels guilty when he does. Naturally, we would ask him why he has this strange moral belief. Now suppose this is his reply. "I don't know why it is wrong exactly. It just *is* wrong!"

We might try to help Joe explain his disapproval to us. "Is it harmful somehow? . . . to the men themselves or to other innocent parties?" "Do men who wear white socks suffer from some character flaw?" "Or do they somehow treat some people unfairly by wearing white socks?"

But Joe has no answer. "No. It is not any of those things. It just *seems* really, obviously wrong to me!" Surely we would not take Joe's moral judgment seriously. The fact that it *seems* really wrong to him would, by itself, be no reason for us to think it is wrong. And that would not change much if there were others like Joe who were also strongly morally opposed to the wearing of white socks by men. More importantly, Joe himself should seriously question whether there really is anything morally wrong with wearing white socks. If he cannot give any reason for why it seems wrong, even after considerable reflection and with prompting from others, then he has good reason to doubt that it is wrong, no matter how it might seem.

Something similar to the moral dumbfounding might be going on with those who remain unconvinced by my Simple Argument for why homosexuality is morally wrong. They might say, "It just *is* wrong. I cannot explain what exactly it is that makes it wrong. It just *seems* very obviously wrong." This is no better reason for moral disapproval of homosexuality than it is for moral disapproval of men wearing white socks. That it seems wrong does not make it wrong. And if that is the only justification for a moral judgment, then there is no justification at all.

As with virtually any argument I will make in this book, things are always more complicated than how I present them. There are some philosophers, for example, who would say that the only way we can know moral properties is through some kind of direct apprehension of rightness and wrongness. In this way, right and wrong are like colors. Suppose I were to comment on the red color of Joe's shirt and he replied that it is not red; it is blue. I insist that it is red and Joe challenges me to prove it. What can I say? "I know it is red because I *see* that it is red." I cannot give any more explanation than that. Maybe moral judgments are like that. Maybe there can be no more evidence for rightness and wrongness than how it seems to us.

This is a view that philosophers refer to as "intuitionism." I will analyze intuitionism more carefully in chapter 6. For now, let me just point out that the color example is different from dumbfounding. If pressed, I could give some indirect support for my belief that the shirt is red, beyond simply that I see it. For example, I could point out that I am looking at the shirt in a well-lit room and that I know that I am not color-blind. I could even get a spectrophotometer and measure the frequency of light reflecting off of the shirt. These extra thoughts about lighting and the use of measuring instruments might not have played any explicit role in why I initially thought that the shirt was red. But they do provide further evidence for my claim. This is very different from simply saying "I just see that it is red, end of discussion."

OTHER MORAL CONSIDERATIONS—THE LESS BAD REASONS FOR THINKING HOMOSEXUALITY IS MORALLY WRONG

Most people who are unconvinced by my Simple Argument probably have some reason for persisting in thinking that there is something morally wrong with homosexuality. Some of them might disagree with my claim (premise 3) that homosexuality has none of the wrong-making features that I list in premise 2. They might claim that homosexuality *is* harmful or that it *does* violates someone's rights. We will examine these claims later, especially in chapter 8.

More likely, I suspect that those who reject my Simple Argument would deny the second premise. They would insist that my list of wrong-making features is incomplete. For example, they might claim that an action is also morally wrong if it is "unnatural" or if it is forbidden by God. They would then claim that homosexuality has one of *these* wrong-making features.

For this reason, my Simple Argument is incomplete. And in some ways it is either necessarily incomplete or else it is controversial. No matter how many wrong-making features I list, someone could always claim that there is another wrong-making feature that I have neglected. Alternatively, I could try to make it complete by adding some further premise like this: "And this is an exhaustive list of wrong-making features." In other words, I could claim that if an action or practice does not have one of these wrong-making features, then it cannot be morally wrong. This would make the argument complete, but now it would be controversial.

Some people have (or claim to have) reasons for thinking that homosexuality is morally wrong, besides only that it seems wrong to them and other members of their group. In order to argue that homosexuality is not wrong, I have to show one of two things. Either I will have to show that the reasons they think that homosexuality is wrong are not good reasons, or I will have to show that homosexuality does not have these (allegedly) wrong-making features. For example, some people claim that homosexuality is wrong because it is forbidden by God; others think it is wrong because it is unnatural. We refute such arguments in one of two ways. First we can show that homosexuality does not have the alleged feature—that is, that it is not forbidden by God or that it is not unnatural. Alternatively, these arguments fail if having that particular feature does not make an action wrong—that is, being forbidden by God or being unnatural is not a good reason to think that an action is morally wrong. In many cases we will be able to show both, thus making an especially strong defense of the morality of homosexuality. The second sort of claim—that having some feature (God forbidden, unnaturalness) makes an action wrong—is a theoretical claim. It is because of the need to assess these theoretical claims that our inquiry into the morality of homosexuality will involve considerations of moral theory and the nature of right and wrong.

SUMMARY OUTLINE

In the next chapter, we will try to define morality (and moral terms like "right" and "wrong"). Some moral opposition to homosexuality is grounded on confused or inadequate conceptions of morality. In chapter 3, I will consider religious objections to homosexuality and the "divine command theory" of morality that these objections assume.

One major dispute that lies at the heart of the gay rights issue is the question of whether homosexuality is biologically innate, the result of environment, or a personal choice. Thus, chapter 4 will consider the relevant evidence. We will also question whether it matters, morally, if homosexuality is chosen or can be changed.

In chapters 5 and 6 we will consider arguments that homosexuality is wrong because it is unnatural or involves a misuse of the human genitals. In chapter 7 we will look at some of the psychological motivations for why some people disapprove of homosexuality. Many of these motives, it turns out, have nothing to do with any morally relevant reasons. Thus, evidence for these motives provides a debunking explanation for the disapproval of homosexuality (or at least the disapproval of some people). In chapters 8 and 9, we will examine arguments that legal recognition of gay rights would be unjust because of their alleged detrimental effects on society or innocent third parties. Chapter 8 will focus especially on "slippery slope" arguments that say that allowing same-sex marriage will establish a precedent that will require acceptance of morally bad practices such as bestiality or polygamy, while chapter 9 will focus on the alleged harms caused by the tolerance of homosexuality and by gay-tolerant policies themselves.

Finally, in chapter 10, we will consider the arguments defending homosexual practices and supporting gay rights.

2

WHAT IS MORALITY?

Homosexuality is not the only issue on which opinions are often guided by emotion and experience rather than by reason. On many moral issues, people hold a certain view because of the way they were raised. But how you happen to have been raised is not a good reason for taking a stand on an important social issue. If and when people change their minds, it is usually motivated by life experience rather than good arguments. I would not claim that life experiences are totally irrelevant to our moral judgments. Maybe knowing someone who is gay will dispel false views of homosexuals as irresponsible, psychologically unstable degenerates. Such experiences, however, should not be *necessary* for revising one's moral judgments. Also, life experiences are not always enlightening; they can also have a perverse, distorting effect. If a woman finds out that her husband is a child molester, for example, she might come to view the crime less harshly. But obviously we should *not* be tolerant of child molesting.

The moral views of most people are shaped by emotional reactions to their very limited experiences more than by impartial rational considerations. One reason for this is that there is so little real public debate on moral issues. Most public discourse on contentious issues like abortion, capital punishment, or military intervention consists of activists shouting slogans. Rarely do we hear, on television talk shows or in political debates, a careful and intellectually honest analysis of the arguments on both sides.

I suspect, however, that there is another reason why opinions on moral issues are so little influenced by debate and argument. Often the two sides of the debate have radically different perspectives and worldviews. In order for those with opposing moral stances to have a meaningful discussion with any hope of a resolution, they must start with something that they can both agree on. The areas where they agree must allow both sides enough resources to make a case for their position on grounds that the other side could accept. Without some minimal agreement, debate dissolves into mere slogans and name-calling.

In debates about certain controversial medical practices, for example, the two sides disagree about the nature of "life," or what it is to be "alive."[1] A large proportion of those who oppose abortion or euthanasia are deeply religious people who believe in the sanctity of life. For these people, the fact that a fetus or a coma patient is alive means something supernatural, such as possessing an eternal, nonphysical soul. On the other hand, many of those who defend abortion or euthanasia have a more secular, naturalistic, scientific worldview. They tend to think of life as being as a cluster of physical, biochemical processes such as heart beat, homeostasis, cellular reproduction, and self-organization. Life in this second sense does not seem especially morally significant. The fetus or the coma patient is alive in the same sense that a chicken or a fish or even a tree is alive.

The persistence of the gay rights debate is a little different. Part of the disagreement is based on different beliefs about certain crucial *empirical* facts—that is, facts that can be determined by observation and good scientific method. For example, some conservatives believe that homosexuality is a choice or that gay people are psychologically maladjusted or that children raised by gay parents are prone to delinquency. Those are empirical claims that can be refuted by scientific and sociological evidence. If all disagreement about gay rights revolved around these facts, we could settle the issue just by looking at the facts. But clearly this is not all there is to the disagreement. Even if we were to settle every one of these empirical questions once and for all, I doubt that that would be sufficient to achieve unanimity on the *moral* question.

So what is it, other than the empirical facts, that supporters and opponents of gay rights disagree about that prevents them from having a fruitful discussion? I suggest that, for at least some people, the disagreement is based on different ideas about the nature of morality. In other words, there is disagreement, or just plain confusion, about what it is for something to be morally right or wrong.

This disagreement might exist on various levels of generality or specificity. On the most general, abstract level, we might disagree over the *concept* of morality or what we *mean* by terms like "right" or "wrong." At the opposite extreme is the *constitutive* question of what particular actions are morally right or morally wrong. In other words, we might disagree on our list of dos and don'ts. In between these two extremes—

the conceptual question and the constitutive question—there is the question of what is it that makes right actions right and wrong actions wrong. This question is about moral *theory*. A moral theory will connect our concepts of right and wrong to the list of dos and don'ts by establishing a criterion to determine whether any given act is right or wrong (or neither).

The disagreement on the morality of homosexuality and gay rights reflects deep differences between gay rights advocates and gay rights opponents in their concept of morality and in their moral theory. These differing ideas about morality are especially recalcitrant since they are largely implicit and rarely come to the fore in the gay rights debate. Thus, before we can analyze and assess the arguments for and against homosexuality, we need to clarify our moral concepts and find some definition of moral terms that both sides could agree to.

DEFINITION AND CONCEPTUAL ANALYSIS

Much of the work philosophers do involves finding clear and precise definitions for the key terms of a given debate. This is important because a lot of confusion and errors in reasoning can result from having concepts that are vague, ambiguous, or incoherent. Consider, for example, the clichéd philosophical question, "If a tree falls in a forest and there is no one there to hear it, does it make a sound?" Some philosophers see this as a puzzle that captures a very deep problem about experience, knowledge, and the nature of reality. Other philosophers, however, think that the puzzle largely disappears if we clarify what we mean by *sound*. If we define "sound" as vibrations in the air (or other gas or liquid medium), then of course the tree makes a sound. The event is taking place in a forest, not on the moon, and so the tree is surrounded by air that will vibrate as a result of its fall. On the other hand, if we take "sound" to refer to an auditory perception, then the tree makes no sound because, *ex hypothesis*, there is no one there to have any auditory perception of it. Even if you disagree that defining the word "sound" *solves* the puzzle, at least it allows us to discuss it more clearly.

Philosophical definitions differ from dictionary definitions. A dictionary definition describes the way people actually use a word. These definitions can be, and often are, ambiguous or incoherent. Sometimes this reflects ignorance of proper use. For example, the Google online dictionary gave me the following definition for the term *jealous*: "Feeling or showing envy of someone or their achievements and advantages."

That is a definition of *envious*, not jealous. Jealousy, properly defined, is envy felt toward one person's relationship with another, combined with a feeling that one's relationship with that other is threatened. So a young boy might be *jealous* when his little sister gets extra attention from their mother, but he is *envious* (not jealous) when his sister gets a cookie and he doesn't.

When philosophers seek definitions, they are not merely looking at the standard usage of words. They are analyzing the concepts that words are used to signify. It does not matter whether the definition I offered is really *the correct* meaning of "jealous." The important thing is that there are two distinct emotions: 1) the simple resentment toward one person who has something you want and 2) the more complex resentment directed at two others—one who has (or is thought to have) a special relationship that you want to have, or think you should have, with the other. Since there are two distinct emotions, we should use two different words to name them.

Searching for a philosophical definition is a matter of analyzing concepts. There are different levels at which we might try to analyze a concept. For example, consider a nonmoral use of the term "good." Specifically, let us consider the notion of "good" as applied to food. What do we mean when we talk about good food?

At the more abstract level is a *conceptual* definition. There are at least two distinct concepts of "good" food. One possibility is that by saying some particular food is "good," we mean that it is delicious, that it tastes good. Another possibility is that by saying some particular food is "good" we mean that it is nutritious, that it is wholesome. These two competing conceptions of good food are abstract in that they contain no reference to any particular kinds of food or to any of the concrete features that make food good. These are *formal* definitions in that they connect one abstract concept, goodness, to other abstract concepts, pleasure or health. A formal definition lacks descriptive content.

At the extreme opposite of the very general *conceptual* definitions are what we might call *constitutive* definitions. While conceptual definitions tend to be abstract, a constitutive definition would be more concrete. It might supply a list of the particular things that the concept applies to. A constitutive analysis of the concept of good food would simply be an exhaustive list of all the foods that are good. There are two problems with this sort of constitutive definition. First, determining whether a particular kind of food belongs on the list will depend on the abstract, conceptual definition. If "good food" means *healthy* food, then tofu belongs on the list and butter does not. If "good food" means *tasty* food, then butter is in and tofu is out. So it is often impossible to give a constitutive account of some concept without first giving an abstract, formal account. Second, constitutive definitions are often not very useful. For example, the Trinidadian restaurant near my home in Washington, D.C., serves up exotic dishes like roti, shark-and-bake, and cow heel soup. Is cow heel good food? If all we have as a definition of good food is a list, then that list would have to be very long. And when a creative chef invents a new dish, it will not be on that list at all (unless the list included every possible dish, in which case it would be infinitely long).

On the other hand, an abstract, formal definition is sometimes even less useful than a constitutive definition. Suppose that by "good food" we mean healthy food. Is cow heel soup good (i.e., healthy) food? We would need some sort of general criteria or principles for what *makes* food healthy. We might do this by listing the basic nutrients essential for maintaining good health—amino acids, dietary fiber, vitamins, minerals, and so on—and the recommended daily allowances (maximum and/or minimum) for each, adjusted for age and weight. We could apply these criteria to any dish, even to strange or novel dishes, and determine whether it is good. These criteria would constitute a *theory* about what makes good food good. Thus, there is a third way to define a concept, one that lies between a purely formal conceptual definition and a purely concrete constitutive definition.

So in analyzing a concept, it usually helps to start with an abstract, conceptual definition, if possible. For example, by "good food" we mean healthy food. Then we can look for some criteria to determine whether particular items fall under this concept. This might be a theory of nutrition. Finally, using this theory, we can give a concrete, constitutive account of the concept—in other words, a list of good and bad foods. Ideally we should try to do the same for morality. We should start by finding a *conceptual* definition of what we mean by morally "wrong" and morally "right." Then we should look for a *theory* about what makes actions right or wrong. This theory could then be used to establish a *constitutive* list of dos and don'ts—in other words, a moral code.

It might not be possible to find one moral theory that everyone will agree on. (But I will suggest a practical theory in chapter 10.) Fortunately, we do not need to find a definitive theory in order to debate particular moral theories about homosexuality. We do, however, need to give a *formal* definition of what we mean when we say something is morally "right" or "wrong." This we will try to do in this chapter. In the rest of this book, we will critically analyze and reject certain especially bad moral theories that serve as the background for bad arguments against homosexuality.

ONE CONCEPTUAL ACCOUNT OF MORALITY: EMOTIVISM

One abstract, formal account of moral concepts, popular among professional philosophers in the 1950s and 1960s, is known as *emotivism*. According to the emotivist account, moral statements like "stealing is wrong" are neither true nor false. This is because they are not genuine statements at all. They may have the grammatical form of a statement, but this is just the literal grammar, or what philosophers call the *surface* grammar.

The surface grammar of a sentence does not always capture the true meaning of what is said. For example, suppose I am carrying something heavy, and I say to you, "Could you open the door for me?" The surface grammar of this sentence is interrogative; it is in the form of a question. But is it really a question? Of course not. I am not seeking information, and if you answered by simply saying "yes," and then stood there doing nothing, I would hardly be satisfied. The true meaning of my sentence "Could you open the door for me?" is not interrogative but imperative. I am issuing a command, roughly the equivalent of "Please open the door for me." We put it in the form of a question for the sake of etiquette. A question sounds less bossy than a command, even though it really is an implicit command.

If a moral utterance like "murder is wrong" is not really a statement, then what kind of sentence is it? The emotivists would say that it is something like an exclamatory sentence. It is the expression of an attitude or feeling, just as "ouch!" expresses pain, "damn it!" expresses anger or frustration, and "woe is me" expresses despair or regret. To say that some action or practice is "wrong," according to emotivism, is merely to express disapproval of it. To say is it "right" is to express approval. Thus, the sentence "murder is wrong" really means something like "boo murder!" The sentence "telling the truth is the right thing to do" really means "hooray for telling the truth!"

It is important to keep in mind that the emotivist theory does not claim that moral statements are covert descriptions of our attitudes. The sentence "murder is wrong," on this theory, is not equivalent to the statement "I disapprove of murder." If I say "I disapprove of murder" then I am making a statement about my own psychological disposition, a statement that is either true or false. That statement does not *express* my attitudes but rather *describes* my attitudes. "Boo stealing," on the other hand, cannot be true or false because it makes no claim about how the world is (not even about that part of the world inside my head). It might be insincere or misleading, but it cannot be *false*. (In the same way, if I say "ouch" when I am not really hurt, I am not stating anything false, though I am saying something misleading and potentially deceptive.)

Does this emotivist theory give the correct analysis of moral discourse and moral thinking? Does it capture the essence of morality and the true meaning of moral terms? The answer is, for the most part, no. There are several problems with this theory. The biggest problem is that it fails to reflect accurately what most of us are trying to convey when we make moral statements. And it does not match up with what goes on in our heads when we engage in moral deliberation. Ask yourself, when you say that a certain action is morally wrong, whether you take yourself to be merely expressing your subjective feelings of disapproval. Or do you take yourself to be saying something more? There may be some times when we use moral terms in a purely emotivist way. For example, when I witness something extremely distasteful—such as an obese, hairy man wearing a speedo—I might say, "That is just *wrong!*" But I suspect that this is very different from how most of us use moral terms most of the time.

Some people who say that homosexuality is morally wrong are probably basing their moral judgment on an emotional reaction, such as disgust. (This is an explanation we will examine in chapter 7.) But I doubt that those people take themselves to be merely expressing those subjective attitudes. They are not simply saying, "yuck homosexuality!" Even if what they say is *motivated* by disgust, what they are saying is more than just an expression of that disgust. And those who claim that homosexuals have a moral right to marry and to be free from discrimination likewise take themselves to be saying something true, not just expressing their feelings. Though there are interesting philosophical arguments defending emotivism (or certain improved versions of the theory), it is not likely to offer a useful account of the meaning of moral terms that both sides of the gay rights debate could agree on.[2]

ONE CONSTITUTIVE ACCOUNT OF MORALITY: PURITANISM

Conceptual analysis ideally starts at the most abstract level, then proceeds to the theoretical level, and then finally to the concrete items to which the category applies. But sometimes this is not possible. Consider, for example, an arbitrary category such as the Ivy League. We may be able to give a formal definition of "league" as a collection of independent colleges that compete against one another in athletics. But we cannot give any formal definition of *Ivy* League. The only way to define the Ivy League is simply to list the eight schools that belong to it.

Perhaps the same is true for morality—or at least for the way that some people think of morality. Some people seem to think of morality in terms of a list of particular dos and don'ts. They have only a *constitutive* account of right and wrong. One such account of morality, one that might motivate anti-gay judgments, is what I will call the *puritanical* conception of morality.

Use of the term "moral" (along with its cognates "morality" and "morally") has come to sound somewhat dated in common use. More often we hear talk of "ethics" or "ethical," though these terms are typically used in the context of professional codes of conduct, such as medical ethics panels or congressional ethics committees. I think this is quite unfortunate. The result is that people associate the term "morality" with old-fashioned conservative prudishness. For example, a recent *New York Times* story on Pope Francis reported him as saying that "the church had grown 'obsessed' with abortion, gay marriage and contraception." The story goes on to say that the new pope "criticized the church . . . for prioritizing moral doctrines over serving the poor and marginalized."[3] When I read this I was quite disappointed to find that the writers and editors at the *New York Times* do not think that feeding the poor is a moral issue![4] They seem to have accepted the puritanical concept of the word "moral."

It is hard to give any general or theoretical definition of this puritanical conception of morality, though H. L. Mencken gave it a shot when he described puritanism as "the haunting fear that someone, somewhere, may be happy."[5] We can describe this puritanical sense of morality by listing some of the things that are considered to be moral or immoral in the puritanical sense. The puritanical code includes general disapproval of sensual pleasure, leisure, bawdy humor or language, revealing or sexy attire, unconventional or nontraditional hairstyles, and so on. When we think of morality in this sense, we have in mind old-fashioned virtues such as chastity, sobriety, and modesty. Immorality in this sense refers to relatively harmless activities like gambling, cursing, drinking, or unmarried women flirting with men in public drinking houses.

In the puritanical view, homosexuality would be considered morally wrong, but so would almost every other kind of sex except for lights-off, man-on-top, strictly procreative sex between married people . . . and even then only if they don't enjoy it. In the puritanical sense of morality, many other things would be considered immoral as well—things that most of us today do not strongly disapprove of. For example, in Victorian days, gambling was considered immoral, and the only two places where organized gambling was legal in the United States were Nevada and Atlantic City. Today, however, Hawaii and Utah are the only states in the United States that do not have some form of legalized gambling.[6] Even Mississippi, where I work, the heart of the Bible Belt and the state with the most churches per capita, has several casinos on the coast. Alcohol consumption was also considered immoral in those Victorian times, and a grassroots campaign to ban all alcohol eventually succeeded in the United States with the Eighteenth Amendment. Today, by contrast, about two-thirds of Americans drink alcohol on a regular basis, and that is significantly lower than in most industrialized countries. Puritanical morality discourages premarital sex, but only about 5 percent of Americans today "save themselves" for their wedding night.

One interpretation we could make of these phenomena is that the world is becoming more and more corrupted and evil. No doubt, some people think exactly that.

But it seems to be a very small minority. Most of us do not feel that there is anything terribly wrong with drinking, premarital sex, or gambling, at least as long as one engages in such activities responsibly and in moderation. If "morality" is taken to refer to these outdated puritanical values of our great-grandparents, then it may be true that homosexuality is "immoral," but most of us today would also say that there is nothing wrong with doing things that are "immoral" in that sense.

I am not arguing that just because drinking and premarital sex are widely accepted, therefore these activities are not morally wrong. That would be a very weak argument.[7] My point is that if few people disapprove of such activities, then it is not very helpful to employ this sense of morality in the gay rights debate. Virtually no one who favors gay rights would accept the puritanical conception, and even most people on the anti-gay side would reject it. Once we have a better definition of moral terms like "right" and "wrong," puritans might still claim that drunkenness and promiscuity are morally wrong. But they will have to give reasons for those moral judgments. They cannot simply say these activities are wrong because that is what the word "wrong" *means*.

I doubt that the debate over homosexuality is a debate over whether it violates the social mores of our Victorian era ancestors. After all, there are many people who think that same-sex marriage should be outlawed, that homosexual couples should not be allowed to adopt children, and that homosexuals are not fit to serve in the military. No reasonable person today seriously advocates re-prohibition of alcohol or outlawing premarital sex, even if they disapprove of those activities. I take it that those on the anti-gay side *do* think that there is something wrong with being gay or engaging in a gay lifestyle and that they think it is wrong in a way that is different from gambling or drinking or (heterosexual) sex before marriage. They also presumably think that those of us who do not disapprove of drinking, cursing, or fornicating (which is most of us), should nevertheless still disapprove of homosexuality. Thus, the puritanical definition of "morality" will not do.

ANOTHER CONCEPTUAL ACCOUNT OF MORALITY: RELATIVISM

Students in my introductory philosophy classes sometimes express support for moral relativism. They may ask, rhetorically, "Isn't morality just opinion?" Or they might suggest that morality depends on culture. "It might be wrong in our society," they will say, "but not in their society." This sort of sentiment is summed up nicely by Bart Simpson when he poses the rhetorical question to Lisa: "In these crazy, topsy-turvy times, who's to say what's right or wrong?"[8] There are different versions of relativism, but let us consider a particularly popular version: conventional relativism. Anthropologist Ruth Benedict defended conventional relativism in the earlier part of the twentieth century. "Mankind," she wrote, "has always preferred to say, 'It is morally good,' rather than 'It is habitual,' and the fact of this preference is matter enough for a critical science of ethics. But historically the two phrases are synonymous."[9] Note that Benedict is not simply claiming that conventional relativism is true. She thinks it is what we *mean* when we make moral claims. "Morally right" and "customary" are *synonymous*, according to her.

To say that morality is *relative* to convention, we mean that whether or not an action is right or wrong depends on whether or not people in our society approve or disapprove. In the nonrelativist view, it is—or at least should be—the other way around. Attitudes of approval or disapproval do not *make* an act right or wrong. Instead, approval and disapproval are supposed to be responses to the objective properties of rightness and wrongness. According to the conventional relativist view, by contrast, there are no objective moral truths. Since people disagree about what they approve or disapprove of, and since approval and disapproval is what makes an action right or wrong, there can be no objective right or wrong. The same action can be morally right from one person's perspective and morally wrong from another person's perspective. Just as beauty is in the eye of the beholder, in this view rightness and wrongness would be in the attitude of the be-judger.

I suspect that my students do not, on reflection, really believe that morality is just opinion or that right and wrong are simply a matter of cultural norms and practices. One possibility is that they are confusing

morality in the puritanical sense with something deeper and more serious. On the one hand, they have adopted the puritanical conception of
morality (thanks in part to usage of the term "moral" in the media); but
then they do not accept those puritanical norms. They cannot say drinking, cursing, and premarital sex are not immoral since that is how morality has—unfortunately—been defined for them. So, instead, they
think they need to reject morality in general.

My response is usually something like this: So you do not think there
is anything necessarily wrong with raping children? You think that it is
just my opinion that it is wrong to torture people for fun? Do you really
think that genocide is wrong "for us" but might be right for some other
culture? When challenged this way, most self-described relativists reply
with surprise: "Oh, *that's* what you mean!" Examples such as these help
point to a different, nonpuritanical sense of morality.

Of course, it is probably true that moral *beliefs* differ from culture to
culture. But that does not mean that what *is* right or wrong varies from
culture to culture. Just because people living in the Sudan think that it
is morally okay to mutilate the genitals of young girls does not mean
that it *is* morally okay for them to do so. And it certainly does not mean
that we have to approve of them doing so.[10] Even if what truly *is* right
or wrong is determined by the beliefs and practices of one's culture, this
is not (pace Benedict) part of the *meaning* of the terms "right" or
"wrong." I think conventional relativism is false. I also think that most
people, on careful reflection, would agree that conventional relativism
is false. But even if it were true, it would not be *true by definition*.

PARADIGM EXAMPLES OF MORALLY RIGHT OR WRONG

Examples of morally wrong actions—such as theft, murder, torture, and
rape—are no substitute for a *definition* of morality. As we saw with the
good food example, such a list would have to be almost endless. More
importantly, with respect to the homosexuality issue, the debate is over
whether homosexuality belongs on the list of don'ts. So we need some
sort of criteria for deciding what *should* be on the list and what should
not. Still, it might be useful to start with these paradigm examples of
morally wrong actions in order to get a rough feel for the concept we
are trying to define. By analogy, if we are trying to define the biological
concept of *bird*, a list of all bird species would not do. Nevertheless, it
might be helpful to start with a few examples of birds—for example,
pigeon, sparrow, owl, and eagle—to get a vague notion of the class of
animals we are trying to define. We can then look at what they have in

common and decide which of these features are essential to being a bird (for example, having feathers) and which are not (for example, the ability to fly). That will help us determine that penguins are birds (even though they cannot fly) and that bats are not birds (since they have no feathers).

So paradigmatic examples of morally wrong actions provide us with an idea of what we mean by "morality," but only a rough idea. It allows us, for example, to see that we are not talking about puritanical taboos. But examples only get us so far. For one thing, these examples will be ones that are obvious and uncontroversial. This does not help to see where the borders of this concept lie. Torturing is morally wrong in this sense, and eating for pleasure is not morally wrong. But what about all those things in between? What about harmless lies or spanking your children? In order to fully understand moral rightness and wrongness, we need to be able to distinguish actions that are wrong-but-not-seri-ously-wrong, from actions that are not wrong at all.

TESTING DEFINITIONS

Suppose we have a candidate definition for morality or for certain moral terms such as "right" or "wrong." How would we test whether that definition captures the correct meaning of the term—or more accurate-ly, the correct analysis of the concept that the term stands for? Here is a simple procedure. Let us use "M" to represent the moral term that we are trying to analyze. Suppose we propose that "M means D," where "D" stands for some proposed definition of M. If D is an adequate definition of M, then to say that "Something is M but not D" would be incoherent or self-contradictory. If we can meaningfully say that some-thing is M and yet deny that it is D, then M cannot mean the same as D. Note that it can be meaningful to say that something is M and yet not D, even if it is true that everything that is M is also D.[11]

This test brings to the fore an important distinction between two sorts of questions that are easily confused. There is a difference be-tween asking "What *is* X?" and asking "What does 'X' *mean*?" If I ask "What *is* the most popular beverage in the Western world?" the answer is cola. But suppose I ask "What do you *mean by* 'the most popular beverage'?" The phrase "most popular beverage" happens to refer to cola, but it does not mean the same as cola. The phrase "most popular beverage" could be defined in various ways. It could designate which liquid (excluding water) is drunk by the most people, drunk in the largest total quantities, or that ranks the highest in surveys. If I were to say "the most popular beverage is not cola," that might be false, but it would not be meaningless or incoherent.

The point is that in order to find a good definition, we typically do not need to check any independent facts. Take, for example, the term "bachelor," which we define as an "unmarried man." To test whether this is a good definition we would not take a survey of men, asking if they are bachelors and then asking if they are married. That would be pointless and unnecessary. If we were to conduct the survey and found less than 100 percent correspondence between bachelors and unmarried men, then it would only show that some of the people surveyed did not understand the question (or perhaps that one of the surveyors recorded the data incorrectly). Instead, we should simply ask whether it would make sense to say that "Mr. Smith is a bachelor and he is married."

TESTING DEFINITIONS OF "WRONG"

So let us apply this test to the proposed relativist definition of moral terms. According to Benedict, to say that something is "wrong" means roughly that it is disapproved of by the speaker's society (or perhaps that it is disapproved of by the society of the person doing the action).

Let us now test this proposed definition of wrongness. If the relativist definition of right and wrong is true, then it *would not make sense* to say, "This action is generally approved of in our society, but nevertheless it is morally wrong." Remember, it is not a question of whether the statement is true, but only whether it is coherent. Clearly the statement makes perfect sense. Societies often find within themselves reformers who challenge the status quo, such as the early abolitionists of the antebellum United States. These opponents of slavery were surely aware that the practice of owning people was generally approved of in their society, but they claimed that this approval was mistaken. By proclaiming slavery to be wrong, the abolitionists were not uttering a contradiction. Their listeners certainly understood what they were saying, and many were even persuaded to agree with them.

Since it makes sense to say something is generally approved of and yet still wrong, the meaning of "wrong" cannot be the same as "approved of by one's society." It is important to note that this does not prove that relativism is false. All that we have proven is that relativism is not true *by definition*. By contrast, the fact that all bachelors are unmarried *is* true by definition. Here is an analogy. It happens to be true that all living organisms that have a heart also have a kidney, and all living organisms that have a kidney also have a heart. It is true, but it is not *true by definition*. The expression "having a heart" does not mean the same as "having a kidney." It makes sense to say "this organism has a heart but no kidney," even though it will be false in every actual case. It would, however, be nonsense to say, "This creature has a heart, but it has no muscular organ that pumps blood through its circulatory system to oxygenate its cells." That is a contradiction. So from the mere concepts of organism-with-heart and organism-with-kidney, we cannot determine that there is a strict correlation between the two.

An important moral of the story is that a good definition does not include everything that is true of the thing defined but only those things that are *necessarily* true of the thing defined. A good definition must be minimalist, especially with an abstract concept like "morally wrong." Whatever definition we give, it must allow us to say not only everything that is true about wrongness, but also everything that is false about wrongness. The only limitation is that a definition cannot allow us to say anything that is meaningless, nonsensical, or logically contradictory about wrongness.

MORALITY AS NORMATIVE

What then do we mean when we say that an action is "wrong"? Well, we could mean a lot of things. When looking for a definition of a term or phrase, we must only look for the minimum of things that we *must* mean, not the maximum of things that we *could* mean. Thus, when I say that an action is wrong, I may have a lot of things in mind, for example that it hurts someone or is unfair or whatever. But what is the bare minimum that I must mean by saying it is wrong?

To get at the essential meaning of moral terms, it might be useful to ask why we have these terms and why we use them. What is the point in having the predicate ". . . is wrong"? It seems to me that, at a minimum, when I say that an action is wrong, I am saying that the action is one that *ought not to be done*. In other words, moral terms are action guiding, or as philosophers say, *normative*. A normative term does not describe how the world *is* but rather how it *should be* or *ought to be*. When we say that something is "blue" or "heavy" or "wooden," we are describing how things *are*. But when we say that something is "bad," we are saying that there should be less (or none) of it; when we say an action is "wrong," we are saying it should be done less often (or not at all). These ought-statements are *norms*. They cite reasons to act, reasons we can appeal to in our deliberation.

Does this proposed definition pass the contradiction test? I think so. Suppose I told you, "this action is wrong; you should do it." Most people would probably think that I was contradicting myself. Maybe people would assume that I was joking, that I misspoke, or that I don't know what the word "wrong" means. At any rate, virtually no one would respond by thinking "that makes sense!" The same goes for other normative terms like *good* and *bad*. If I said, "Mr. Smith is a good person; we should discourage others from following his example," that would be baffling.

On this proposed definition, all moral terms are action guiding. An essential part of their meaning is to say something about what we *ought* to do or how we *should* act, think, or feel. To say that an action is wrong means that one ought not to do it. But there may be more to it than that. We probably also think that to say an action is wrong means that we ought to disapprove of the act and disapprove of those who intentionally do it. But all of that is still a matter of what we *ought* to do, say, think, or feel. The same is true of other moral terms. To say an action is morally right means that one ought to do it and to approve of others who do it. To say it is one's duty to perform some action means it would be wrong not to do it. And so on.

MORAL OUGHTS VERSUS NONMORAL

Although moral claims are about what we ought to do (or ought to think, feel, or say), not every claim about what we ought to do is a moral claim. There are other kinds of norms beside moral norms. Let us consider some of the nonmoral senses in which we use terms like "ought," "should," or "must." These different kinds of norms represent different reasons an agent might have for performing an action.

First, there are *legal* norms. For example, in the United States you must drive your automobile on the right (on two-way streets). Then, there are norms of *etiquette*, such as when Miss Manners says, "You ought not to chew with your mouth open." Yet another kind of norm is *prudence*. Prudence means doing what is in your own best interest. When I say to my students that they ought to study for the upcoming exam, or when I say to a friend that he ought to quit smoking, I am making a prudential claim. It would be in the students' best interest to study; it would be in the best interest of my friend to quit smoking.

So our definition of morality in terms of what we ought to do (or not do), or what we have reason to do (or not do), is insufficient. "Oughtness," or normativity, is a necessary part of the definition of morality;

but in order to distinguish moral concepts from other normative concepts, we need more in the definition of moral terms than just normativity.

Some norms can be defined in terms of their content, that is, in terms of the different *kinds* of reasons for action. That is how we would define prudence. To say that a certain behavior is prudent means that 1) you ought to do it and (or because) 2) by doing it you benefit yourself or prevent some harm to yourself. So prudence, by definition, cannot involve behavior that does not affect the agent in some way. If I were to say, "Giving to charity is prudent, even though it will not benefit you in any way," I would not be making any sense. If an action does not benefit the person doing it, then *by definition* the act is not prudent. Thus, we can only define prudence with reference to the kind of content prudential oughts have. This definition is still fairly abstract and formal. It leaves open questions of exactly what counts as a benefit or a harm to oneself. But there is still some definite content. Only certain kinds of reasons will count as prudential reasons to act.

Other norms could probably also be distinguished in terms of their content. Legal norms, we might say, are those rules that originate in legislative acts of some legitimate political authority with the power to enforce them. Etiquette norms are rules, based on social conventions and traditions, that involve expressions of respect and avoidance of causing offense or disgust.

So it might be tempting to do something similar with moral norms. We might try to distinguish them from other sorts of norms by describing their content. Moral norms, for example, might be defined as things we ought to do in order to avoid or prevent harm, benefit those in need, respect individual autonomy, repay debts, and keep promises.[12] Morality, we might say, is about benefits and harms, fairness, and individual rights.

I think it is true that morality consists of those kinds of norms and only those kinds of norms. This is one of the central arguments I will make throughout this book when critiquing claims that homosexuality is morally wrong. Yet this is not part of the *meaning* of moral terms. It might be true that morality involves those things (harm, fairness, and rights) and only those things, but it is not true *by definition* that morality involves only those sorts of reasons to act.

If we were to agree that what it means for something to be morally wrong is that it causes harm, is unfair, or violates someone's rights, then it would be easy to prove that homosexuality is not morally wrong. All we would need to do is to show that homosexuality has none of those properties. It does not (normally) harm anyone, is not unfair, and does not violate anyone's rights. That would be easy, but maybe a little too easy. (Some people who are morally opposed to homosexuality might claim that it is harmful, to the gay people or to innocent third parties. But this can be shown to be false. We will look at those arguments in chapter 9.)

Many opponents of homosexuality would say that there are other things that can make an action or practice morally wrong. For example, they might claim that an action is wrong if it is unnatural or forbidden by God. I argue that those claims are false. Being unnatural or forbidden by God does *not* make an action wrong. But I cannot base my claim simply on the meaning of the word "wrong." Even if I were to insist that this is part of the meaning of the word "wrong," my opponent could simply point out that he means something different by "wrong." I need to give some argument for why my conception of wrongness is better than his. I must give good reasons supporting my claim that being God forbidden or unnatural does not make an action wrong. (I will give such arguments in chapters 3 and chapter 5, respectively.)

DEFINING FEATURES OF MORAL NORMS

We cannot define moral norms in terms of their content—as norms involving harms, fairness, rights, and autonomy. But there are other ways to distinguish moral norms from other sorts of norms, such as law, etiquette, or prudence. We should first observe that there is much overlap in these different kinds of norms. There are many things that we ought to do for several reasons. For example, suppose I am considering robbing my neighbor's house while he is away on vacation. Obviously that is something that I should not do. But what sense of "ought" or "should" am I using here? There are several reasons not to do it. First of all, it would be rude to rob my neighbor. But most people would probably say that there are much more compelling reasons not to do it than mere etiquette. There is also a law against robbing people's houses. The simple fact *that* it is a law is not very compelling, but it is also a good law and one that is enforced rather heavily. For that reason, it is also against my own interest to rob my neighbor. There is a significant chance that I will get caught and thrown in jail.

Thus, different kinds of norms are often in agreement. Robbing my neighbor's house would be rude, illegal, and imprudent (and presumably also morally wrong). Other times, however, norms can conflict. We ought to do something, in one context, while having no reason to do it or even reason not to do it, in another. For example, suppose I am at a fancy dinner party with the Queen of England. Just after taking a rather large bite of beef Wellington, I notice that another guest is about to drink absentmindedly from a can of Sterno. It would be rude for me to talk with my mouth full, and so, from an etiquette standpoint, I should say nothing until I finish chewing and swallow my food. On the other hand, I have a moral obligation to prevent harm. So, from a moral perspective, I should shout at him to stop (or shout at someone else to stop him).

What should I do in this case? Should I follow the rules of etiquette and swallow my food before I speak? Or should I warn my dining companion, even though doing so would be rude? It seems pretty obvious that in this case the norm to prevent harm far outweighs the norm not to talk with food in my mouth. I propose that this is part of what we mean when we say that I *morally* ought to warn the diner. Moral norms are those norms that outweigh other norms, such as prudence, etiquette, and law.

It is especially important to distinguish legal norms from moral norms. Some laws are arbitrary. For example, in the United States, traffic laws dictate that we drive on the right. In the U.K. the law says to drive on the left. Neither one is better or worse than the other. There are good reasons to have *some* rule dictating that cars must drive on one side or the other, but it does not matter which. All that matters is that there is consistency. Of course, when I am driving in the United States, I may have a moral obligation to stay on the right. But the moral obligation is not just because it is the law. I have a moral obligation to obey traffic laws because disobeying (e.g., driving on the wrong side of the street) would risk harm to other drivers and pedestrians.

More importantly, there can be bad laws. In those cases we might be morally obligated to break the law. For example, in 1850 the U.S. Congress passed the Fugitive Slave Act, which made it a crime to aid an escaped slave. Suppose that I were living in the antebellum South and had a friend who was an escaped slave. The law requires that I should turn him in. But that is an unjust law. The morally right thing to do is to help him escape (or at least not hinder him from escaping). Moral norms override legal norms when they conflict.

Couldn't a very serious law sometimes outweigh a trivial moral duty? Yes and no. If the legal ought is *only* a legal ought, then it could never outweigh a moral ought. But most of our important legal oughts are also moral oughts. Wearing your seat belt is probably not a moral duty, but it is not a very serious crime to drive without buckling up. More serious laws, with greater punishments attached, forbid things like robbery, murder, and rape. And of course there are also good *moral* reasons not to do these sorts of things (and moral reasons to prevent others from doing them). This is why the example of slavery works well in illustrating the difference between law and morality. There is really no moral justification for slavery or for returning an escaped slave into bondage. Suppose that the law against abetting escaped slaves was a very serious one, with a very serious punishment (such as life in prison or execution). The moral duty would still override the law, and we should disobey it (even though we might not *blame* people who obey the law out of fear).

Remember that we are trying to find a definition of morality and moral terms. A good definition is one that virtually every competent speaker would agree on. Would the slave owner agree that moral obligations outweigh legal ones? He would probably not agree that I should help my friend escape—but only because he would not agree that slavery is wrong or that the law requiring me to turn my friend in is unjust. The slave owner would, however, probably agree that moral oughts override legal ones, that we should disobey unjust laws. We agree on the concept of morality. We agree that our moral duties, whatever they may be, override legal demands. Our disagreement is only about which particular practices are morally right or wrong.

OTHER FORMAL FEATURES OF MORALITY: UNIVERSAL, NONARBITRARY, AND BLAMEWORTHY

There may be other features of moral norms that distinguish them from norms of prudence, law, or etiquette. One is that moral norms are seen to have a kind of inescapable authority.[13] To say that moral demands are "inescapable" means that they do not depend on the agent's desires, values, or goals. In this way, moral norms are very different from prudence. Suppose I tell one of my students that he needs to study more, and he replies that he really does not care about his grade. He does not need to earn a degree because of his family's wealth. He is only taking classes for fun. There is little I could say to convince him that he should study. In fact, I am not so sure that he *has* any reason to study. It is a different matter, however, when it comes to moral claims. Suppose I say to my neighbor that he should not beat his children, and he replies that he is not interested in being a decent father. That would hardly let him off the hook. He should not beat his children because of the harm it causes them. Whether beating them conflicts with any of his goals or preferences is irrelevant.

Moral norms also have a kind of authority that distinguishes them from norms of etiquette or legal rules. Rules of etiquette have their authority from conventions, and laws have their authority from legislative procedure and codes of enforcement. But moral norms do not depend on some other authority. Moral norms are authoritative on their own. When the United States outlawed alcohol in 1920, the manufacturing, sales, and consumption of alcoholic beverages became illegal. When Prohibition was repealed thirteen years later, alcohol became legal again. But whether it is morally okay to make, sell, or drink liquor did not change. Etiquette can likewise be quite arbitrary. In Japan, the proper way to eat soup is to raise the bowl to your lips and slurp. That would not be considered proper in our society, where etiquette demands eating soup with a spoon. The polite way to eat soup thus can change between lunch at a French restaurant and dinner, a mere six hours later, at a Japanese restaurant.

It would be ridiculous to think that some rules of etiquette are *the correct* ones, independently of the customs and practices or the group. No reasonable person would think it is rude for an Indian family in Hyderabad to eat their rice with their hands, just because that is not how we eat rice in the United States. On the other hand, imagine a society in which slavery is nearly universally accepted. Even the slaves themselves accept the practice, though of course they do not like being slaves. It would make sense to say that people in that society ought not to own slaves, even if none of them would agree to that claim. That is because the people who make that claim have *reasons*—moral reasons—not to practice slavery; and these reasons do not depend on them thinking they have a reason. Moral norms thus seem to have a kind of universality. They apply to all people everywhere, regardless of custom or law or convention.

Moral norms differ from norms of prudence, etiquette, and law in another important way. We tend to think that people who intentionally violate moral norms deserve punishment, even if it's only a cold shoulder. That is we why tend to feel guilty when we believe we have done wrong and feel anger or resentment toward others when we believe they have done wrong. Guilt is, in part, a feeling of being worthy of punishment, while anger and resentment are tied to desires to punish or chastise others.

When someone violates a rule of prudence, their imprudent behavior is its own punishment. We don't feel guilty when we act imprudently, and we do not usually feel anger or resentment toward others who act imprudently. Imprudent behavior tends to evoke pity, and we think imprudent people need instruction or assistance rather than sanctions. Even violations of etiquette and law do not necessarily cause guilt, resentment, or punishment. Someone who acts rudely might be socially ostracized, but only insofar as their rude behavior is also morally offensive. Harmless violations of etiquette, such as eating with the wrong fork or replying in first person to an invitation written in third person, do not evoke censure even by the fussiest of etiquette sticklers. Laws, of course, have sanctions built in. But even violations of laws do not necessarily call for punishment if there is no moral violation. If I ran out in the middle of the street to save a child from being run over, what police officer would give me a ticket for jaywalking? It is only with moral violations that we believe people deserve punishment. And punishment is only punishment if it is inflicted because of some (alleged) wrongdoing. Thus morality and punishment seem to be conceptually linked.

CONCLUSION

Morality is about reasons to act—reasons that 1) are independent of the agent's goals or preferences, 2) are independent of political authority or convention, 3) override other sorts of norms such as prudence or law, and 4) warrant sanctions. There are many reasons to think that most people would accept this analysis, or something very close to it. For one thing, seeing moral norms as overriding reasons to act that have a certain inescapable authority helps to explain the force of moral judgments and the meaning of moral debates. If we say that "stealing is wrong," we mean that people have some reason not to steal, that these reasons would apply equally to anyone in a similar situation, and that these reasons (whatever they may be) override other kinds of reasons such as prudential reasons (since it might sometimes be in your best interests to steal). If the wrongness of stealing did not involve reasons not to steal, then why would anyone care whether it was "wrong"?

We cannot define moral norms in terms of their content—that is, norms involving benefits and harms, fairness, or rights. Doing so would be controversial. In order to fairly assess the arguments against homosexuality, we need to define moral terms in ways that those on the anti-gay side could agree to. Both sides should agree that actions that are morally wrong are ones that we should not do, regardless of our goals and inclinations and regardless of the customs of one's community. Since this is a definition of morality that both sides can agree on, we cannot settle the issue simply by appeal to the meaning of moral terms. Nevertheless, this analysis is helpful. It tells us what must be shown in order to defend the claim that homosexuality is morally wrong. To justify moral disapproval of homosexuality, one would have to show that homosexuals have a reason not to engage in same-sex relations, that these reasons do not depend on convention, and that those who engage in homosexual activities are worthy of some form of social sanction.

3

MORAL THEORY AND DIVINE COMMAND

So now we have a formal definition of morality. Morality involves how we—meaning everyone—ought to act in certain situations. To say that an action is wrong is to say that people ought not to perform that sort of action (in that sort of circumstance). That is to say, we have compelling reasons not to act that way. These reasons are not based on convention or authority, and they override other kinds of norms such as law, prudence, and etiquette.

Does this solve the debate over the morality of homosexuality and gay marriage? Of course not. That is because it is a merely formal definition with no specific content. We still need to describe the particular features that *make* actions right or wrong. Nevertheless, it does clarify the debate. At least now we can determine what it would mean to say that homosexuality is morally wrong. It would mean that people should not perform homosexual acts or live homosexual lifestyles. They ought not to do so because they have compelling reasons not to. These reasons are ones that apply to everyone (homosexual people as well as straight people). They are not based on convention or authority and they are more important than norms of etiquette or law.

We have clarified the debate, but defining our terms is not enough to decide whether homosexuality is morally right or wrong. To do that we must find out what constitutes these convention-independent, over-riding reasons to act. We have a pretty good idea of what constitutes a legal reason. There is a statute of some sort, usually codified in some available text, that is enforced through sanctions. These laws might come from a dictator or from a legislative body or from a direct vote by the citizens, depending on the form of one's political system. We might not agree with the laws, but we can usually all agree on what the laws are, or at least on how to find out what they are. We also have a pretty good idea of the dictates of etiquette and what is in a person's best interest. But what sorts of considerations constitute *moral* reasons? What makes something morally right or wrong? The answer to that question is what philosophers call *moral theory*.

It might be that when some people say homosexuality is wrong, they simply mean that they do not like it or they are simply expressing discomfort with the idea. These people may be using the predicate ". . . is wrong" in a purely emotive way. It is highly doubtful, however, that most people who disapprove of homosexuality would say that their disapproval is nothing more than their own subjective discomfort. Most people mean something more, and I think that most of them would agree that when they say it is wrong, they mean that in the sense of "wrong" that we defined in chapter 2. They think that all people, even homosexual people, have good reasons to avoid engaging in sexual activity with people of the same sex. They think that these reasons are not mere conventions like etiquette, that they are not simply matters of prudence (which depend on the individual's goals and preferences), and that these reasons override reasons in favor of having sexual or romantic relations with members of the same sex (such as the fact that they might enjoy it).

So to answer the question of whether or not homosexuality is morally wrong, we must consider questions of moral theory. What is it that makes right actions right and wrong actions wrong? Moral theory is the search for some general criterion or principle that would determine the right thing to do in all circumstances. This is no easy task. Every time a philosopher thinks he has discovered the one thing that makes all right actions right and all wrong actions wrong, someone will come along and present a counter-example—an action that has the essential right-making feature but is nevertheless obviously morally wrong (or vice versa). But we do not need to discover *the* correct moral theory in order to decide whether homosexuality is morally right or wrong. There are several good moral theories that would agree in claiming that homosexuality is morally permissible. We do not need to show which of these theories is better than the others in order to defend the morality of homosexuality. (I will demonstrate that in chapter 10.) On the other hand, there are several moral theories that support the claim that homosexuality is morally wrong. I will show, in the course of this book, why those theories are not very good and should be rejected, starting in this chapter with the divine command theory.[1]

DIVINE COMMAND THEORY OF RIGHT AND WRONG

Judging from the frequency with which we hear biblical references in the slogans and propaganda of the anti-gay activists—such as the now clichéd "Adam and Eve, not Adam and Steve"—much of the moral opposition to homosexuality seems to be driven by religious faith. These people seem to be operating with a moral theory that philosophers refer to as *divine command theory* (DCT). We might formulate a DCT of right and wrong this way:

> *DCT (right/wrong)*: An action is morally wrong if (and only if) it is forbidden by God. An action is morally required if (and only if) it is commanded by God.

We could likewise formulate a DCT of (morally) good and bad:

> *DCT (good/bad)*: An action, character trait, or state of affairs is morally good if (and only if) God approves of it, endorses it, or recommends it. Something is morally bad if (and only if) God disapproves of it or condemns it.

Of course, it is possible that those who have moral objections to homosexuality on religious grounds would deny that they accept anything like DCT. But then their objection would be very puzzling. If the divine command theory is false, then homosexuals could ask why God's disapproval has any relevance to the moral question of homosexuality.

In assessing the religiously based moral objection to homosexuality, we need to ask two questions. First, is DCT itself true? And secondly, if DCT were true, would it support the claim that homosexuality is morally wrong? In other words, do we have good reasons to think that God does in fact disapprove of homosexuality? For the religiously based argument against homosexuality to work, the answer to both questions must be "yes." If the answer to either question is "no," then the religiously based argument fails. It fails if God's will is not what determines right or wrong. It also fails if God does not in fact disapprove of homosexuality.[2] We shall begin with the second question first. Is there any reason to think that God does in fact disapprove of homosexuality?

Before we even ask whether God disapproves of homosexuality, we have to first assume that God exists. An implication of DCT is that if there were no God, then nothing would be morally right or wrong. The theory says that an action is wrong if and only if God forbids it or disapproves of it. If there is no God, then there could be no action that is forbidden or disapproved of by God. So no action could be wrong.

Obviously, those who accept DCT take it as a given that there is a God. Most people who doubt God's existence would also reject DCT. It is perfectly *consistent* to accept DCT and yet deny the existence of God. But if you deny the existence of God and also accept DCT, you would also have to deny that there is any moral right or wrong.[3]

Let us therefore assume, for the sake of argument, that there is a God, and that this God commands and forbids certain sorts of actions. The next question is, What does God *in fact* command and forbid? This is a very difficult question. Even among the faithful, it is hard to find an uncontroversial answer. Believers cannot even agree on *how* to answer this question.

There are some people who claim to be God's authority on earth. They claim to receive messages directly from God. Unfortunately, there is no vetting process to test the legitimacy of such claims. Some of these people are harmless. Others start cults and convince their impressionable followers to do terrible things. Many of them are clearly mentally ill. How can we determine with any reliability whether any one of these self-proclaimed mouthpieces of God *really is* God's appointed spokesperson? Since a large number of them are either frauds or schizophrenics, we need to come up with a better way of determining God's will than through the testimony of individual human beings.

Fortunately for our assessment, most people who make claims about what God commands and forbids appeal to something more tangible than a voice from the heavens that only they can hear. Most of them appeal to scripture. The good thing about scripture is that it is available to everyone, even to the nonbelievers. Scripture gives us something we can use to verify the claims people make about God's will. If someone claims that scripture forbids abortion, we can read through the books and see whether that is actually the case. (It turns out that abortion is not forbidden, at least not in the Bible.)[4] Of course, here we have a new problem: which scripture? No doubt Christians will say that the Bible contains the word of God, while Jews will say only a part of what Christians call the Bible (specifically, the first five books of the Old Testament) contains the word of God. Some will say that the Koran is the word of God, straight from God's mouth, no less. Hindus will point to the Vedas, Sikhs will cite the Guru Granth Sahib, and Zoroastrians will refer to the Avesta. Now it might be that all of these texts will agree on some points, but they disagree on a great many others. Since they are not consistent with each other, they cannot all express the will of God— at least not if we assume that God, being perfect, should be able to make up his mind about these sorts of things.

Perhaps we could put these various scriptures to the test and determine which ones are better. For example, we might test the reliability of the scripture by judging the veracity of the other things claimed in their pages, things other than the claims about what God says, does, or thinks. What about the historical events depicted in these scriptures? Are these stories true? Or do they tell of events that could not have happened or are so fantastic as to be very unlikely to have happened? If a scripture says many things that are false or probably false, then that would seem to be a mark against it. But this will not work. Many of these texts, like the Vedas and the Koran, are strictly doctrinal. There are no historical events described in them. They contain only descriptions of the nature of God, his commands, and our relationship to Him. Even for those scriptures that do contain things other than doctrine, believers will object to this proposed test. At first glance, many of the stories will contain fantastic and unbelievable events. But that is because many of these stories involve miracles. Miracles by their very nature are fantastic and unbelievable. It is the essence of religious scriptures that they tell of events that seem unlikely to have occurred. Miracles, as they say, do not happen every day. A miracle that was very easy to believe, and consistent with everyday experience, would not be a very impressive miracle.

I am at a loss for any test to determine which scripture is more likely to be true. But we can set that question aside for now. Since this book is in English, we can assume that most of the readers (outside of the Indian subcontinent) live in a predominately Judeo-Christian society. That means that most of the anti-gay people we encounter will appeal to the Bible, if they appeal to any scripture at all. So let us assume, for the sake of argument, that the Bible (or major parts of it) is true and expresses God's commands for how we humans should live. As a philosopher, I must point out that we are now assuming a great many things for the sake of argument. We have assumed that the divine command theory is true, that God exists, and that the Bible expresses the word of God. On the other hand, many people in our society, whether anti-gay or pro-gay, already accept those last two claims.

THE BIBLE AND HOMOSEXUALITY

Our next question then is whether the Bible does, in fact, condemn homosexuality. It sure seems to. Anti-gay religious folks tend to point to six passages in particular—the Sodom and Gomorrah story (in Genesis), two pronouncements in Leviticus, and three mentions in the doctrinal parts of the New Testament. Does this mean—assuming that the Bible is the word of God—that God therefore forbids homosexuality? I am no biblical scholar, but some biblical scholars have provided alternative interpretations to these passages.[5]

Let's start with the Sodom and Gomorrah story, which goes something like this: God intends to destroy Sodom and Gomorrah (S & G) because the people there are so wicked. He first sends two men (angels) to seek out any virtuous people and encourage them to flee. Lot sees the two men entering the gates of the town and offers them refuge from the wicked inhabitants who want to sodomize the two strangers. Some have interpreted this to mean that God disapproved of the men of S & G because they wanted to have sexual relations with other men, viz the strangers in Lot's house. Presumably this is something the men of S & G did routinely, and that is why God was so disappointed in them. (The story gives no indication why the women and children of S & G were wicked, but we can ignore that for our purposes.)

How could this story be interpreted so that God does not disapprove of homosexuality? The people were condemned by God because they were wicked; that is pretty clear. But the Bible does not explicitly say that God disapproved of them because they were gay or that their wickedness consisted in them being gay. Maybe their wickedness was meant to be illustrated not by the fact that they wanted to have sex with the men in Lot's house but by the fact that they wanted to *rape* the men in Lot's house. In fact, the Bible itself says, in other passages, that the men of S & G were wicked because they were inhospitable, not because they were gay (Ezekiel 16:48–49, Matthew 10:5–15).

What about the three condemnations of homosexuality in the New Testament? All three of these occur in letters by Paul. These were letters he sent to specific churches responding to specific questions and were meant to guide those people in those places at that time. Some biblical scholars insist that these letters were not intended to be doctrine for all people at all times. For example, in the First Epistle to the Corinthians, Paul tells the people that circumcision is not a requirement for joining the Christian church. It might not seem important now, but at the time Christianity was essentially a Jewish sect. There were some uncircumcised Gentiles, however, who wanted to join. The question was really about whether Christianity should be open to all people or limited only to Jews. It was a very contentious issue at that time, but it is not important to us now. Perhaps the same is true about Paul's condemnations of homosexuality. Maybe there were good reasons to discourage the practice among those people at that time, but those reasons are not relevant for us today. Also, a close reading of the original Greek shows that Paul condemns homosexuality using words that are different from the words he uses to condemn actions that are obviously wrong, like theft or murder. For example, in Romans 1:18–32 the terms used are *atimia* and *aschemosyne*, which are best translated as "unseemly," "dishonorable," or "rude"—or so say the Greek scholars.[6] To be honest, it's all Greek to me.

What about the two places in Leviticus where homosexuality is condemned? Some biblical scholars say that if you look at the context in which the condemnations took place, you find that the surrounding text is banning followers of "The One True God" (i.e., the Jews) from going to pagan temples and making offerings there. Apparently some of these pagan temples engaged in ritual orgies with all sorts of unconventional sexual acts. (Those kinky pagans!) Perhaps the practice being condemned was not engaging in gay sex but engaging in kinky pagan orgies (whether gay or straight). These condemnations take place in the context of purity rules, such as not eating seafood that doesn't have scales or not mixing two different kinds of seeds together. It is safe to say that the God of Abraham probably disapproved of his chosen people attending pagan orgies. He disapproved because it was *pagan* sex. Maybe his disapproval had nothing to do with it being pagan *gay* sex.

Some biblical scholars also question the alleged condemnation of homosexuality on semantic grounds. There was no word "homosexual" in ancient Hebrew (the language of the Old Testament) or ancient Greek (the language of the New Testament). If we were to insist on interpreting the Bible literally, then we could not say that it condemns homosexuality because it does not anywhere explicitly, literally condemn *homosexuality*. Those passages in the Bible that are taken to condemn homosexuality are rather coy about what exactly is being condemned. The text describes these practices in very roundabout ways, such as "lying with a man as one would with a woman." It is unclear to me exactly what that means.

Some scholars also point out that Jesus never condemns homosexuality. There is even one story indicating that Jesus tacitly approved of same-sex relations (Matthew 8:5–13; Luke 7:1–10). A centurion comes to Jesus asking that he heal his "servant." Jesus agrees to go to the centurion's house, but the centurion wants to save Jesus the inconvenience and suggests that he do the healing remotely. Some historians and scholars claim that the Greek word translated as "servant" really meant *same-sex concubine*. Jesus would have known this, but apparently he did not care.

Some people, particularly fundamentalist Christians, object to the notion that we should interpret the Bible. They think that the Bible must be taken literally. But it is very difficult, if not impossible, to understand the Bible without interpretation. Rarely is anything in the Bible univocal and completely unambiguous. Take even the most obvious commandment, "Thou shalt not kill." That seems to be a pretty straightforward condemnation of killing. (We will just assume that it means that thou shalt not kill *people*, and that it was not advocating some kind of vegetarianism.) But there are two obstacles to the simplistic reading of this command. For one thing, the Bible does not consistently forbid killing. In fact, the Bible condones killing in many situations—even as punishment for relatively minor infractions such as adultery. So, according to DCT, we should not kill. And also, according to DCT, we should execute adulterers and blasphemers. Given that execution is a form of killing, then either the Bible is flatly contradictory or we cannot interpret "Thou shalt not kill" as a blanket prohibition of killing.

The other obstacle to this simplistic reading of the commandment not to kill is that, although it is obvious that killing people is generally wrong, it is not at all obvious that killing is always wrong. If an axe-wielding serial killer breaks into your home and is about to attack your family, and the only way to stop him is with deadly force, then I think most of us would agree that killing would be morally okay. Even some pacifists might agree that it is morally permissible to kill in self-defense. (The pacifist could say that absolute nonviolence is an ideal, but it is an ideal that is too demanding to be strictly required. Thus, it is morally *permitted* to use violence if necessary for self-defense, but it would be morally *better* to abstain from violence, even in self-defense.)

Some fundamentalists suggest that this problem could be solved by a more precise translation from the original Hebrew. It should read "Thou shalt not *murder*." But this is no help at all, for the word "murder" simply means *wrongful* killing. In that translation, the commandment is entirely uninformative. Of course thou shalt not wrongfully kill. Duh. One should not *wrongfully* do *anything*. What we need to know, if we are to guide our behavior by this commandment, is which acts of killing are murder (wrongful killing) and which acts of killing are not murder (permissible killing).

Much more could be said on the issue of interpretation and translation, both generally and on the specific passages condemning homosexuality. I do not claim to be especially qualified to have the final word on biblical interpretation. Then again, most of the people who point to the Bible as evidence that homosexuality is morally wrong are not biblical scholars, either. That being said, I suspect that the consensus among experts would be that it is a bit of stretch to claim that the Bible does *not at all* condemn homosexuality. Some of the condemnations can be reinterpreted, but the more straightforward reading of the Bible seems to be at least moderately anti-gay.

Thus, it seems that we can formulate a simple argument against homosexuality based on DCT. If we assume . . .

1. The Bible is the word of God and its doctrines express his divine will.

. . . and we add that . . .

2. The Bible condemns homosexuality.

Then from (1) and (2), it seems to follow that . . .

3. Therefore, God disapproves of, and explicitly forbids, homosexuality.

If we take (3) and add the divine command theory of morality . . .

4. If God forbids or disapproves of an action, then it is morally wrong; if he commands or approves of an action then it is morally right, etc.

. . . then we get the conclusion:

5. Therefore, homosexuality is morally wrong.

That seems to be an open-and-shut case.[7]

But not so fast. There is a problem with this argument, over and above the dubiousness of the many assumptions required. The problem is not that there are any gaps or inconsistencies within the argument itself. The problem is that we could take this same basic argument and apply it to other issues to get absurd results. This critique of the DCT argument against homosexuality uses a method that philosophers call a *reductio ad absurdum* (literally, reducing to absurdity). The reductio ad absurdum works this way: First we start with some theory or argument, in this case DCT or the DCT argument against homosexuality. Then we follow this theory or argument to further conclusions. Eventually we find some conclusions that are obviously false. If a theory entails something that is obviously false, then the theory itself must be false. Similarly, if an argument can be used to derive conclusions that are obviously false, then the argument is not very good.

Here is an example. In an episode of the animated television comedy, *King of the Hill*, Hank's doctor tells little Bobby that the intestinal tract of the average human being is long enough to circle the earth. Hank scoffs, pointing out that if that were true, then in order to digest a meal in twenty-four hours, the food would have to pass through the intestines at over one thousand miles per hour. Hank's objection is a perfect reductio ad absurdum. At the risk of being pedantic, we would formulate the argument this way:

1. If the human intestines were long enough to circle the earth, then food would have to pass through our digestive tract at over

1,000 miles per hour (given that the circumference of the earth is about 24,900 miles).
2. It is obviously not the case that food passes through our gut anywhere near that fast (thank goodness).
3. Therefore, it cannot be the case that our intestines are long enough to circle the earth.

Now let's examine some of the absurdities that can be derived from DCT.

We start by assuming that DCT is true and that the Bible is the word of God. This would mean that everything that is forbidden or condemned in the Bible is morally wrong and anything that is commanded is morally required. The problem is that the Bible forbids many other things besides homosexuality. Some of the things that the Bible forbids are obviously not morally wrong. For example, the Bible explicitly commands that that one should not wear clothing of mixed fibers (Deuteronomy 22:11). (To be precise, it forbids wearing mixtures of wool and linen. Back in those days, before polyester and Lycra, those were about the only two materials for making cloth.) If we start with the assumptions that the Bible is the word of God and that DCT is correct, then we could apply the same argument against wearing fabric blends as we did against homosexuality.

1. The Bible is the word of God, etc.
2. The Bible condemns wearing clothing of mixed fibers.
3. Therefore, God disapproves of, and explicitly forbids, wearing clothing of mixed fibers.

When we combine this with the divine command theory . . .

4. If God disapproves of an action, then it is morally wrong, etc.

. . . we get the following conclusion.

5. Therefore, it is morally wrong to wear clothing made of mixed fibers.

If this conclusion is false, if there is nothing morally wrong with wearing mixed-fiber clothing, then the argument must be flawed. So the question is whether it is morally wrong to wear mixed-fiber clothes. That is a question that the reader will have to ask his or her own conscience. Do think you should avoid wearing such clothes? Should you feel guilty for times in the past when you wore such abominations? Should you punish others who wear mixed fibers?

The religious anti-gay person might point out that the Bible does not condemn wearing mixed-fiber clothing nearly as strongly as it does homosexuality. But that is neither here nor there. Let us grant that, according to DCT, wearing mixed-fiber clothing would be less wrong than homosexuality. It seems pretty obvious to me, however, that wearing mixed-fiber clothing is not wrong *at all*. I don't see how there could be anything morally objectionable about it.

Of course, just because it *seems* obvious that it is not wrong to wear mixed-fiber clothing does not mean that it is not wrong. It might seem odd or silly to be morally opposed to wearing mixed-fiber clothes, but is it crazy? Maybe not. But one does not have to dig very deep into the Bible to find commands that *are* crazy. The ban on mixed fibers is simply a matter of condemning something that seems morally neutral. But there are many places where the Bible condemns actions that seem to be morally right and praises actions that are morally wrong. For example, the Bible says that it morally okay to sell your daughters into slavery (Exodus 21). A virgin who is raped can be forced to marry her rapist (Deuteronomy 22). Adulterers should be stoned to death (Deuteronomy 22). We should not make oaths or vows (Matthew 5).

ARE GOD'S COMMANDS ALWAYS MORAL COMMANDS?

So far, we have defined "morally wrong action" to mean actions that everyone—regardless of his or her own values, preferences, or cultural background—has strong, even overriding, reasons not to do, that these reasons are universal rather than conventional, and that violators deserve punishment. So now the question is, If the Bible condemns homosexuality, does *everyone* have reason to follow the Bible's condemnation? Even homosexuals? What if they are not Christians (or Jews)? What if they are atheists? What reasons can we give these people for obeying the scriptures of a religion they do not accept? It would make no sense for a Muslim to tell me that I must make a pilgrimage to Mecca. I do not practice Islam and I do not believe the writings of the Koran. So what reason would I have to make a hajj, given that there are countless ways I would rather spend my vacation time?

In exploring the religiously based argument against homosexuality, we had assumed (for the sake of argument) that God exists, that the Bible expresses his divine will, and that the divine command theory is true. With all of those assumptions in place, it might seem that everyone would have a reason to obey what it says in the Bible—even atheists. If God exists and the Bible is true, then atheists have good reason to convert. If God exists, then the atheist ought to change his beliefs about the existence of God. But that does not necessarily mean that the atheist (or the former atheist) should also convert to the religious *practices* set forth in the Bible. At any rate, it is not at all clear that he would be a bad person if he does not.

At first glance, it seems that DCT would imply that if God exists, then we all should worship him and follow his commands. God's will determines what is right and wrong; and it is God's will that we should worship him and perform these various rituals and practices. Thus we are morally obligated to do so. Or so it would seem. But what if the Bible itself said that one could be morally a good person without practicing the religious faith of the Bible? If we assume that the Bible is the last word on what is morally right and wrong, and the Bible itself says that we do not have to be practitioners of the faith in order to be morally good, then someone who does not practice the religion of the Bible can still be a good person. And in fact the Bible, or at least the New Testament, says exactly that in the story of the Good Samaritan (Luke 10:29–37).

In this familiar story, a man is attacked by bandits, robbed, beaten, and left for dead by the side of the road. A priest and another man pass by the poor victim but do nothing. Then a Samaritan—a pagan who does not recognize or worship the "One True God"—comes along. It is the nonbeliever who does the right thing, going out of his way to help the man. I take it that the main message of the story is that practicing the proper religious faith is neither necessary nor sufficient to make you a good person. You can practice the faith and yet not be good (as shown by the holy man who passed by the injured victim without helping), and you could be a morally good person without practicing the proper religious faith (as the Samaritan's actions show). An atheist who is a faithful spouse, nurturing parent, hard worker, and honest person and who helps those in need, avoids harming others, and is fair in all of his dealings with strangers is a good person, even though he does not say grace before dinner or go to church on Sundays.

It is possible then, that not everything that the Bible directs us to do is a *moral* command. In other words, not every command in the Bible is meant to give *everyone* an overriding reason to act. Consider, for example, the Ten Commandments. The fifth commandment says, "Thou shalt not kill," and the seventh commandment says, "Thou shalt not steal."[8] Apart from some vagueness and possible exceptions, these are pretty good rules. We might need to qualify them, for example by allowing killing in self-defense, but certainly stealing and killing are almost always morally wrong. It is not unreasonable to think that *every-*

one has an overriding reason not to kill or steal, barring very unusual circumstances.

Now let us contrast that with the third commandment, "Thou shalt keep the Sabbath," and the first (the second part), "Thou shalt not make graven images." Are these *moral* commandments? Does everyone have a reason to keep the Sabbath? Even non-Jews who live in non-Jewish communities? If so, do these reasons override other non–moral reasons? Suppose that I am the only doctor in town and my neighbor breaks a leg on a Saturday? Should I tell him that he will have to wait until sundown before I can set it for him? Or suppose that I am a sculptor by trade and my family is very poor. The only way that I can support them is by making graven images. (I have no other marketable skills, and no one wants to buy my abstract sculptures; they only want sculptures of pagan gods.) Should I let my family go hungry? *Even if* I am not a Christian (or a Jew)?

It seems reasonable that many of these rules are not moral rules but *religious* rules. These include rules about circumcision, abstaining from shellfish, avoiding clothing of mixed fiber, fasting, making burnt offerings, and so on. They only pertain to a certain class of people: the practitioners of that religion (in the case of the Old Testament, the "chosen people," also known as the "Israelites"). If I work on Saturday or make a graven image in my basement, does that make me a bad *person*? Or just a bad *Jew*? (By "bad Jew" I simply mean *not fully observant Jew*, or deficiently Jewish.) These rules can be thought of as the rules that pertain to members of a club, as when a fraternity imposes strange burdens and difficult tasks on new pledges in order for them to demonstrate their commitment to the organization. Some of these rules were created by God so that practitioners could show that they are serious in their worship. The rules are meant to weed out the half-assed practitioners, just as hazing is intended to weed out those pledges who are not willing to make sacrifices to belong to the group.

It is possible that rules concerning homosexuality are meant to be religious rules, like avoiding shellfish or keeping the Sabbath, and not a moral rule. It is meant hypothetically. If you want to be a good Jew (or Christian), then you should not engage in homosexuality . . . or wear mixed-fiber clothes or work on Saturday or whatever. Maybe it is not intended as a moral rule that everyone should follow, regardless of the practices of their community or their religious orientation.

If this interpretation is correct, then homosexuality would not necessarily be morally wrong *even if* we assume that DCT is true and that the Bible is the word of God and that the Bible condemns homosexuality. It would depend on what kind of command it is meant to be. Unfortunately, the Bible is not clear on which rules are moral rules and which rules are intended only for members of the faith. Perhaps this is because the writers of the Bible were not expecting nonbelievers to read it. Paul, in writing his epistles, was not acting as an advice columnist for anyone and everyone who would solicit his opinions. He was acting as an authority for the practitioners of the newly founded religion, Christianity.

To make a DCT against homosexuality work, we would have to prove that when the Bible disapproves of homosexuality, it is meant as a moral command, not just as a special rule for membership of the faith. One could insist that *all* of the rules in the Bible are meant as moral commands without exception, even stuff like not wearing mixed fibers (and so I am a morally bad person for wearing synthetic/cotton blends, regardless of my religious faith). That claim is quite implausible.

The other way to go would be to interpret the biblical ban on homosexuality as one of the moral commands and not one of the merely religious rules. Then the question is how we could determine which commands in the Bible are meant to be moral rules and which are just rules that are intended for members of the faith. Well, in the case of killing and stealing there are obvious reasons why we should not do those sorts of things—reasons that are independent of what God happens to forbid or disapprove. By contrast, there does not seem to be any reason—independently of God's commands—for why we should not eat shrimp, wear cloth blends, or work on Saturday. That is why it is most reasonable to think that these rules are the ones that God made up so that we can show our obedience to the scripture. The seeming arbitrariness of these rules is good reason to think that they are meant as religious obligations and not moral obligations.

If we think that God's forbidding of homosexuality is supposed to be on a par with the moral rules, then we should be able to find some other reason why homosexuality is wrong, other than arbitrary divine fiat. This we will consider in subsequent chapters. But notice that if we take this route, then we are abandoning DCT. If we can find other compelling reasons why people generally would have overriding reasons not to be gay, then it does not matter whether God forbids it or not. It would be wrong anyway. Or it would be wrong even if there were no God or if God had not explicitly disapproved of it.

THE "EUTHYPHRO" OBJECTION TO DCT

The whole question of whether or not the Bible condemns homosexuality, and whether these condemnations were meant to be moral rules or just rules for joining the club, was premised on the assumption that

DCT is the correct theory of what makes an action right or wrong. We accepted DCT for the sake of argument, in order to assess the theory in light of its implications and to test whether it would make a good case against homosexuality, *if* it were true. The results were mixed at best. As we saw, the DCT argument against homosexuality has some weak spots. These problems include the many texts other than the Bible that claim to represent God's will, the wacky and even reprehensible biblical commands, the lack of reasons for atheists or non–Judeo-Christians to follow the rules laid out in the Bible, and the possibility that the biblical condemnation of homosexuality is only a religious rule for members of the congregation. Now we must consider whether we have any reason to accept DCT as a reasonable theory of right and wrong.

DCT says that an action is morally wrong if and only if it is forbidden by God. Presumably, if God is indifferent to some action, then it is neither right nor wrong. For example, if God does not care whether I eat oatmeal or grits for breakfast, then the choice is morally neutral. I am free to eat either one (or both or neither). According to DCT, all moral truths are thus determined by the divine will.

Let us suppose that there is a God—a necessary condition for DCT to be meaningful. Suppose that He is all knowing and all powerful, that He created the entire universe out of nothing, and that He cares about each and every one of us like a father (like a *loving* father, not a deadbeat dad). If all of that were true, then it seems as though we would have good reason to try to make him happy and follow his advice. One reason is that it would be in our interests to do so. If someone is all powerful and all knowing, then it would probably be a good idea for us to do what he says. If you don't do it, he will know. And since he is all powerful, he could make things very unpleasant for you. On the other hand, if you make him happy you might be rewarded. But these are only *prudential* reasons, not moral ones.

Here is an analogy. Suppose a man has a gun to my head and orders me to hand over my wallet. It is in my best interest to do as he says, but that does not make me *morally* obligated to give him my money. Suppose I really don't care about eternal life or whatever other reward God might promise to his faithful. Then I don't have much reason to obey his orders. Machiavelli, for example, said that he would rather go to hell than to heaven because in hell he would be in the company of kings, popes, and princes, while in heaven there would be only beggars, monks, and apostles. One might think it crazy to prefer hell over heaven, but some people also prefer hamburger over lobster, which seems equally crazy to me.

There might, however, be genuinely moral reasons to do as God says. It does not seem unreasonable to say that I have a moral duty to obey the commands of God, assuming that He created me and cares for me, just as I have duties to my parents because they raised me and cared for me. I owe him gratitude and respect, if nothing else. Yet far from supporting DCT, this line of reasoning assumes that DCT is false. That is because it assumes that we have duties to repay kindness and to respect the wishes of those who have cared for us. It would be this duty—a duty of gratitude or a duty to honor one's creator—that would be what gives God's commands their moral authority. This duty, not God's will, would be the ultimate source of morality. Supporters of DCT, however, would have to say that there is no duty to respect and honor those who have cared for us *unless* God commands that we respect and honor those who have cared for us. Thus, the divine command theory cannot be rationalized or supported with any *other* moral considerations. It must be bedrock. According to DCT, we have a duty to follow God's commands simply because they are God's commands and because God's commands constitute what is right and wrong. There can be no further external reasons why we should follow them. Why is killing wrong? Because God said so, and according to DCT, that has to be the end of the explanation.

It is important to understand that, according to this theory, God's approval and commands are what *make* something right or wrong. Nothing is right or wrong until God decides that it is so. What God forbids us to do is wrong, according to DCT, not because God perceives that it is wrong, and then passes that information along to us. If that were the case, then right and wrong would not be determined by God's will but rather God's will would be tracking some morality that exists independently of his will. DCT is not based on God's omniscience but on his omnipotence. He does not figure out or discover what is already wrong. He *decides* what will be right and what will be wrong.

There is a famous objection to this sort of theory that originates with Plato. In one of his dialogues, a character named Euthyphro is discussing piety with Socrates (the hero of most of Plato's dialogues). Euthyphro advocates an account of piety that is very similar to the DCT account of right and wrong. Piety, he says, is whatever is loved by all the gods. Socrates then presents Euthyphro with a challenge: "Is an action pious (or morally right) because the gods love it? Or do the gods love those actions because they are pious (morally right)?" Both Socrates and Euthyphro seem to think that the first option is absurd and so they pass it over rather quickly. Instead, they focus on the second account. The argument against the second definition of piety is not that it is false but that it does not capture the essence of piety. If the gods love things because they have some property of piety, then being god-loved is a mere side effect of piety. The gods' love might be an indicator of whether or not something has this property, but we still have not described what this property is.

More importantly for our purposes, taking the second option amounts to denying DCT. If God approves of certain actions *because* they are morally right, then God's approval is a mere side effect, or indicator of moral rightness. His approval would not make it right but would only reliably track what is right. Since the first option is essentially what DCT claims, we need to consider it a little more carefully than Plato did. What would it mean to say that an action is morally right *because* God praises it, and not the other way around?

One implication of DCT is that God could forbid *anything*, and it would be wrong just because he forbade it. And likewise he could approve of anything, and it would be right just because he approves of it. Any constraint on the sort of things that God could command or forbid would amount to there being some morality that exists independently of God. DCT entails that there is no right and wrong existing independently of God's will.

So if there is no limit to what God can command or forbid, then the only reasons that killing and stealing are wrong, according to this view, is that it *just so happens* that God forbids it. But, if there is no independent morality constraining what God can approve or disapprove of, then he could have commanded or forbidden different things. In that case, different things would be right and wrong. That means that God could conceivably command us to rape our children and torture the innocent, and it would be morally right to do so. God could forbid us from helping the poor or keeping our promises, and it would thereby be wrong for us to help the poor or keep our promises.

The defender of DCT cannot say that God would not do such a thing because he is good. That is to assume that those sorts of things are already morally wrong whether or not God condemns them. (It is no help to say that God approved and disapproved of certain things since the beginning of time. When I say that certain things were morally wrong before God forbade them, I do not mean that they were wrong at an earlier time. I am talking about logical priority, not temporal priority.)

In fact, according to DCT, it does not even make sense to say that "God is good." Since goodness, in this view, is determined by God's approval, saying that God is good would simply mean that God approves of himself or that God follows his own commands. When people say that God is good, I think they mean something more than that. But in order to mean something more than that, we would have to reject DCT. For this reason, even those who believe in God have good reason to reject DCT.

4

DESTINY OR CHOICE? BIOLOGY, SEXUAL ORIENTATION, AND RESPONSIBILITY

Much of the debate today about gay rights and the morality of homosexuality revolves around the question of whether people are born gay or whether they become gay, either through personal choice or environment. For much of the twentieth century, it was assumed that human beings were not born with any particular sexual orientation. Humans were thought to be sexual blank slates. Anyone could grow up to be straight or gay. The standard view, influenced by Sigmund Freud, was that children acquire their heterosexual orientation through family dynamics and a complex process that eventually leads to identification with the parent of the same sex. Homosexuality in males was thought to be the result of overprotective mothers, distant fathers, or overbearing mothers who dominated their meek husbands. Lesbianism was given similar explanations. Of course, if sexual orientation were the result of upbringing, then it would not be chosen, since we do not choose our parents or how we are raised. But it would not be innate. If one could be made to be gay, then one could be made un-gay. The influence of Freudianism has gradually faded, due to the total lack of scientific evidence supporting it, and is now regarded by most scientists as pseudoscientific mythology. Nevertheless, the notion that the sexual orientation of children is up for grabs persists among many lay folk.

This question of whether sexual orientation is innate and inborn or something that can be acquired is taken to be of crucial importance by those on both sides of the debate. Anti-gay activists seem bent on assuming that homosexuality is either chosen or is caused by one's environment. For example, *Conservapedia* (a right-wing Christian conservative rip-off of the ubiquitous *Wikipedia*) has this to say about homosexuality: "The causes of homosexuality are attributable to man's sinful nature, nurture and environment, and personal choice." If homosexuality was the result of choice or the result of upbringing, it would not be innate and so could be reversed. *Conservapedia* denies any biological cause of homosexuality, presumably because that would mean that God intended for some people to be gay.

Supporters of gay rights are more divided on the question of whether homosexuality is, or can be, acquired or chosen. On the one hand, many welcome the idea that their sexual orientation is something that they were born with. For one thing, that would mean that they cannot be blamed for being gay. Nor would it make sense to try to pressure gay people into trying to become straight. A belief in biological causes of homosexuality might also make coming out to one's family easier. Parents won't wring their hands pleading, "What could we have done differently?"

On the other hand, many gay rights activist worry that this whole approach concedes too much to the anti-gay crowd.[1] It could be taken as a denial of responsibility, or even a kind of apology. It is almost as if gay people were saying, "If it *were* a choice we'd change, but it isn't, so we can't." Furthermore, some gay rights activists worry that if we were to discover a biological cause for homosexuality, then people might use this scientific knowledge to try to prevent homosexuality and eliminate homosexuals from society by preventing future generations of homosexuals. If we were to discover a gene for homosexuality, for example, expectant mothers could screen their early-stage embryos and abort fetuses that have the gay gene.

Regardless of these concerns, most people believe that a biological cause of homosexuality would support the case for gay rights.[2] Public opinion is almost equally divided over the question of whether homosexuality is biological or caused by one's environment. About 37 percent think sexual orientation is genetic and fixed at birth while about 37 percent think sexual orientation is malleable and can be chosen or shaped by environment. (About 12 percent believe it is a roughly equal combination of both.) This is quite a shift from thirty years ago when about 56 percent thought it was mostly environmental. Belief in a biological cause of sexual orientation has been found to be highly correlated with acceptance of homosexuality. Sixty-one percent of those polled believed that finding a biological cause of homosexuality would help the cause for gay rights. Along with fostering more sympathetic attitudes about gay people, a biological source might also strengthen the legal case for antidiscrimination laws. Arguing for protected group status would be easier if the group could be identified by objective, scientific criteria.

Those who think that sexual orientation is mostly biological tend to be more tolerant of homosexuality, have better opinions of gay people, and are more supportive of gay rights. Of course, many other factors are positively or negatively correlated with approval of homosexuality and support for gay rights, including religious affiliation, liberal or conservative ideology, and personal acquaintance with someone who is gay. But of all these, the biggest factor is one's belief about the origins of sexual orientation. Thus, it would seem that the best way to get people to accept homosexuality and to support gay rights would be to convince them that homosexuality is biological. That would be a lot easier than getting them to adopt an overall liberal political ideology, curtailing their church attendance, or outing some of their loved ones. Conversely, the best way to get people to disapprove of homosexuality and oppose gay rights is to get them to believe that homosexuality is the result of environment or choice.

In this chapter, we need to consider two questions. First, is sexual orientation innate or can it be shaped by environment or personal choices? Second, what implication does the answer to the first question have for the morality of homosexuality? If homosexuality is not chosen, does that make it morally okay? Conversely, does homosexuality need to be outside of one's control in order for it to be morally okay?

WHAT, IF ANYTHING, IS A "HOMOSEXUAL"?

It might be useful here to pause for a moment to try to define just what it is to be a homosexual. This is not as easy to do as it might seem. The obvious answer is that a homosexual is someone who is sexually attracted to people of the same sex. We might want to add "exclusively," in order to distinguish homosexuals from bisexuals, though folks who morally disapprove of homosexuality are likely to be just as disapproving of bisexuality, or at least the same-sex attractions of bisexuals. But exclusivity seems too strong. If someone is 98 percent attracted to people of the same sex and only 2 percent attracted to members of the opposite sex, I would be inclined to say that that person is gay. So maybe we should say homosexuals are sexually attracted *predominately* to members of the same sex.

However we draw the boundary of homosexual attraction—attracted *only* to members of the same sex, *predominately* to members of the same sex, or having even the *slightest* attraction to the members of the same sex—there are bigger problems with this way of defining homosexuality. For one thing, it is not clear that it must involve attraction.

Also, it is not obvious that it has to be sexual. Consider someone who willingly engages in same-sex *behavior* but is not sexually *attracted* to members of the same sex. This might be someone who is not repulsed by same-sex relations and who willingly engages in gay sex for reasons other than sexual desire. For example, it is a rite of passage for all boys of the Sambia people of Papua New Guinea to perform fellatio on the elder men of the community. It is not really a sexual thing; instead, these rituals are tied to magical beliefs about acquiring manhood. Should we include the boys and men of this community in the category of "homosexual"?

On the other hand, what about people who prefer to be with members of the opposite sex romantically, but are sexually attracted to members of the same sex (or both sexes)? They prefer to have intimate partners of the opposite sex and so are not inclined to live a gay lifestyle, but they nevertheless want—or even prefer—gay sex. These people might have celibate marriages, or they might have open marriages where sex is not an important part of the relationship. Should we call these people homosexuals? The answer to this question is not obvious. What that shows is that our concept of homosexuality is not as clear as we might have thought.

Another difficulty with categorizing people as "gay" or "straight" is that different cultures (or subcultures) define homosexual differently. As some people see it, two men could engage in homosexual activity without both of them being gay. A man who performs fellatio on another man would be considered gay, while the man who receives fellatio from another man would not be considered gay.

For reasons such as this, some people have argued that the concept of homosexuality, as well as other labels for sexual orientation, is an arbitrary social convention.[3] On this social construct theory, "homosexuality" is an artificial category invented to label a set of thoughts, practices, or dispositions. We, as a society—or perhaps influential authority figures in our society—lumped together a certain number of practices and preferences and gave them a label. Once this arbitrary category gets a label, it comes to take on an artificial importance.

This process of labeling is potentially distorting in two ways. One way is that these categories are arbitrary conventions but falsely thought to be real, objective, and universal. We could have lumped together different practices and preferences in different ways, giving us a very different set of sexual-orientation concepts. Or we might have resisted categorizing sexual orientation altogether, in which case we might see sexual preference as more of a continuum. Without rigidly defined categories, sexual preferences might not seem especially important or deep. But once we give labels to these sexual orientation categories, they dictate how we see the world and influence how we interpret the beliefs, attitudes, and activities of others. Categorization creates an artificial reality, which becomes even more real when people try to conform to these categories by adjusting and prioritizing their preferences and practices to fit them.

The other way that this labeling can distort reality is that, once they come to be widely accepted in society, these categories are taken to be defining features of individual identity. Sexual orientation comes to take on an exaggerated importance. With a label, we now think of a homosexual as a kind of person, a way of being, as opposed to simply a guy who likes other guys. We think that homosexuality has a kind of essence, that it pervades the person, in a way that other sexual preferences—such as a preference for brunettes, small-breasted women, or hirsute men—don't. What was originally just a label for a certain set of preferences or practices comes to be constitutive of an individual's identity.

In this socially constructed view, there were no homosexuals, as least not in our sense of the term, until the phrase "homosexuality" was coined in the late 1800s. There were no gay people in Ancient Greece, and therefore no straight people either. This is not just because there were no labels for the term. After all, if that were the argument, then we could easily say that there were no dinosaurs. (There was never a term for those beasts at the time they existed.) The concept of homosexuality does not simply label something that already existed. Rather, in some sense it creates what it labels by changing our perceptions and expectations. People now try to conform to the label by adopting it as a lifestyle or by avoiding all associated thoughts and overcompensating in the opposite direction in order to distance themselves from it.

Of course, the socially constructed theory of sexual orientation is not without its critics. And even if it is true, it would not mean that there are no such things as homosexuals. After all, a socially constructed reality is still real. That means that people who belong to our society and who have been enculturated to our worldview cannot deny that there are homosexuals in this society, even if there are no such things in other cultures with other conceptual schemes. (We will return to the idea of sexuality as a social construct in chapter 5.) Also, even if our categories of sexual orientation are arbitrary, they are not *completely* arbitrary. Maybe we could define the categories differently, or try to avoid categorizing altogether, but some ways of categorizing people into sexual orientations would be incoherent, useless, or simply false. This is in part because there is *some* objective reality onto which we impose our categories, even if our categories distort that objective reality. And it might be that this objective reality has a biological basis. It might be that some people are biologically determined to be into members of the same sex, whether or not we label them as "homosexual."

COMMONSENSE EVIDENCE REGARDING HOMOSEXUALITY AND CHOICE

First, let us consider the phenomenology of sexual orientation and commonsense evidence for or against the claim that sexual orientation is innate. (By "phenomenology" I mean an examination of subjective, first-person experiences.) If sexual orientation were a choice, then presumably it would be a choice either way. That is, gay people chose to be gay while straight people chose to be straight. Also, if homosexuals could change and become straight, then heterosexuals should be equally capable of choosing to be gay. Speaking personally, I do not recall ever having made a choice to be straight. And I doubt that I could choose to be gay, even if (for whatever reason) I had strong incentive to do so. I suspect that most heterosexual people would agree. For me, being straight was not chosen and could not be unchosen.[4] Furthermore, interview-based studies of gay men reveal a consistent pattern of innateness. Most of them report knowing from very early on that they were different from other boys in certain ways and that they could not make themselves straight no matter how hard they might try.[5] It is the same with many, though perhaps not all, lesbian women.

There are also some commonsense reasons to think that we cannot choose our sexual orientation. Homosexuality consists, at least in part, in having sexual desires and romantic feelings for members of the same sex. If homosexuality—as an orientation or disposition—is a choice, then it would have to be possible for us to choose our desires and feelings. But it certainly does not seem that our desires and emotions are voluntarily chosen. A desire or emotion is not something that *you do*; it is more like something that *happens to you*. If I am hungry I may be able to choose not to eat, but I cannot simply decide not to *want* to eat.

It might not even be conceivable that we could choose our desires, at least not all of them. At least some of our desires are simply given and are not subject to choice. That is because what we choose is ultimately based, at least partly, on our desires. (This should not be controversial as long as we take "desire" in a broad sense, one that includes values, intentions, and goals.) Here is an illustration. Suppose you are on a road trip and come to an exit on the open highway. You are faced with a choice. Should you pull over, or should you keep going? The choice you make will be based on your desires. If you are hungry or sleepy, then you might decide to exit for one of those reasons. On the other hand, you may decide to keep driving, despite your hunger or fatigue. But you would do this only because of some other desire you have, such as the desire to get to your destination on time. How would this work if you could choose your desires? Should you choose to be hungry or sleepy? Or should you choose to want to get where you are going as soon as possible? It is hard to see how you could have any basis on which to make *that* decision. At least some of our desires cannot be subject to choice. They serve as basic motives from which all of our deliberation and choices ultimately derive.

On the other hand, it is not as if our desires are completely out of our control. Not only can we usually control whether or not to act on our desires, but sometimes we have at least indirect control over the desires themselves. We might not be able instantly to desire at will, but we can do things to influence our desires, thereby bolstering good desires and gradually extinguishing bad ones. Anyone who has successfully quit smoking can testify to this. Quitting smoking would be easy if one could simply choose not to want to smoke. Obviously, it does not work that way. But if we could not change our desires at all, then quitting smoking would be impossible, at least in the long run. Even if a former smoker were nicotine free for years, he would forever have to worry about relapsing.

Several years ago I stopped smoking. This was not something that just happened overnight. I did not simply wake up one morning with no inclination to smoke. It was my intention to stop smoking, and it happened as a result of concerted efforts. My effort to quit smoking was not merely a matter of choosing different behavior. Part of the aim, and (thankfully) part of the result, was to no longer have any desire for cigarettes. Thus, in some important sense, I chose not to desire cigarettes. It was a choice because 1) my aim was no longer to have the desire, 2) I made an effort to extinguish the desire, and 3) that effort was successful.

Though we might have control over some of our preferences, it would be impossible for us to choose *all* of our preferences since we would have no basis on which to choose them. But we can, and sometimes do, modify some of our preferences voluntarily. The question now is whether sexual orientation is one of those preferences that we can change. Suppose sexual orientation were a matter of choice. If that were true, then gay people (or at least some gay people) consciously cultivate sexual desires for those of the same sex. But why would anyone choose to be gay? What other desire, goal, or intention could possibly motivate that kind of choice? I had many good reasons for wanting to be rid of my desire for cigarettes. I was motivated by desires to save money, to be free from addiction, and to live a long healthy life. What motive would someone have for trying to be gay, given the stigmatization of homosexuality in our society, the rampant discrimination, and the family conflict most homosexuals inevitably face (whether they stay in the closet or come out)? The only reasonable explanation is that gay people (or at least most gay people) do not choose to be gay.

These reasons for thinking that homosexuality is not and cannot be chosen are based on first-person experience (most of us could not choose to have a different sexual orientation) and on commonsense intuition (there would be no motive for choosing to be gay). But there is also empirical evidence that sexual orientation is not so malleable.[6] While growing up, most gay people experience plenty of incentives to try to be straight: social pressure, religious beliefs, and family obligations, just to name a few. Many young gay people try to make themselves straight and try to live a straight life. But most of them fail, and those who manage to live a straight life are generally not very happy. Some conservative psychotherapists offer "conversion therapy," to try to help gay people become straight. But there are good reasons to think that these "therapies" do more harm than good.

In 2003, psychologist Robert Spitzer made a big splash publishing an article reporting the success of conversion therapy.[7] Of the 200 individuals studied who had undergone the therapy, Spitzer reported that 66 percent of the men and 44 percent of the women were successfully living heterosexual lifestyles. There were, however, many problems with the study. In particular, the subjects studied were overwhelmingly politically conservative Christians with strong motivation to exaggerate the success of their therapy. Spitzer made no attempt to measure deception or self-deception. Also, Spitzer did not interview any of his subjects prior to therapy. (For all he knows, most of them might have been bisexual before the therapy.) And there were no follow-up studies to test the long-term effects of the therapy.[8]

Meanwhile, there are plenty of reasons to think that conversion therapy is snake oil at best. No mainstream psychological or psychiatric organizations recognize the treatment as legitimate. There are also many high-profile cases of its failure. One especially notable example is the case of George Rekers. He was one of the most well-known practitioners of conversion therapy and one of its biggest advocates—until he was caught returning from vacation with a gay male escort. Former "patients" have successfully sued practitioners on the basis of fraud and abuse. One prominent practitioner, Arthur Goldberg, who is not a licensed therapist, founded his conversion therapy organization, Jonah, after finishing a prison sentence for financial fraud. The plaintiffs in these cases report humiliating techniques. One form of "therapy" required them to strip naked and beat effigies of their mothers. Another victim reported that conversion "therapist," Alan Downing (Goldberg's business partner), "had him remove his clothes and touch himself, saying it would help him reconnect with his masculinity."[9] The state of California has banned the use of "conversion therapy" on minors, and in 2013, a federal appeals court, in a unanimous decision, upheld the law on the basis of the ineffectiveness and potential harm of the practice.[10] New Jersey has since also banned the practice on minors. In the summer of 2013, Alan Chambers, conversion therapist and president of the Christian ex-gay group Exodus International, admitted that ex-gay therapy had about a 99.99 percent failure rate. Mr. Chambers had the moral decency to shut down the practice and even offered an apology to the gay community.[11]

SCIENTIFIC EVIDENCE I: THE GENETIC CASE

Common sense and introspection give us reasons to doubt that sexual preference is under a person's control. But commonsense intuitions are sometimes false and introspection is often unreliable. It is possible, however unlikely, that I am deluded in believing that I could never have chosen to be gay. It is also possible that failures of conversion therapy are due to weakness of will, or maybe we just have not yet found the proper methods. A stronger case could be made for the claim that sexual orientation is innate and fixed if we could demonstrate biological causes. (Most of the evidence I will review explores the causes of male homosexuality. This is partly because less research has been done on homosexuality in women but also because the results of studies of women are more complicated. I discuss the special case of lesbians in a separate section below.)

The biological evidence indicating innateness of human sexual orientation comes in two forms: genetic evidence and physiological evidence. The genetic evidence involves patterns of inheritance of homosexuality. If homosexuality tends to run in the family, then there is good reason to think that it is genetic. And if it is genetic, then obviously it is innate, since we cannot choose our DNA, and the environment cannot change our DNA. Physiological evidence consists of physical differences between gay and straight men or between gay and straight women. In particular, physiological evidence for sexual orientation should involve differences in the nervous system or the endocrine system, since those

structures have the most influence over our thoughts, desires, and behavior.

Of course genes do not cause our desires and dispositions directly
but only through some intermediary causes. The only thing that genes
do is make proteins. DNA can affect our thoughts, dispositions, and
behaviors only by causing our bodies to develop or to function in certain
ways. So if there is a genetic cause of homosexuality, then there must
also be a physiological cause. Nevertheless, the genetic *evidence* is independent of the physiological evidence. We can be fairly certain that a
trait is genetic even if we don't know the exact physiological mechanisms through which the gene causes the trait. On the other hand, it is
possible that there are physiological differences between straight and
gay men that are not caused by genetic differences. And it is possible
that there could be more than one cause of homosexuality, even when
we consider male or female homosexuality exclusively.

Let us start with the genetic evidence. The rate of homosexuality in
the general population is probably about 8 percent.[12] The prevalence of
homosexuality within the population is important in genetic studies because it establishes a baseline. When we say that a trait runs in the
family we mean that when one family member has the trait, others in
the family are more likely to also have that trait. "More likely" means
more likely *than the general population*. For this reason, we will assume
that the rate of homosexuality in the general population is 10 percent,
even though it is probably a little lower than that. By assigning a relatively high number, we make it harder to find a genetic link. That way,
if we find evidence that homosexuality runs in the family, we can be
fairly certain that it is because of a genetic link and not the result of
chance or sampling error.

Let us start with statistics for siblings who are not genetically related—in other words, adopted children who were raised together. If
homosexuality is caused by environment and not genes, then there
should be a higher rate of homosexuality among biologically unrelated
siblings, since they will have shared roughly the same environment
growing up. It turns out that the genetically unrelated siblings of gay
people are no more likely to be gay than anyone else. This is a strong
indication that being gay is not caused by one's upbringing. So much for
the Freudian view.

What about siblings who are genetically related? If biological relatives of homosexuals are more than 10 percent likely to be gay, then
there is probably some genetic cause. Let us start with identical twins,
since they have exactly the same set of genes. Statistically, if one male
identical twin is gay, then his twin brother is about 50 percent likely to
be gay.[13] In technical terms, we say that the *concordance rate* of homo-

sexuality among identical twins is 50 percent. That is five times more than the baseline and so we have very good reason to think that homosexuality is genetic. When we look at non–identical twins, we see that there is about a 20–25 percent concordance rate. This fits rather nicely with the 50 percent concordance rate found with identical twins. Since non–identical twins have about half of the same genes, their concordance rate should be about half that of identical twins, who share all of the same genes.

Further studies of family patterns show that gay men are also significantly more likely to have maternal uncles who are gay. This is a common inheritance pattern that indicates an X-linked genetic source. Since men have only one X chromosome, which they receive from their mother, the maternal uncle pattern suggests that at least some of the genes involved in homosexuality are located on the X chromosome. A DNA analysis of non-twin gay brothers found a statistically significant correlation between homosexuality and shared genes on a particular portion of the X chromosome, a region labeled Xq28.[14] It would be oversimplifying to say that Xq28 is the "gay gene." But this is evidence that genes in this region might have some role in sexual orientation. Follow-up studies on the role of Xq28 have yielded mixed results. But that does not weaken the evidence that homosexuality is *somehow* genetic.

WOULDN'T EVOLUTION SELECT AGAINST A GAY GENE?

One puzzle about the genetic explanation is that, if homosexuality were genetic, we should expect that the genes for homosexuality would eventually be eliminated from the human population through the process of natural selection. Gay men and women would be likely to produce fewer offspring since they are disinclined to engage in reproductive (i.e., heterosexual) sex. Even in societies where opposite-sex pairings are mandatory—as for example, in societies with arranged marriages— gay people in opposite-sex relations would presumably be much less enthusiastic about performing their marital duties. Though they could probably manage to produce children, they would still have fewer children on average than heterosexuals. Over multiple generations, gay genes would eventually be eliminated from the population.

Just because a certain trait is selected against, however, does not necessarily mean that the genes that cause that trait are also selected against. There may be other factors that select in favor of that gene. Consider sickle cell anemia, a painful and debilitating condition caused by abnormal red blood cells. This potentially fatal condition should certainly be selected against, especially when modern medical treatments are not available. But the *genes* for sickle cell provide fitness-enhancing benefits, and thus they have been favored in natural selection. This is because those who are carriers for sickle cells (those who inherit one sickle cell gene and one normal gene) have a greater resistance to malaria. That is why sickle cell anemia is found almost exclusively in those whose ancestors lived in tropical Africa.

As with sickle cell anemia, there is some reason to think that the genes that cause homosexuality might provide some fitness-enhancing traits to those people who are not gay. Women with gay brothers, for example, tend to have more children than women without any homosexual relatives.[15] It seems that those genes that tend to make a man gay also tend to make a woman more fertile. Thus, the genes for homosexuality will avoid elimination by natural selection as long as the increased fertility of the sisters of gay men outweighs the decreased number of offspring sired by their gay brothers.

WHY NOT 100 PERCENT?

Another puzzle for the genetic theory of homosexuality involves the 50 percent concordance rate between identical twins. If being gay were genetically caused, then shouldn't the concordance rate for identical twins be 100 percent? (And shouldn't the concordance rate for nonidentical twins be about 50 percent?) After all, identical twins have exactly the same genes, so if one of them has the gay gene, then the other must have the gay gene as well. The 50 percent concordance rate seems too high for homosexuality not to be genetically caused but too low for it to be entirely genetic. Perhaps having the gay gene is only a necessary, but not a sufficient, condition for being gay. Those who lack the gay gene simply grow up straight, while those who have the gay gene could grow up either straight or gay. If genes only made homosexuality possible but not inevitable, then we would still need an explanation for why a certain individual with the gay gene become gay while another with the gay gene does not. It could even be that those with a genetic predisposition for homosexuality become gay because of environment or personal choice. Some anti-gay conservatives have argued exactly that, insisting that the lack of 100 percent concordance for homosexuality among identical twins is evidence that sexual orientation is not biologically determined, even though there is some genetic influence.[16] This argument, however, relies on ignorance about biology.

It is not unusual for a condition to be genetic and yet have a less than perfect concordance rate. For example, type 1 diabetes occurs in childhood when insulin-producing cells in the pancreas spontaneously die off. Unlike type 2 diabetes, this is a genetic condition that has nothing to do with diet or environment—and obviously children do not choose to be diabetic. Yet the concordance rate for type 1 diabetes in identical twins is even lower than it is for homosexuality. The fact is that identical twins are not usually truly identical, even at birth.

The expression "identical twins" refers to twins that started out as one zygote—one egg cell fertilized by one sperm cell. Sometime after the zygote has multiplied into a small colony of a few dozen fetal stem cells, and before any of the cells start to form anatomical structures or differentiate into specialized tissue types, the blob of fetal cells divides into two blobs of fetal cells, which then go on to grow into two different fetuses, two distinct babies, and eventually two separate people. Since identical twins came from the same original egg and sperm combination, they should have exactly the same set of genes—*theoretically*. But biological facts are rarely as neat and clean as that. Since identical twins are never literally identical, we should avoid confusion by using the more technical term, *monozygotic* twins.

Sometimes monozygotic twins deviate from each other genetically.[17] This, however, is very rare and so it could not explain how monozygotic male twins could be 50 percent discordant for homosexuality. Recent work in biology has revealed another way that identical twins can be born differently, even if their DNA is the same. There are complex molecular processes that control the *expression* of genes. Discoveries of these processes have resulted in a newly emerging field of study in biological referred to as *epigenetics*. Epigenetics are modifications of our genetic material that switch genes on or off without altering the underlying gene sequence itself. This is done by the use of various epigenetic "markers"—molecules that are attached to the chromosome at specific places and instruct the cell whether or not to use nearby genes.[18] It might be helpful to think of the genes in a cell as a textbook and the epigenetic markers as the highlights and marginal notes that a reader might add. Some epigenetic changes are relatively permanent (like notes written in pen or text marked with a highlighter) while others are more temporary (like notes written in pencil or on sticky notes).[19]

Cell specialization is one of the phenomena controlled by epigenetic mechanisms. The early embryo consists of stem cells that have the potential to develop into any cell of the human body. This is because virtually all the genes are switched "on" in the early embryo. As cells develop into particular kinds of tissues—nerve cells, blood cells, skin cells, and so on—epigenetic markers essentially shut down the genes for all biological functions except those performed by that type of cell. Other epigenetic changes, however, are more subtle.

Shortly after fertilization, most of the epigenetic markers contained on the DNA of the egg and the sperm are erased, effectively changing the egg cell into a stem cell. Occasionally, however, some epigenetic markers escape erasure. For example, pregnant women who are extremely malnourished during their first trimester tend to give birth to children of normal weight. This is because epigenetic markers, in response to the lack of nutrients, were put in place to alter the fetus's metabolism, allowing it to squeeze more energy out of the few available calories. When these children grow up, these epigenetic modifications tend to result in obesity. What is really interesting, however, is that women with this epigenetically modified metabolism tend to give birth to children of higher than average weight. The epigenetic modifications altering their metabolism were passed down to their children. Nevertheless, there has been no change to the genetic code itself.

Epigenetic mechanisms could easily explain how homosexuality could be 100 percent genetic[20] even though there is only a 50 percent concordance for homosexuality in identical twins. It could be that about half of the men who have the genes that cause homosexuality are not gay because those genes are not *expressed* in that individual. To put it in somewhat oversimplified terms, it could be that the gay gene is turned "off" in about half of the people who have it.

SCIENTIFIC EVIDENCE II: THE PHYSIOLOGICAL CASE

The evidence for genetic causes of homosexuality is fairly strong, though more work needs to be done to find the exact genetic causes. A more complete theory should involve physiological differences between gay and straight people as well as genetic differences. So let us now turn to empirical evidence for physiological causes of sexual orientation.

Some of the physiological differences are subtle, only weakly correlated with sexual orientation, and lack any obvious causal connection with sexual or romantic desires. For example, gay men and lesbians are both about 50 percent more likely to be left-handed than straight men and women. About 25 percent of gay men have a counterclockwise hair pattern on the back of their head, as opposed to about 8 percent of the general population. Also gay men, like most straight women, tend to have index fingers that are longer than their ring fingers. For most straight men, and many lesbians, the ring finger is longer.[21]

Of course, this does not mean that if a man is left-handed or has longer ring fingers, then he is gay. Although the correlation is statistically significant (in other words, unlikely to be mere coincidence), it is still far less than 50 percent. Plenty of gay men, most of them in fact, have clockwise hair patterns; and some straight men have counterclockwise hair patterns. By contrast, there is approximately 100 percent correlation between being sexually and romantically attracted to members of the same sex and being homosexual. Although these physiological differences between gay and straight people have nothing to do with sexual orientation, the fact that there are such statistically significant differences is evidence of a biological cause of homosexuality, which in turn is evidence that sexual orientation cannot be chosen. After all, we cannot choose our finger lengths or the whorl patterns on our head. If these things are linked to homosexuality, then it is likely that homosexuality is likewise not something we choose.

Not all of the physiological correlations with homosexuality are unconnected with romantic attraction or sexual desire. The most interesting difference between gay and straight men involves a region of the brain referred to as the *interstitial nucleus of the anterior hypothalamus*, or INAH3. This is a tiny region located in the hypothalamus, a grape-sized structure that links the brain to the endocrine system.[22] The hypothalamus is made up of many smaller structures, each of which is involved in regulating activities of the body that are not under conscious control. Functions of the hypothalamus include control of heart rate, blood pressure, sweating and shivering (heat regulation), feelings of thirst and hunger, menstrual cycles, and sexual desire and arousal. It is because of the hypothalamic involvement in sexual desire and other basic drives[23] that the biological difference between of the INAH3 of gay and straight men is especially interesting.

The average size of the INAH3 in men is significantly larger than the average size in women. Examining the brains of gay men, neurologists have discovered that the size of the INAH3 in gay men seems to be closer to that in average women. The original study was widely criticized at the time, in part because all of the gay men studied had died of AIDS (making it possible that the smaller brain structure was the result of the disease). Follow-up studies, however, have generally tended to support the original finding.[24]

It is important to keep in mind that homosexuality is a sexual orientation. It may be *caused* by biological differences, but it is not *constituted* by these biological differences. If a man has all of the physiological and genetic factors associated with homosexuality (in particular, the Xq28 gene and the smaller INAH3), but he is not physically or romantically attracted to other men, then he is not a homosexual. These biological and physiological features are only *correlated* with being gay. It is conceivable that the difference in the human brains of gay and straight men is not the cause of homosexuality but the result of homosexual activities or lifestyles.

The brain is surprisingly flexible; it can change shape through our lifetimes as a result of our actions, thoughts, and experiences. Neuroscientists refer to this as *plasticity*. For example, London taxi drivers develop a significantly larger hippocampus than other people. This is because the hippocampus is involved in spatial memory and because London is a huge city with a very chaotic, random arrangement of streets. The observed difference in INAH3 size between gay and straight men, however, is almost certainly not the result of their different thoughts and behaviors. Laboratory experiments have shown that sexual behavior does not alter the size or structure of the INAH3 specifically or the hypothalamus generally (though it may be affected by prenatal environment). So the far more likely explanation is that *all* of the anatomical differences, both in the brain and in the more incidental features like finger lengths and hair whorls, are mostly the result of genetics rather than experience or choice, especially given the independent evidence for a genetic link (viz, inheritance patterns and twin concordance).

MALE BIRTH-ORDER EFFECT

Although there is good evidence that sexual orientation is genetic, there is also evidence that homosexuality might have nongenetic causes. One interesting piece of evidence is the observed correlation between birth order of males and their sexual orientation.[25] Basically, each son born of the same woman is 33 percent more likely to be gay than the previous son.[26] (This effect applies only to males. There is no observed pattern of birth order and homosexuality in women.) Some researchers go so far as to claim that this is the strongest predictor of sexual orientation. The effect is found only in biologically related brothers, regardless of whether they were raised together. It is not found in adopted brothers, stepbrothers, or in half-brothers with different biological mothers and raised together. If having older brothers with the same mom is what causes a man to be gay, then homosexuality would not be genetic, since birth order cannot affect one's genes. The male birth-order effect is also independent of childhood experiences, parental treatment, or any other aspect of one's environment growing up. That leaves only environmental factors in the womb.

At this point, scientists can only speculate about the causal mechanisms that explain this phenomenon. The most popular theory is that each time a woman is pregnant with a male fetus, there is a chance that her body will recognize the presence of male hormones in her womb. If her body recognizes these hormones and takes them to be foreign materials, it might take steps to reduce or eliminate them by creating antigens. Though hormones cannot pass through the placental barrier, antigens can, and if anti-testosterone antigens enter the fetal bloodstream, it could reduce the level of male hormones in the developing fetus. This in turn might lead to a smaller INAH3, which could then influence sexual orientation (as well as some of those incidental physiological differences between straight and gay people).

Male birth order, however, cannot explain all cases of male homosexuality. For one thing, there are some first-born sons who are gay. Maybe other factors can influence fetal hormone levels besides anti-testosterone antigens; or there may be multiple causes of (male) homosexuality, some genetic and some prenatal. But either way, the birth-order effect adds to the evidence indicating that sexual orientation is innate. It is just as impossible to choose one's birth order as it is to choose one's genes. And since the effect is seen in biological brothers who are raised separately, it must have something to do with fetal development in utero, not in one's environment growing up. Whether caused by genes or by environmental factors in the womb, it seems that gay men are born that way.

SCIENTIFIC EVIDENCE III: THE EPIGENETIC THEORY

There is a new theory of the biological causes of homosexuality, one that might help to unify the seemingly conflicting evidence of genetics, hypothalamic structures, and birth order. According to the new theory, homosexuality is primarily epigenetic.[27] It is the result of epigenetic modifications to the genome that alter the fetus's sensitivity to hormones.

Human fetal development into male or female is caused by hormones in the fetal environment. In an XX fetus there is usually a greater relative proportion of estrogen to testosterone, while in an XY fetus there is usually a greater relative proportion of testosterone to estrogen. Though that is how it usually works, hormone levels in the womb can vary for many reasons, including stress or medical conditions of the pregnant mother. Interestingly, this does not generally affect the sexual development of the fetus. An XX fetus can still develop as female even if there are unusually high levels of testosterone, and an XY fetus can still develop as male even if there are unusually low levels of testosterone. So hormone levels do not tell the whole story. There are also epigenetic changes that make most XX fetuses extra sensitive to estrogen and less sensitive to testosterone. Epigenetic changes to XY fetuses do the reverse.

Homosexuality, according to this new theory, results when these epigenetic markers survive erasure during conception. In male homosexuals, some of the epigenetic markers that reduce sensitivity to testosterone, inherited from the mother's DNA, are still present on the male fetus's DNA. Likewise, female homosexuality could be caused by epigenetic markers for increased sensitivity to testosterone, inherited from the father's DNA, that escape erasure. (Some news stories and blog entries on the new theory contained the misleading headline "Homosexuality is not Genetic," indicating that scientists have concluded just that. In a narrow sense of "genetic," that is correct. This theory makes no reference to a gay gene or genes. But homosexuality would still be caused by the *expression of* genes.)

The beauty of this theory is that it might be able to unite empirical evidence for conflicting explanations of homosexuality. These epigenetic markers are inherited, so homosexuality might run in the family, even if there is no gay gene. This theory also claims that homosexuality is caused by response to hormones in the fetal environment, so birth order could play a role as well. Although scientists are still working to find a compete explanation, all of the empirical evidence points to innate biological causes occurring before birth. Sexual orientation, at least for most people, is biological and innate.

BUT HOW DO ANY OF THESE THINGS MAKE SOMEONE GAY?

There is still a puzzling gap in these biological explanations of homosexuality. How is it that genes or tiny differences in a tiny brain structure could actually cause one to be gay? Genes do not cause thoughts, feelings, or behaviors, at least not directly. They only make proteins, and proteins are not the kinds of things that can represent the content of our desires and emotions. Thus, sexual orientation cannot be coded in one's genes. This is not to deny that genes could be part of the ultimate cause, but it could be only a remote link in a very long causal chain.

The brain is a much more proximal cause of our thoughts, feelings, and actions. And, unlike the genome, the brain is able to represent the contents of our thoughts and preferences (coded in patterns of neural activity). Nevertheless, there still seems to be something missing. It is hard to see how the contents of our sexual desires and romantic feelings could be coded in the brain already at birth. How could a newborn baby's brain already be preprogrammed to prefer romantic intimacy with men before the baby has had any experience of men and women? There probably are some innate sexual drives that arise around puberty, but children are not born knowing the physiological difference between men and women. And much of what we take to be markers of gender are cultural and superficial, such as hairstyle or dress. Inborn emotions, desires, and drives, by contrast, tend to be very basic. We are all born with systems in the brain that make us desire food, but no one is born with a preference for pizza, rogan josh, or beef teriyaki. Our particular tastes can only be developed through experience.

There are, however, explanations that can fill this causal gap between structures in the brain and sexual orientation. The most prominent and most plausible theory is the *exotic becomes erotic* theory (EBE).[28] The general idea behind the theory is that what is caused by inborn physiological differences (such as the smaller INAH3) is not sexual orientation itself, which requires at least some experience in order to learn about gender differences. Instead, the subtle differences in the hypothalamus influence some basic disposition or temperament in early childhood. The child's temperament affects the sorts of activities and experiences he or she will have growing up, which in turn will eventually direct his or her sexual desires and romantic feelings one way or the other.

According to EBE, boys and girls have innate preferences for different sorts of activities. Because of this, the typical boy will play mostly with other boys and will come to identify with boys. Girls will be seen as different or alien. The same is true for girls. They will play mostly with other girls, and boys will come to be seen as alien. That which is unfamiliar tends to arouse tension and fascination. As puberty approaches, this fascination is transformed into infatuation and sexual arousal. There also seems to be an innate mechanism causing people to be sexually unattracted to those who were familiar during childhood. This is why children who were raised together are usually not sexually interested in each other when they reach puberty.[29] This innate psychological mechanism probably evolved as a way to prevent incest and keep the gene pool broad. Boys are familiar to the boy, and so he is not aroused by them; girls are strange and exotic, unfamiliar, exciting. This excitement translates into romantic feelings and physical attraction. The same is true for most girls.

The explanation of homosexuality is thus indirect. The genetic and physiological determinants of homosexuality do not cause a preference for men or women per se. They only cause certain dispositions and temperaments. In the case of boys, something in the genes or in the brain may cause an aversion to roughhousing. These boys do not enjoy the aggressive physical play—wrestling, punching, and contact sports—that most boys do. Instead they prefer gentler pursuits. These boys will be more inclined to play tea party with the girls than to play dodgeball with the boys. They then come to feel at ease with the girls, while the other boys are seen as alien and strange. This exoticness of the boys becomes "eroticness" once puberty starts. Similarly, some small difference in the brain of the young lesbian-to-be makes her prefer rough play. She hangs out with the boys and so other girls seem exotic.

Empirical evidence for this theory is compelling. Sixty-three percent of gay men and gay women report having engaged in non–gender conforming behavior as children, compared to only 10–15 percent of straight men and women. On a more anecdotal level, many gay people say that they knew they were "different" from a very early age. But it is unlikely that prepubescent children could know they were gay when puberty was still several years away. This theory explains that phenomenon. Gay men were different from their boyhood peers, not in sexual orientation but in their interests and temperaments.

It is important to note that this does not mean that sexual orientation is caused by experience, only that the causes of mature sexual orientation are mediated by experience. If a boy is already predisposed to be straight, then playing with girls will not make him gay. A boy could play with girls without necessarily feeling that he belongs among them. Similarly, if a boy is predisposed for homosexuality and has a preference for "girlish" activities, making him play roughly with other boys is unlikely to prevent him from growing up gay. He can play contact sports without it feeling natural, and without identifying with his male peers for whom rough play is a deeply ingrained drive. If, in a misguided attempt to mold their sexual orientation, parents force children to engage in activities that feel highly unnatural to them, it will almost certainly do more harm than good. Instead of growing up gay, these children are likely to grow up to be loners and misfits . . . and still gay.

DON'T FORGET THE LADIES

One might wonder why most of the scientific evidence for biological causes of homosexuality involves male homosexuals. What about lesbians? This is a difficult question, and I can only suggest a few possible answers. Part of it is that we live in a male-dominated society and so women are routinely understudied in medical and biological research.[30] But there is more to it than that. The scientific research that has been conducted on women's sexuality has yielded confusing results. The data from studies of male sexuality, by contrast, is pretty straightforward and easy to interpret.

Here is one example. When male test subjects view heterosexual pornography, lesbian pornography, gay male pornography, and ape pornography (films of chimpanzees having sex), the straight men get physically aroused by the straight and the lesbian sex while the gay men get aroused by the gay sex. Neither gay nor straight men are aroused by chimpanzee sex. Also, the subjective reports men give of what turns them on tends to match very closely their physiological response. What is going on in their heads reliably tracks what is going on in their pants.

Things are very different, however, with women. First, most women, straight or gay, become physically aroused by films of straight sex, lesbian sex, gay male sex, and even chimpanzee sex. More importantly, what women say they find sexually arousing deviates significantly from their physiological response.[31]

One possible explanation for the deviation of self-report from physiological response is that, traditionally and even in today's society, women are discouraged from fully and freely expressing their sexuality. Thus, they have repressed many of their true sexual desires or interests, which are revealed by the physiological responses. Another explanation is that, because the male sex organs are external, men are constantly aware of when they are aroused. Thus men are more in touch with their sexual desires and preferences. Either explanation implies that the physiological response is the true expression of what women really want sexually. But if that were the case, we would have to conclude that most women want to have sex with apes, and that is not plausible. Instead, we should assume that a woman's report about her sexual arousal in response to stimuli is accurate, unless we have good independent evidence indicating otherwise. On that assumption, women's physiological responses are not closely related to their sexual desires.

Perhaps the best explanation for the mismatch of physiological and psychological arousal in women is that a woman's physical arousal has a very different function from a man's physical arousal. The biological function of a man's erection is for him to act on his sexual desires. Thus his psychological feelings of lust are highly correlated with his physical erection. The biological purpose of physical arousal in women (in particular, lubrication of the vaginal walls) might have a very different biological purpose. It is to prevent injury during coitus.[32] Thus a woman's physical arousal might be a response not to her own lustful desires but to the anticipation of intercourse, even unwanted intercourse.[33]

This explanation, if true, is still incomplete. It would explain why women are aroused physically by gay male sex and even chimpanzee sex. Seeing an erect male penis causes an anticipation of penetration. But that does not explain why most women are physically aroused by girl-on-girl sex, whether they are lesbians or straight. The best explanation for physiological arousal to lesbian sex is that women's sexuality seems to be more flexible than men's.

Studies based on interviews with lesbian women reveal two distinct patterns of sexual identity.[34] Many lesbians experience their sexual orientation as fixed, permanent, and innate. They report having been "different" from other girls early on. This is very similar to the experience of most gay men. Other lesbians, however, describe their sexual orientation as a self-conscious choice. These reports are supported by anecdotal evidence of famous women who chose to be lesbians. In the late 1990s, for example, Ellen DeGeneres dated actress Anne Heche, who had previously been heterosexual. Melissa Etheridge spent twelve years with a woman who had had been previously married to a man. The mayor of New York, Bill de Blasio, is married to "former lesbian" Chirlane McCray. This is not to say that all or even most women can simply choose their sexual orientation, or that all or most women are really bisexual. Many heterosexual women and many lesbians do not and cannot choose to go the other way. But it does seem that, for at least some women, sexuality is more fluid and more flexible than it is for men.

IS CHOICE RELEVANT TO THE MORALITY OF HOMOSEXUALITY?

Now the question is to what extent it matters, morally, whether homosexuality is voluntarily chosen. People who believe that homosexual orientation is innate and has a biological source tend to be more accepting of homosexuality and more supportive of gay rights. Conversely, people who believe that homosexuality is not innate tend to disapprove of homosexuality and tend to oppose gay rights. This implies that most people believe, at least implicitly, that *if* being gay were not innate, then it *would be* morally wrong. The question that we need to ask at this point is, What is the connection between voluntary choice and the rightness or wrongness of actions?

At first glance, it might seem obvious that something cannot be morally wrong if it was not chosen. We can only be responsible for things we do voluntarily. We do not generally hold people responsible for things they cannot choose or that are beyond their control. For example, if a man robbed a bank while sleepwalking, we should not hold him accountable and would not punish him (though of course, he would still have to give the money back). There are exceptions to this. Someone under the influence of drugs or alcohol might not be acting voluntarily, but we still hold him responsible. But that is only assuming that he made a voluntary choice to get intoxicated. If someone slipped drugs into his coffee without his knowing, we should not blame him for anything that the drugs made him do.

We must, however, distinguish the wrongfulness of actions from the blameworthiness of the person doing it. Consider a kleptomaniac, who steals against his own desires and intentions. Assuming that he truly cannot control his compulsive behavior, we should not hold him accountable for his theft. He may need therapy or medication, but he does not deserve punishment. That does not mean, however, that what he did was not wrong. Even though it would be unfair to punish him for doing it, stealing is still morally wrong. So the fact that homosexuality is innate and not chosen does not imply that homosexuality is not wrong, only that one cannot be blamed for being a homosexual. (I will argue throughout this book that homosexuality is not wrong. The reason why it is not wrong, however, has nothing to do with it being involuntary.)

There is an ambiguity in the notion of what it is to be a homosexual. On the one hand, when we say that someone is a homosexual, we mean he or she is sexually or romantically attracted primarily to people of the same sex. These feelings and desires, or the disposition to have such feelings or desires, is what is innate. That they are not chosen does not matter morally since we do not normally think of thoughts, feelings, or preferences as being morally wrong.[35] Wrongness is a feature of actions, not mental states or dispositions. No one chooses to be gay, but people do choose to engage in homosexual activities. And I should think that supporters of gay rights would want to do more than just say that gay people should not be *blamed* for their behavior. They should want to say that there is nothing morally *wrong* with the behavior itself.

Is there any reason to think that homosexual behavior is not chosen? Actions that are not chosen are those that are done by accident, due to ignorance, or out of compulsion. These are the conditions under which we do not hold people responsible for their actions, even if the action per se is morally wrong. But it is hard to imagine how anyone could engage in homosexual behavior by accident or due to ignorance. There may be some bizarre scenario in which it would be possible, but most homosexual behavior is performed consciously and knowingly.

It is also unreasonable to think that most homosexual behavior is compulsive. Certainly we do not think that normal heterosexual activity is compulsive. Many heterosexuals find themselves with sexual desires or romantic feelings that, for whatever reason, they believe they should not act on—whether in order to be faithful to a spouse, to save one's strength for athletic performance, or just to avoid an awkward moment afterward. Even when the opportunity is available, when a seductive tempter or temptress is ready and willing, most of us are able to refrain—at least under the proper circumstances. Everyone is subject to weakness of will, and certain circumstances (like loneliness or alcohol) might make it much more likely that we will succumb to our desires, against our own best judgment. But most normal human beings are not mindless animals, ruled by our genitals, humping anything that we find attractive when the opportunity arises. There is no reason to think that homosexuals are any different from heterosexuals in this regard. Gay people, on average, are no less in control of their behavior than heterosexuals. There may be certain aspects of gay culture that give the impression otherwise—such as the exhibitionistic practices of some participants at gay pride parades. But the fact that you rarely see people act or dress that way outside of those contexts indicates that the behavior is not compulsive but part of the celebratory atmosphere, not much different from the behavior of straight people at a Mardi Gras parade.

Since homosexual behavior is generally voluntary, it is irrational to think that it matters, morally speaking, whether homosexual orientation is biologically determined. Only the feelings, inclinations, and desires are involuntary. But it is actions, not desires or feelings, that are morally right or wrong. If homosexual behavior is not morally wrong, as I argue, then it does not matter whether it is intentionally chosen or not. And if homosexual behavior is morally wrong, it would still be wrong even if it were not chosen, though homosexuals would not be blameworthy. The fact that polls show a high correlation between belief in a biological cause of homosexuality and support for gay rights only shows that most people in our society have irrational views about the connection between the biological source of homosexual inclinations and the morality of homosexual behavior. Either they falsely think that people should be morally responsible for their desires and emotions, or they falsely think that a biological source of homosexual inclinations would render homosexual behavior involuntary.

HOW HOMOSEXUALITY CAN BE A CHOICE—
EXISTENTIALISM AND AUTHENTICITY

A review of the scientific evidence has shown that sexual orientation is, at least for most people, innate and relatively fixed. Most of us did not choose our sexual orientation and most of us could not change it even if we wanted to. Thus people should not be held morally responsible for their sexual orientation, only for their sexual behavior. This, however, only pertains to homosexuality as an orientation. It is a different matter with engaging in homosexual practices or living a gay lifestyle. Since these activities usually involve voluntary choices, people can and should be held responsible for them.

It could be argued, however, that gay people are responsible, or should take responsibility, for their sexual orientation, even if it is innate. We might even say that gay people can *choose* to be gay, even if they could not choose otherwise. This idea of radical choice and complete responsibility can be found in the writings of existentialist philosophers of the early twentieth century, especially the works of Jean-Paul Sartre and Simone de Beauvoir.[36]

Existentialism has been caricatured as the view that life is meaningless. Though that is a misleading oversimplification of the view, there is a kernel of truth to it. The existentialists claim that human life in general, and every particular human life, is devoid of any *inherent* meaning. The "meaning of life," or the purpose of a given person's individual life, is not some objective fact to be discovered. But that does not mean that life cannot have any meaning. It can be given meaning. There is no one "meaning of life" that holds for all people universally; each individual has to find the meaning of her own life. The meaning of an individual's life is not discovered but is constructed by one's choices. We determine the meaning and purpose of our own lives by the decisions we make and the projects that we take up. And we establish values and the meaning of life for ourselves as individuals through our actions, our attitudes, and the way we interpret the world around us. The value of a particular goal, project, or preference is determined by our choices. Your choosing it is what gives it value. Values and meanings are created by human choices and attitudes.

According to existentialism, our character traits are not simply given. No one is born brave or cowardly, honest or dishonest, compassionate or coldhearted. You become the sort of person you are by the way you live your life—the choices you make and the attitudes you adopt. A brave person is not someone who possesses some deep internal property of bravery but simply someone who does courageous deeds. Although we have free will and real choices in life, these choices take place in a world that we did not choose, a world that often resists our will. Our freedom is always situated. Sometimes your circumstances leave many options open to you; other times your options might be severely restricted. But no matter how limited the available alternative courses of action are, you are still free to choose the *attitude* you take to your situation. A man who is laid off from work, for example, can view his unemployment as a personal failure, an insult to his dignity, or an opportunity to start a new career. Which attitude he takes and the corresponding plan he adopts determine his values, his character, and even the meaning of his life—be it a search for material comfort, a struggle for respect, a passion for some cause, or just marking time.

Since you choose what attitude to take and assign meaning to your life, you can be responsible for who you are—even for those aspects of your existence that are beyond your control. You may not choose those facts about who you are—your race, gender, nationality, or sexual orientation—but you can choose how to deal with them. For example, I was born in the United States. I did not choose to be an American and I cannot choose not to be an American. Even if I choose to emigrate and change my citizenship, I would still be an ex-American. I cannot entirely escape my American-ness. But although I cannot choose never to have been American, it is still up to me to choose what it means to be an American. I can adopt a cosmopolitan view and decide that being an American (for me at least) is to be connected to a broader global community. Or I can adopt a nationalistic attitude and decide that being American distinguishes me from the citizens of other countries. Either way, I choose to be American in that I choose *what it means* (for me) to be an American. And for that reason, I am responsible for being American. I can be responsible for it, even though I could not choose otherwise.

This entails a heavy burden of responsibility, which serves as temptation to try to avoid choice. One response to this burden is to try to escape responsibility through what existentialists refer to as *bad faith* or *inauthenticity*, a kind of self-deception whereby we ascribe an external source to our values, meanings, and choices. This can take many forms. One form of inauthenticity involves conformity with the larger group, allowing society to define the meaning of our lives for us. Another form of inauthenticity is to assume that the facts of one's life are exhaustive of one's identity. For example, one might identify entirely with a social role, seeing oneself as *just* a wife or *just* a teacher or *just* an American and nothing more. Authenticity may also take the opposite form, as when you deny that an important fact of your existence has any bearing on who you are. An example might be one who denies that his nationality plays any part of his identity. For example, I might say, "There are no Americans, Germans, or Russians. There are only people." Either way, there is a kind of alienation, an attempt to distance yourself from an important part of who you are. The inauthentic person alienates herself from the facts of her existence or from her freedom and responsibility.

Seeing one's sexual orientation as unchosen and as something that one is not responsible for might be, according to the existentialist, a kind of inauthenticity. Sexual orientation is, like it or not, an important part of who you are. Even if the social constructivist view is correct, and categories like "homosexual" are arbitrary and artificial, these categories are part of the social reality we live in. You cannot deny that you live in a society where these things are viewed as important. It might not seem to straight people that sexual orientation is an important part of one's identity, since heterosexuality is often assumed as the norm. Since heterosexuality is taken for granted, the sexual orientation of straight people is less salient to them. But it is hardly a trivial matter like being flatfooted or left-handed. Being gay or straight shapes many of life's choices and projects, as well as many of one's day-to-day activities.

It is delusional to think of one's sexual orientation as merely given. Desires and feelings are usually ambiguous and stand in need of interpretation. How to interpret one's desires and feelings is partly a matter of choice, though of course interpretation is limited by facts. I might decide that the excitement I feel when I am with a female friend is infatuation, fear, lust, or social anxiety. But I cannot pretend that I do not feel it. Even if some desires and feelings are unambiguous and need no interpretation, they would still need to be unified, integrated, and prioritized. This integration of our emotional lives involves a transition from having a sexual orientation to having a sexual identity, from being merely a cluster of sexual desires to being a sexual person. Identity is a self-conscious project of construction and integration—or at least it should be. And, for that reason, we can be responsible for who we are. Even if you inauthentically take your identity as simply given, you are still responsible for it in that you are negligently allowing the facts to decide for you who you are.

Most importantly, interpreting one's situation, making choices (when possible), and adopting attitudes are what determine one's values. Denying responsibility for your sexuality is thus alienating yourself from an important part of your personal identity. Seeing one's sexual orientation as a simple fact that cannot be chosen is, in a sense, to devalue it. It is only by embracing one's orientation as something worthy of choice that we give it value. By viewing homosexuality as a choice, a gay person affirms his or her sexual orientation as having positive worth.

RELEVANCY OF BIOLOGY

We have seen that there is overwhelming evidence that sexual orientation, for most people, has a biological source and is relatively fixed early on. I have argued, however, that this is irrelevant to the morality of homosexual behavior and the gay lifestyle, because behaviors and lifestyles are (or at least can be) chosen. I have even suggested that homosexuals should view their orientation as a choice in order to value it and integrate it in their personal sense of self. That does not mean, however, that the biological facts are irrelevant to the issue of gay rights. It is important to acknowledge, in forming public policy, that changing one's sexual orientation is not a realistic option for most people. Some conservatives, for example, oppose legal recognition of gay rights on the grounds that it will result in an increase in the proportion of homosexuals in the population. There are many problems with that sort of argument; but the biggest problem is that it is simply false. Being raised by same-sex parents or living next door to a gay couple will not turn a straight person gay. And encouraging gay people to live a heterosexual lifestyle is a pointless endeavor that will only lead to misery for those gay people and the straight partners in their sham marriages.

5

HOMOSEXUALITY AND MORALITY I— THE NATURAL LAW ARGUMENT

Many who voice disapproval of same-sex relations do so for reasons that are irrelevant to the morality of homosexuality and the gay rights issue. Some who disapprove of homosexuality are merely expressing their subjective attitudes. This is the emotive use of moral expressions. Even if the emotivist theory of moral language were correct, such moral claims cannot be taken seriously in the gay rights debate. Morality is about reasons to act. The fact that some people don't like the idea of same-sex relations, however, is no reason for homosexuals, who *do* enjoy same-sex relations, not to engage in them.

Others oppose homosexuality and gay marriage on the basis of biblical (or other scriptural) condemnations. As we saw in chapter 3, however, this religiously inspired disapproval should be dismissed for a number of reasons. For one thing, the Scriptures make all sorts of outrageous demands (like the ban on wearing clothes of mixed fibers) and even morally appalling claims (such as condoning slavery). Why think the Bible's condemnation of homosexuality is any more legitimate than its ban on wearing jewelry or its ban on contact with menstruating women? Furthermore, it is unclear whether the biblical ban on homosexuality is intended as a moral claim or merely as a religious obligation. If it is a mere religious requirement, like circumcision, then it would not be relevant to those who are not members of that faith. It would be outrageous, in a free country, to legally require all babies—even the babies of parents who are atheists, Hindus, or Buddhists—to be circumcised, just because the Bible requires it.

Most importantly, the religiously based disapproval of homosexuality assumes a divine command theory of ethics—a theory that even the devout believer should reject. God's forbidding something does not make it wrong. There must be objective right or wrong, good and bad, independently of God's will, otherwise we could not meaningfully praise God as being good. If homosexuality is wrong, then there must be something about it that makes it wrong, other than God's arbitrary fiat. This wrong-making feature would constitute a reason that would apply to everyone, not just believers in a particular faith. In that case, we should be able to find what these reasons are without relying on Scriptures that many reasonable people do not accept as true.

In this chapter and the next, we will examine the most prominent nonreligious arguments that have been given against the morality of homosexuality and gay rights. In this chapter, we will look at claims that homosexuality is unnatural. In the next chapter, we look at claims that homosexual activities violate the proper function of the reproductive organs and that same-sex marriage conflicts with the true nature of marriage. Two questions will need to be answered in assessing each of these arguments. The first question is whether homosexuality *really is* unnatural or whether it *really does* involve a misuse of the sexual organs. The second, more important question is whether being unnatural or misusing one's organs really is a wrong-making feature of actions. If the arguments against homosexuality fail either of these tests, then the arguments fail. As we shall see, these arguments, for the most part, fail both tests. [1]

THE UNNATURAL ARGUMENT AND MEANING OF "UNNATURAL"

One common argument against homosexuality is that it is "unnatural." I will call this the "Simple Natural Law" (SNL) argument to distinguish it from the "New" Natural Law argument, which we will examine later in this chapter. One example of this argument was put forward by Dr. James W. Holsinger Jr., George W. Bush's nominee for surgeon general, who wrote a paper in 1991 that made the purported medical argument that homosexuality is unnatural and unhealthy. [2] The argument has also been made by at least one professional philosopher. [3] But this is an argument that is made by many ordinary folks and seems to have significant intuitive appeal to those who are morally opposed to homosexuality. Often the argument takes a very simple form.

1. Homosexuality is unnatural.
2. Therefore, homosexuality is morally wrong.

Put in this simplistic form, the argument is not very convincing. First of all, the conclusion does not follow. There is an unstated assumption here, namely that everything that is unnatural is morally wrong. Without this crucial premise, the argument fails to get off the ground.

Those who use the SNL argument might complain that I have formulated the suppressed premise too broadly by saying that *everything* unnatural is thereby morally wrong. We could instead formulate this principle more narrowly by claiming only that things that are unnatural *in certain specific ways* are thereby morally wrong. But then the argument fails again. The argument would no longer support the conclusion that homosexuality is morally wrong because the stated premise (1) claims simply that homosexuality is unnatural. It does not say *in what way* it is unnatural. To make the argument work, it would have to be claimed that homosexuality is unnatural *in that specific way that makes unnatural things wrong*. It would be easier and clearer instead to simply formulate the hidden premise as claiming that *everything* that is unnatural is wrong and then give a more specific, narrower definition of "unnatural."

This leads to the other weakness of this argument. It is unclear in what sense homosexuality is thought to be unnatural. The terms "natural" and "unnatural" are highly ambiguous. They have several distinct meanings. We cannot assess the truth or falsity of the claim that homosexuality is unnatural until we know exactly what it means to be natural or unnatural. Homosexuality might be unnatural in some sense or other but might be quite natural in another sense.

Here are some of the various things that might be meant by the term "unnatural." When we say an activity is unnatural, we might mean that it is unhealthy, abnormal, awkward or uncomfortable (as in "he has a very unnatural walk"), unfamiliar (as in "Chinese music sounds very unnatural to me"), contrary to instinct, not innate, artificial (i.e., being the product of human invention), or contrived. Some of these senses of "unnatural" overlap, but many of them do not.

To assess the SNL argument, we must first go through the various senses of "unnatural" and ask whether homosexuality is unnatural in any of these various senses—and if so, which ones. Then we must ask whether any of these senses of "unnatural" are morally relevant. The SNL argument against homosexuality fails *either* if homosexuality is not unnatural *or* if being unnatural does not necessarily make something wrong. But it especially fails if we can show *both* that homosexuality is not unnatural and also that being unnatural (in that particular way) does not make something morally wrong.

IS HOMOSEXUALITY UNNATURAL?

One thing we sometimes mean when we describe a certain behavior as "natural" is that the behavior comes easily, as when we say, "Jane is a natural athlete" or "Singing comes naturally to me." Behavior that is unnatural in this sense would be awkward or counterintuitive. A similar, but slightly different, meaning is that the behavior is innate or instinctual, as opposed to being the result of training. For example, we might say that "John has a natural inclination to help people" or that "human beings are naturally cooperative." Behavior that is unnatural in this sense might feel forced or counterintuitive—at least initially, without some kind of conditioning or desensitization. Obviously homosexuality, in this sense, is very natural for some people, though not others. People who are gay, and who have never lived in self-denial about their orientation or struggled to hide it from others, might find engaging in same-sex relations to be very natural—much more so than engaging in heterosexual relations. Homosexuality per se is clearly not unnatural in this sense, but this is obviously not what those who disapprove of homosexuality mean when they say it is unnatural.

Another sense of the term "natural" is used to distinguish natural things from artificial. Artificial things are intentionally and consciously created by humans and do not exist apart from human invention. Natural things, by contrast, exist "on their own," in the wilderness. So, for example, we talk about foods as containing natural ingredients, like sugar or butter, or unnatural ingredients, like aspartame or margarine. Of course, this is somewhat arbitrary. Sugar and butter do not really exist without human invention. Sugar *cane* exists in nature. Refined sugar, however, is a human product requiring elaborate processing. Likewise, cow's milk exists in nature, but butter requires churning. (And even cow's milk is not entirely natural since the cow is a domesticated animal.) Still, there does seem to be a difference between products like sugar and butter that are mere extractions or modifications of natural products and chemicals like aspartame and margarine, which are created in the laboratory. Is homosexuality natural in this sense, or is it artificial? That is hard to say.

Some postmodern philosophers would argue that gender, sexuality, and sexual orientation are all social constructs.[4] (A brief account of the social constructivist view is given early in the previous chapter.) According to this view, societies determine what is "feminine" and "masculine" as well as what is sexual or nonsexual. In some societies, for example, wearing makeup and skirts could be considered masculine while playing sports and roughhousing could be considered feminine. The point is that masculinity and femininity are not innate or fixed categories. Sexuality, in the postmodern view, is also defined culturally. In our society, female breasts are sexualized. But in certain low-tech tropical societies where women routinely go topless, breasts might be seen as relatively mundane. In those topless societies, a man who gets sexually aroused by a woman's breasts might be seen as some kind of perverted fetishist.

If gender and sexuality are both socially constructed, then obviously so is homosexuality, since is it involves sexual attraction to members of the same gender. There is something to be said for the claim that homosexuality is culturally defined. In ancient Greece, for example, same-sex relations between men were routine, at least among members of the upper class. But men who engaged in these relations were not seen as homosexual or even bisexual. As long as a man was married, or intended eventually to get married, he would be considered normal. A man who wanted nothing to do with women sexually or romantically might have been seen as abnormal, but even then he would not have been labeled a homosexual since they did not actually have a concept for homosexuality.[5] Nevertheless, the claims of these postmodernists do not hold up well against scientific findings. More importantly, in the postmodern view, homosexuality and heterosexuality are both *equally* artificial. So this could obviously not serve as a basis for any argument that homosexuality in particular is unnatural. The upshot of the post-modern claim that gender and sexuality are socially constructed is that gender differences and sexual preferences do not exist independently of how we conceive of them. We could conceive of gender and sexuality differently; or we could refuse to categorize people into rigid categories of "men" and "women" and simply view them as individuals on a contin-uum with various gender traits. This is all intended to be very subver-sive and makes it impossible to even make sense of the question of whether homosexuality is morally wrong.

Sometimes those who claim that homosexuality is unnatural follow this claim by pointing out that homosexuality is not found among non-human animals. For example, the Anglican archbishop of Nigeria, Peter Akinola, has said, "I cannot think of how a man in his senses would be having a sexual relationship with another man. Even in the world of animals—dogs, cows, lions—we don't hear of such things." Presumably this is evidence that homosexuality is not natural for humans in the sense that it is not innate, or at least not innate in normal humans.

In this interpretation of "unnatural," the argument against homosex-uality goes something like this.

1. Homosexuality is not practiced by nonhuman animals.
2. Whatever is not practiced by nonhuman animals is wrong for humans.

3. Therefore, (human) homosexuality is morally wrong.

It would be very odd to think that being "unnatural" for humans means that it is not natural for other animals. That would amount to claiming that there can be no natural human traits that are not found in other animals, which is obviously false. There are innate behaviors that are uniquely human, such as language. The capacity for language seems to be hardwired in the human brain.[6] Even chimps, smart as they are, cannot master language.[7] By contrast, there has never been a human community without a very rich and complex language. Other activities that are uniquely human include farming, domestication of animals, storytelling, division of labor, political governance, and religious worship. It would be strange to claim that all of these practices should be considered morally wrong. It is especially ironic that a bishop would make this sort of comment. We could make the same kind of argument against religion by replacing homosexuality with worshiping God: "I cannot think of how a man in his senses could worship God. Even in the world of animals—dogs, cows, lions—we don't hear of such things."

Perhaps the claim that nonhuman animals do not engage in homosexual behavior is intended only as evidence that it is probably not innate in humans. Still, the claim that homosexuality is nonexistent outside of the human species is in fact false. Homosexual behavior has been observed in many animal species. One of our closest relatives, the bonobos (pygmy chimps of the Congo jungle), frequently engage in same-sex liaisons. Male lions also occasionally have sex with each other. In fact, some sort of homosexual activity has been observed in over fifteen hundred species. These animals that engage in same-sex relations are predominantly heterosexual and would be better described as bi/curious. There are, however, animals that form long-term same-sex bonds. This is especially common among black-headed gulls. About 10 percent of the females of this species are homosexual. There are even entire species that are gay. Some species of whiptail lizards, for example, are all female and reproduce by parthenogenesis (a process in which the female's egg cells spontaneously develop into offspring that are genetically identical to the mother). Interestingly, these lizards still need to have sex to stimulate reproduction. Thus, virtually the entire species consists of homosexuals.[8]

Of course, proponents of the SNL argument against homosexuality might insist that these animals are not *truly* gay. They may engage in same-sex relations, but not in the ways that humans do. That is probably true. But this fact works more to undermine the SNL argument than to support it. For the same can be said for heterosexuality. Nonhuman animals may engage in heterosexual activities but not in the same ways that humans do. (For one thing, these opposite-sex nonhuman animal couples do not get married.) Most human behaviors—such as eating, grooming, playing—differ in significant and important ways from analogous behaviors in nonhuman animals. Thus, the claim that homosexuality is unnatural, in the sense of not existing in nonhuman animals, fails one way or another. It is either false, incoherent, or morally irrelevant.

Perhaps when people claim that homosexuality is "unnatural," what they mean is that it is *abnormal*. But the term "abnormal" is itself ambiguous. It might mean "unusual" or "uncommon," or it might mean "unhealthy." Let us consider the first option, the claim that homosexuality is relatively uncommon. This sort of argument was articulated by the cartoon character Homer Simpson. When asked why he has a problem with gays, Homer replies, "It's not . . . *usual!*"[9]

It is commonly claimed that 10 percent of the human population is homosexual. This number is controversial. Those opposed to homosexuality typically claim that this figure is inflated. But it is hard to know exactly what percentage of the population is homosexual since some gay people are not open about their sexual preferences, and some are in denial. Also, the prevalence of homosexuality will depend a lot on exactly how it is defined. (As was discussed in the beginning of chapter 4, we might define it primarily in terms of sexual preferences or in terms of preferred partner for intimacy. We may want to include bisexual people or only exclusively homosexual people.) But that does not matter for this argument. Even at the highest estimates—10 percent of the population—homosexuality is relatively uncommon.[10] If this is what is meant by the claim that homosexuality is "unnatural," then we can agree that homosexuality is unnatural. In the next section I will argue that being uncommon does not make something bad or morally wrong (which is probably so obvious as not to need any argument), and so this is probably not what is meant when people say that homosexuality is unnatural.

More likely, those who think that homosexuality is unnatural because it is abnormal, think it is abnormal in the sense that it is unhealthy. This is the sense of "abnormal" that is used when a psychologist describes a schizophrenic patient as having "abnormal thought processes and behavior," or when a doctor describes a cancerous tissue growth as "abnormal." Is homosexuality abnormal in this sense? This is a hard question to answer. Not because there might be some truth to the idea that homosexuality is unhealthy, but because we sometimes use the term "unhealthy" simply to express disapproval. In this way, what is called "healthy" or "unhealthy" is often a subjective matter. My wife, for example, thinks that I have an *unhealthy* obsession with football. This is because I spend (what seems to her) an inordinate amount of time watching football, and it seems to cause me more grief than pleasure.

She is not misusing the term "unhealthy," and she is right that I do watch a lot of football. But many people would think that my interest in football is perfectly normal. Even my wife would concede that I do not need to see a shrink or take medication because I watch a lot of football. In this subjective use of "unhealthy," some people will say homosexuality is unhealthy and others will disagree. There is no objective truth to whether something is "unhealthy" in this sense. Thus, this use of the term "unhealthy" is like the emotive use of "right" and "wrong." It is merely an expression of one's attitudes.

To find an objective answer to the question of whether homosexuality is healthy, we need some objective sense of "healthy" or "unhealthy." Here is one that should be relatively uncontroversial. An activity can be unhealthy in two ways. First of all, an activity is unhealthy if it is detrimental to a person's health. Something is detrimental to one's health if it leads to, or is likely to lead to, significant pain, loss of function, or shortened lifespan. In this sense, smoking is unhealthy. (It can cause lung disease, which is painful and potentially fatal. It also diminishes one's endurance in the short term.) Second, a behavior is unhealthy if it is compulsive or caused by delusions or causes significant anxiety or stress in those who engage in it. This kind of behavior is unhealthy, not because it leads to poor health but because it is a symptom of some unhealthy condition, especially a mentally unhealthy condition such as obsessive-compulsive disorder or depression.

Some people might be tempted to argue that homosexuality is unhealthy in the first sense (as leading to poor health) because of its association with AIDS. But this argument fails for several reasons. (In order to assess this line of reasoning, we will consider only the transmission of AIDS through sexual conduct and ignore the other ways that people can get AIDS, such as by sharing hypodermic needles.) The only way one can contract AIDS sexually is by having sex with a partner who is already infected with the HIV virus. And the only way that the partner could be HIV positive is for him or her to have had sex with yet another person who was HIV positive. It is also important to keep in mind that HIV can be contracted from heterosexual contact as well as homosexual. Thus, what is unsafe is not gay sex but only *promiscuous* sex (whether gay or straight). Two monogamous gay men, with no prior partners, would have virtually zero chance of contracting HIV. And when you compare straight sex with gay sex (ignoring lifetime monogamy), the form of sex that is least likely to spread HIV is lesbian sex. Furthermore, even for promiscuous gay men (as well as straight men or women), there are very effective ways to avoid contracting and transmitting STDs—namely latex condoms (especially those with spermicidal lubricant). So the only thing that is unhealthy, with regard to sexual transmission of HIV, is sex that is both unprotected and with promiscuous partners—and it does not matter much whether one's sexual partner is the same or the opposite sex. (We will take a closer look at the claim that homosexuality is bad for one's health in chapter 9.)

The other way in which homosexuality is supposed to be unhealthy is that it is symptomatic of some deeper mental-health problem. For example, Marilyn vos Savant, who claims to be the world's smartest person, says, "I suspect that some apparently homosexual people are really heterosexuals who deeply phobic [sic] about the opposite sex or have other emotional problems."[11] The claim that homosexuality is a mental illness has a long history, but it is demonstrably false. To assess this version of the "unnatural" argument, we will need to examine the history of psychological theories of homosexuality.

A BRIEF HISTORY OF HOMOSEXUALITY AND PSYCHOLOGY

There was a time when modern professional psychology officially considered homosexuality to be a mental illness or a symptom of mental illness. But we should not take past claims of psychology too seriously. The short history of modern psychology is littered with examples of quackery—from phrenology to primal scream therapy to the Rorschach test.[12] Most legitimate sciences have embarrassingly unscientific origins, and modern psychology is no exception. The science of astronomy, for example, has its origins in astrology. Even the great Johannes Kepler made his living mostly through fortune-telling.[13] Similarly, the much younger field of psychology has its origins in the very unscientific and largely debunked theories of psychoanalysis. Homosexuality was abnormal according to the Freudian theory because it failed to fit with the oedipal story of "normal" child development. Let us think about that for a minute. That means—according to Freud and his followers—that it is normal to want to murder your father and have sex with your mother; but it is abnormal to want to have a romantic relationship with someone of the same sex. Surely that can't be right.

Modern psychotherapy relies on the *Diagnostic and Statistical Manual of Mental Health* (*DSM*) for defining metal illnesses and disorders. The *DSM* was designed to give clear definitions of mental-health disorders, list criteria of symptoms for the purpose of diagnosis, and provide standardized terminology. As the science of psychology has developed, the *DSM* has changed. But traditionally, the changes to the *DSM* have tended to lag behind cutting-edge progress in psychology and neuroscience.

When the *DSM* was originally published in 1952, homosexuality was described as a personality disorder. It was included in a list of so-called sexual deviancies. There was no description of what homosexuality is and no explanation of why it should be considered a disorder.[14] (The sketchiness was due to the fact that the original *DSM* had fewer than one hundred pages and gave only the briefest description of most disorders. Today it contains almost one thousand pages.) The listing of homosexuality as a mental illness was modified in later versions of the *DSM*. In particular, only those who were unhappy about their homosexual orientation were considered to be suffering from a mental illness. It was not until 1974 that homosexuality was finally removed entirely from the *DSM* and no longer officially considered a mental illness.

Social conservatives typically chalk up this change in the *DSM* to "political correctness" and pressure from gay activists. Although there might have been such pressure from gay activists, it is unlikely that they had that much influence back in the early 1970s. But whether political pressure had anything to do with the elimination of homosexuality from the official list of mental illnesses is irrelevant. What matters is not what actually motivated the change but whether the change was justified by good science. Removing homosexuality from the list of mental illnesses in the *DSM* might have been scientifically sound even if it was done for unscientific reasons.

The scientific evidence for the claim that homosexuality is not a mental illness starts with the remarkable work of Evelyn Hooker. Hooker was a psychologist at UCLA back in the 1940s and 1950s. She was heterosexual and happily married (the second time around). Professor Hooker proposed to study "normal" heterosexual men. At the time, "normal homosexual" was considered an oxymoron, like "compassionate psychopath" or "humble narcissist." But that was merely an untested assumption on the part of the psychologists and psychiatrists of the day. Hooker set out to put this assumption to the test with carefully conducted, impartial experiments.

Using funding from a National Institutes of Health grant, Hooker recruited thirty gay and thirty straight men as test subjects. Each man was given three of the most widely used tests for psychological evaluation at the time. The results of the tests for each of the men were then grouped into thirty gay-straight pairs, matched for similar age, IQ, and education level. Each matched gay/straight pair was then given to experts in psychology who were asked to assess the test results and to determine for each pair, which of the test subjects was gay and which one was straight.

The results were that the gay and straight men had the same average psychological score and the same distribution of scores. Also, the experts were not able to distinguish the gay test subjects from the straight test subjects. The conclusion was that gay men are not significantly different psychologically from straight men, except of course for their different sexual preferences. The tools Hooker used for evaluating the mental health and well-being of the men—Rorschach inkblots, make-a-picture-story test, and so on—have since been shown to be quite useless. That is not, however, a critique of Hooker's methods; she was using the tests that were considered the best diagnostic tools at that time. It turns out that it does not matter that those personality tests were deficient.[15] Hooker's studies have been replicated several times using more advanced, scientifically sound personality tests. Every time Hooker's test is replicated with better mental health and personality measures, the results are the same. Homosexuals are not generally different psychologically from heterosexuals. There are, of course, homosexuals who are mentally unstable or suffer from various diagnosable mental illness or personality disorders, but the same is true of heterosexuals. And the prevalence of mental illness in each group is no more or less than in the other group.[16] (Any tests that show otherwise are not sufficiently controlled or have some other obvious scientific flaws.)

IS UNNATURAL BEHAVIOR MORALLY WRONG? THE SIMPLE NATURAL LAW THEORY

So it seems that homosexuality is not unnatural in most senses of the term "unnatural." It is not unhealthy, not unique to humans, and not awkward or counterintuitive (at least not for most homosexuals). On the other hand, homosexuality could be said to be unnatural in some senses. It could be argued to be artificial in some ways—in the same ways that human heterosexual behavior is artificial—and it is abnormal in the sense of being atypical. We can already see that the SNL argument is pretty weak. Homosexuality is not unnatural in most senses, and the few senses in which it is unnatural are obviously not morally relevant. But let us assume, for the sake of argument, that homosexuality *was* unnatural (in any or all of these ways). We must now examine the question of whether being natural or unnatural, in any of the various senses of the terms, is morally relevant.

When people claim that homosexuality is "unnatural," and use that claim as part of an argument for denying certain rights, liberties, or privileges to homosexuals, they are making certain general theoretical claims about what makes an action right or wrong. This Natural Law theory basically claims that if an action (or disposition, inclination, or practice) is unnatural—under some specific definition of "unnatural"—then it is morally wrong or bad. This SNL theory is a crucial premise in the unnatural argument. Without it, the unnatural argument fails.

The Natural Law theory, or some version of it, was very popular in the Middle Ages and the Renaissance. It has since fallen out of favor for various reasons. Though it is still popular within the hierarchy of the Catholic Church, it is not very popular in philosophy today. It has also, though to a lesser extent, fallen out of favor among ordinary folk. Though people often appeal to natural law when discussing homosexuality, you rarely hear anyone making a natural law argument when discussing other social and moral issues such as capital punishment, gun control, or even abortion. Those who argue that abortion is wrong, for example, usually claim that the fetus has a right to life, or they claim that abortion has bad consequences (for the pregnant woman or for society at large), or they appeal to some supernatural quality like "sanctity of life."[17] But I have never heard anyone argue that abortion is wrong because it is *unnatural*.

I think the reason for its lack of popularity outside of philosophy is due at least in part to the emergence of science and the scientific understanding of the universe. Among contemporary philosophers, it is unpopular because it has been refuted by very convincing arguments. One of the first, and still one of the best, arguments against the natural law theory of morality comes from a philosopher named David Hume (1711–1776). Here is a brief summary of Hume's argument, in his own words. (Pardon the anachronistic spelling and the weird eighteenth-century punctuation!)

> Nothing can be more unphilosophical than those systems, which assert, that virtue is the same with what is natural, and vice with what is unnatural. For in the first sense of the word, Nature, as opposed to miracles, both vice and virtue are equally natural; and in the second sense, as oppos'd to what is unusual, perhaps virtue will be found to be the most unnatural. . . . As to the third sense of the word, 'tis certain, that both vice and virtue are equally artificial, and out of nature. For however it may be disputed, whether the notion of a merit or demerit in certain actions be natural or artificial, 'tis evident, that the actions themselves are artificial, and are perform'd with a certain design and intention; otherwise they cou'd never be rank'd under any of these denominations.[18]

In most of the analysis that follows, my critiques of the SNL theory borrow heavily from Hume.

Let us start with the notion of "natural" as referring to the totality of the observable, physical universe. Nature in this sense refers to everything that can be studied by the sciences. Given this sense of natural, unnatural things and occurrences would have to be *supernatural*. But obviously supernatural actions, if there were any such actions, would not necessarily be morally bad or wrong. After all, God's miracles (if there were such things) would be supernatural, and we do not think that they are morally bad or wrong. When we are told that Jesus cured a leper or restored sight to a blind man (assuming these events should be interpreted as supernatural), we think it to be very morally good. So on this interpretation the argument obviously fails. But it is unlikely that this is what people intend when they claim that homosexuality is unnatural.

What about the notion of unnatural activities as activities that are not innate? Are such activities thereby morally wrong or bad? This is highly implausible. Playing the guitar, for example, is clearly not innate. Even for one who has a natural talent for it, it still has to be learned. It might not even be innate in the weak sense in which we say that "it comes naturally to him" meaning that he has a knack for it. I personally have very little innate musical skill, but I still managed, with significant struggle, to learn to play guitar. So it is very unnatural for me. But obviously there is nothing morally objectionable about me playing the guitar, even if I play it poorly.

One could argue that, to some extent, performing music is natural, or innate, in that the *capacity* for music is hardwired in the human brain.[19] Even those who lack a natural talent for music still have a natural *ability* to play music, even if not very well. Contrast my innate capacity for music playing with that of my cat. It might be very hard for me to learn to play music well, but it would be absolutely impossible for my cat to learn to play music at all.[20] In that sense, music might be said to be natural to all humans generally. But this argument is no help to the SNL theory. To say that all normal humans have a basic capacity for listening to and playing music simply means that it is *possible* for us to do so, even if it might be difficult. If that is what is meant by natural, then for an act to be unnatural it would have to be one that we humans have *no* capacity *at all* to perform. Unnatural acts are those that it would be impossible for us to perform—like breathing underwater (without any sort of special diving apparatus) or flying under our own power. Is it morally wrong to do things that are impossible? That question does not even make sense. If a particular action cannot be done, then it does not matter whether it is right or wrong. It would be no help to try to say that an act that is impossible to do *would* be wrong *if* it could be done. That would not work as an interpretation of SNL theory because it would amount to saying that an unnatural act would be wrong to do if it were natural.

Another sense of "unnatural" is roughly synonymous to *artificial* or *the product of conscious human intention*—the sense in which sugarcane and milk are natural while aspartame and hydrogenated vegetable oil are not. What sort of activities and behaviors would not be "natural" in this sense? It would seem that every intentional action done by a human being is the product of conscious human intention. The action is consciously intended by the human who performs it. Otherwise it would not be a voluntary action (and we cannot be held morally responsible for involuntary acts). So if natural means "not human made," then it would be impossible for a human being to intentionally perform any natural activity. If there are any activities performed by humans that are natural in this sense, they could only be things like digesting food or sweating or the beating of one's heart. These are not things that we *do*; they are not under our control. They are processes that occur in our bodies whether we want them to or not.

Perhaps there is a narrower sense of artificial that will allow for some intentional actions to be natural and others to be artificial. For example, there seems to be something very natural about certain activities, like eating and drinking. They might be human made in that we bring about these actions through our conscious intentions. But they are still natural in important ways. What makes these actions natural cannot be that other animals do them. For that would make language use and other uniquely human activities artificial or unnatural. Still, it might be said that they are "natural" for several reasons. First, they involve activities necessary for survival and for the maintenance of physical health and well-being. Second, they are innate or instinctual. Human babies, for example, are born with an instinct to nurse. And feral children do not starve to death because no one has taught them how to eat. It is just obvious to any hungry person that food goes in the mouth where it is chewed (if necessary) and then swallowed. No one would think that the hunger he feels could be satisfied by shoving food into his ear, even if he has never been shown the proper way to consume food.

So there might be activities that are natural in this sense. But it would be a very short list of behaviors. Most of the things we do on a daily basis would be considered artificial. Brushing our teeth, wearing clothes, cooking food, driving a car or riding a bicycle, typing on a computer keyboard, and talking on a telephone are all artificial activities. So are skiing, scuba diving, horse riding, and surfing. If all artificial activities are unnatural, and unnatural activities are morally wrong or bad, then all of these activities are morally wrong or bad. This is absurd. None of these activities could reasonably be said to be morally objectionable. So the SNL argument based on the notion of "unnatural-as-artificial" fails.

Yet another sense in which we say something is unnatural is to say that it is abnormal. But what does *abnormal* mean? If we take *abnormal* to mean wrong or bad, then the Natural Law theory would be circular. It would amount to this.

1. An action is wrong if it is unnatural.
2. Unnatural actions are those actions that are abnormal.
3. By "abnormal" we mean wrong.

Since being unnatural entails being wrong, according to (1), we can substitute "wrong" for "unnatural" in (2), without loss of meaning. And since abnormality is equated with wrongness in (3), we can substitute "wrong" for "abnormal" in (2). The theory then turns out to be equivalent to the claim that actions are wrong because they are wrong. That may be true, but it is vacuous—it does not say anything about which actions are wrong or why. And it would be of no help in moral reasoning.

It would not necessarily be circular or vacuous to say, as the SNL theory claims, that all unnatural actions *are* morally wrong—but only as long as "unnatural" *means* something different from simply "being wrong." Here is an analogy. To say that "organic things are those things that are comprised of organic substances" is circular and vacuous. To say that "organic things are those things that are comprised of carbon, oxygen, hydrogen, and nitrogen," by contrast, is not at all circular or vacuous. That is because "carbon," "oxygen," and the other elements can be defined on their own, without reference to organic things or substances. Similarly, for SNL to avoid circularity or vacuity it must define "unnatural" independently of any moral terms. And if we define *unnatural* in terms of abnormal, then abnormality must also be defined independently of moral or evaluative terms.

So here might be a definition we can give of the term "abnormal" that is not morally loaded. "Abnormal" can mean *unusual* or *atypical*. For example, we can say that a human being who has more than five fingers on one hand is abnormal. That is because most humans have exactly five fingers on each hand—barring accidents or injuries, in which case they usually have less than five, not more. As was discussed above, homosexuality is probably abnormal in that sense. It is atypical, or relatively unusual. But does that make it morally wrong? Many things are unusual or atypical for humans. For example, having an IQ above 130 is very unusual. (Only about 2.5 percent of the human population has an IQ in that range.) These days, waiting to have sex until you are married is also very unusual, at least in our culture. Only about 5 percent of Americans abstain from sex until marriage.[21] Donating blood on a regular basis is another thing that is quite uncommon. Less than 10 percent of Americans do so.[22] Are these activities morally wrong? One might make a case that abstaining from sex until marriage is *imprudent*, but it sounds very odd to say that it is morally *wrong*. Having a high IQ is generally thought to be a good thing, and donating blood certainly seems to be morally praiseworthy. So to claim that what is abnormal in this sense (unusual or atypical) is thereby morally wrong or bad is clearly false.

Thus, none of the usual senses of *unnatural* are morally relevant. I have tried to examine every sense of the terms "natural" and "unnatural" that I could think of. There may be other senses of unnatural that I have not considered. But I am confident that any other sense would either be morally loaded (unnatural = bad) or would be morally irrelevant.

THE NEW NATURAL LAW ARGUMENT

The SNL argument, like most of the anti-gay arguments discussed in this book, is one that is presented by ordinary folk, not experts or scholars. But there are also some professional scholars in theology, political science, and jurisprudence who have formulated a fancier version of the Natural Law argument, which I will call the "*New* Natural Law" (NNL) argument.[23] There are three key features of the NNL argument: 1) claims about the intrinsic nature, or essence, of marriage and sex, 2) a list of basic goods that constitute human flourishing (which includes marriage or those goals inherent in the nature of marriage), and 3) the view that the role of government is to promote and facilitate the achievement of these basic goods.[24] While NNL theorists argue specifically against gay marriage, their argument is also intended to support anti-sodomy laws and other laws discouraging homosexual activity and gay lifestyles. We will focus on the first two claims here. Assessment of the third claim, what is sometimes called "perfectionism," will be postponed until chapter 8.

NNL theorists argue that whether you support same-sex marriage or oppose it, you must accept that there is some objective essence to what marriage is. In order to argue against same-sex marriage, one would have to argue that the essential nature of marriage excludes same-sex unions; to argue for same-sex marriage, one would have to argue that the nature of marriage is such that it does not exclude same-sex unions.

Either way, they argue, the issue should be settled by objective facts about what marriage is. If we deny that there is any objective essence to marriage, then we would be left with anything-goes relativism, and we could not make any argument either way.

This "true essence" of marriage, according to NNL theorists, is captured by what they call the *conjugal* conception. According to the conjugal conception, marriage has a dual purpose of uniting two people in a comprehensive sharing of their lives and of bringing healthy, well-adjusted children into the world.[25] Furthermore, NNL claims that conjugal marriage is, or promotes, one of the basic goods that collectively constitute human flourishing. When NNL theorists talk about human goods, they do not mean that these things necessarily contribute to our happiness, bring us pleasure, or satisfy our desires. Human goods are distinct from happiness, though happiness might be *one* of the many human goods. For the NNL theory, human goods are determined by objective facts about human nature, not subjective pleasure or personal desires. These natural goods contribute to a successful human life, even if we do not want them and do not enjoy them. According to NNL, we *should* want them and *should* enjoy them. Sexual relations have value, according to NNL, only insofar as they instantiate and consummate the basic good of conjugal marriage, which is union and procreation. Sex is good, according to NNL, only if it is *marital* sex. By "marital" sex, they mean only that activity that can result in pregnancy (i.e., penis-in-the-vagina sex) and only when conducted by two people married to each other trying to have kids. Other kinds or sexual relations or activities (nonmarital sex) do not instantiate any such basic goods and are thus morally wrong. That includes premarital sex, masturbation, the use of contraception, and oral sex (even oral sex between married partners).

DEFINITION OF MARRIAGE AS A TRUE ESSENCE OF MARRIAGE

An essential part of marriage, according to NNL, is biological reproduction. Since people of the same sex cannot reproduce naturally, marriage of the conjugal sort is impossible for same-sex couples, no matter how devoted they are to each other.[26] Same-sex marriage, they say, is incoherent because marriage is a relationship aimed at reproduction, and it is impossible for two people of the same sex to reproduce sexually. This argument against homosexuality and same-sex marriage relies on the assumption that there exists some essential, intrinsic nature to marriage. NNL thus assumes a kind of realism about marriage.

This idea that there is a *real* essence of marriage is also seen in arguments, offered by laypeople, that same-sex marriage is wrong because marriage is *by definition* a union between a man and a woman. It would be hard to see why anyone could object to redefining marriage unless they believed there was an objective essence of marriage. Changing the meaning of words is a common phenomenon, and people usually don't make a big fuss about it. For example, take the word "nurse." Today this refers to trained healthcare providers who monitor patients, take tissue samples, and perform other basic medical services. But the term originally referred to a woman who breastfed another woman's children. It would be absurd, however, for someone to claim that a nurse who works in a hospital is not a "true" nurse because she does not breastfeed the patients, or that the idea of a male nurse is incoherent because he lacks mammary glands. Presumably, those who object to allowing same-sex marriage because it would involve redefining the term "marriage" do so because they think that there is a real essence of marriage captured by the term. Their complaint is not merely semantic. They think that we are not free to redefine "marriage" so as to allow same-sex unions in the same way that we cannot redefine "carbon" as an element whose atoms have seven protons.

Realism about a given subject matter means that facts about that subject matter are neither subjective nor a matter of convention. Realism about marriage would mean that there are *mind-independent* facts, "out there" in the world, that constitute what marriage truly is. In this view, we do not and cannot *decide* what marriage is; we *discover* what marriage is. And on the NNL version of marriage realism, part of the very essence of marriage involves activities aimed at procreation. That would make it impossible for same-sex relations to be genuine marriages.

The question now is whether realism about marriage is plausible, or even coherent. There are two ways that marriage could have an objective nature independently of our beliefs or social conventions. One possibility is that there is some Platonic essence of marriage. Another possibility is that marriage is a *natural kind*. Let us consider natural kinds first. A *natural kind* is a category of things that share important, natural properties and these properties explain certain observable phenomena. One example of a natural kind is chemical elements, like sodium, oxygen, or carbon. All carbon atoms have exactly six protons in their nucleus. That's what makes it a carbon atom and not some other kind of atom. Also, the fact that carbon atoms have six protons in their nucleus explains why carbon has certain other properties and why it reacts with other elements the way that it does. Another example of a natural kind is a species of animal, like dogs. Although dogs can vary in size, shape, and color, there are certain essential features that any animal must have for it to be a dog.

Natural kinds are based on real facts. We do not invent natural kinds, we discover them. For example, that water is not an element is an objective fact. Water is comprised of two clearly distinct atoms (hydrogen and oxygen). If we simply *decided* to categorize water as an element, we would be making a mistake. Contrast this with the notion of a *planet*. A planet is a large celestial body orbiting a star. The problem is that asteroids and comets are also celestial bodies that orbit a star. What distinguishes a planet from those other sorts of objects is that a planet is bigger than an asteroid, and its orbit is less elliptical than a comet's. But how big does something have to be to be a planet? How circular does its orbit have to be? The answer is that we—or more precisely, certain astrophysicists among us—*decide* where to draw the line. That is why the International Astronomical Union could *decide*, in 2006, to downgrade Pluto to a dwarf planet or planetoid. (It also explains why this decision was not unanimous.)

One problem with thinking of marriage as a natural kind is that natural kinds are usually thought to be purely descriptive. The NNL conception of marriage, however, is not descriptive; it is evaluative. It is not so much a claim about how marriages are, but how they should be. Yet there may be a way that natural kinds can be evaluative. We might think that concrete particulars can be judged according to how well they exemplify their natural kind. For example, we might judge that a zebra without black and white vertical stripes is an imperfect zebra because the natural kind, the species *equus zebra*, has bold vertical black and white stripes.[27] An unstriped zebra, we might say, is less of a zebra, or not a *true* zebra. In the same way, if marriage is a natural kind, and biological reproduction is a defining characteristic of that natural kind, then a same-sex "marriage" would not be a good marriage (even if it brings happiness and fulfillment to both partners) because it would deviate from true marriage.

Even if we allowed that natural kinds serve as evaluative standards, however, they could only serve as standards of what it is for something to be *good-of-its-kind*. But something can be good-of-its-kind without being good *tout court*. For example, a zebra without stripes might not be a very good zebra, but that does not mean it is not a good *thing*. Similarly, a good burglar (one who is good at burgling) is someone who is stealthy, good at picking locks, and knows where valuables are likely to be found in a house. But a good burglar is a bad thing. The world would be a better place if there were fewer good burglars. So even if conjugal marriage were the best or truest marriages, that does not mean that we should encourage "good" marriages. Maybe some other arrangement, one that includes same-sex unions, would be better. If NNL theorists want to insist that this other kind of relation would not truly be marriage, then we can call it *schmarriage*. The NNL theorists would then have to argue why we as a society should adopt the institution of marriage rather than the institution of schmarriage.

An even bigger problem with seeing marriage as a natural kind is that natural kinds can be defined through observation; and their features can be explained by, or reduced to, more basic natural/physical kinds. For example, a species of animal can be defined by its genome. Elements like carbon and oxygen can be reduced to a specific combination of protons, neutrons, and electrons. Furthermore, we can discover the genetic properties of an animal species, or the atomic properties of elements, through careful observation and good scientific methods. But how could we *discover* the "real" essential features of practices, institutions, or social roles? It might be reasonable to say that the social roles of certain animals, such as the worker bee, are natural kinds. But that is because the worker role is hardwired in the honeybee and is found universally in all bee hives. By contrast, there is too much variation in marriage practices among different human cultures, and even among different people living in the same culture, to think that conjugal marriage is somehow built into the human species. Though there may be some psychological need for companionship that is innate in a normal human being, it is grossly implausible to think that forming a conjugal marriage is part of our biological destiny, any more than the drive to form a labor union or a bridge club.

The other possibility for realism about marriage is that there is a Platonic essence, or "form," of marriage. A Platonic form is an abstract concept or idea that exists objectively, independently of anyone thinking of it. Particular concrete instances of the concept are approximations of the form, which represents a sort of ideal. Consider, for example, a geometric object such as the triangle. According to Platonic realism, the essence of triangularity, or what-it-is-to-be a triangle, is something that really exists independently of anyone drawing shapes or doing geometry. One reason for thinking that the form of a triangle exists independently of our thinking about triangles is that there are certain necessary truths about triangles that we can discover. For example, the sum of the three angles of any triangle (in Euclidean space) equals 180 degrees. It is not up to us to *decide* whether the sum of the angles is 180 degrees; it is an objective fact that can be proven deductively.

Now consider social institutions such as marriage. Is there any reason to think that there are forms (immutable, real, abstract essences) of what it is to be a marriage? First, if marriage has an essential nature, then we should expect that other social institutions would also have essential natures. (It would be odd to say that marriage is different from all social institutions in having an essential form.) Is there also such a thing as a *real* book club, or a *true* chamber of commerce, or a *real* labor union? Do sewing circles and fantasy football leagues also have objective, essential features? Such an idea might seem silly, but no sillier than the idea of essential features of any other social institution, including marriage. NNL theorists would argue that marriage enables a biological need or essential bodily function—that of reproduction. But there are other social institutions that fulfill equally vital biological needs, such as co-op food stores (which provide food to members) or sewing circles (which provide clothing). There are other, possibly better, ways to provide food and clothing. And there are certainly other ways for human beings to reproduce.

Even if it made sense to say that there are objectively real essences of social institutions, in what sense would they be evaluative? The problem is that, just as with natural kinds, Platonic essences are evaluative only in that they determine what it is for something to be good-of-its-kind, not necessarily good *tout court*. A good triangle with straight lines is a better triangle than one with slightly curved lines, but it is not a better *thing*. Consider the institution of slavery. Is there some Platonic form that determines what *real* slavery is? If so, would real slavery be better than some kind of pseudo-slavery, such as indentured servitude? It seems to me that indentured servitude is better—or more accurately, less evil—than slavery. And it is less evil *because*, and insofar as, it deviates from pure slavery.

SOCIALLY INVENTED ESSENCE

One might be tempted to say that there are essential features that define what it is to be a book club. For a group to be a book club there must be at least two members, they must agree to read the same book, and they must meet to discuss the book. But that simply means that the phrase "book club" has some more or less definite meaning in English. NNL theorists make the mistake of supposing that either marriage must have some eternal essence or that the term "marriage" cannot have any meaning at all. But that is obviously false. There may be limits to what counts as a book club, even though there is no real, objective essence to what a book club is. And the same might be true of marriage. The institution of "book club" is merely a social invention, created by people. We can redesign the institution in any way we want. For example, if the members were to read plays or short stories instead of books, would it still be a book club? There is no objective answer to that question. We can decide either way, though if we redefine it too much, we might want to rename it, if only to avoid confusion. The essential features of social institutions such as book clubs or marriage are based on social practice, habit, and linguistic intuition. There may be some essential features of marriage, but the essence of marriage is not *real* in the sense of there being objective facts about it that obtain independently of our beliefs, values, and social customs.

Thus we can ask what the essential features of marriage are without assuming that marriage has an objectively real, Platonic essence. Philosopher Ralph Wedgwood, for example, defines the essential features of marriage as those features that explain general facts and norms surrounding the institution. The test, for him, of whether any feature of our current cultural understanding about marriage is essential, is whether we (in our modern Western society) would still view a relationship as a "marriage" if it lacked this feature.[28] The essence of marriage is constructed by a society through the practices, values, and expectations of (most) members of that society. Thus, the essence of marriage can differ from one society to the next and can change over time.

This socially constructed essence of marriage is evaluative. But since a socially invented essence can be modified, the evaluative judgments go both ways. On the one hand, we do tend to judge marriages as better or worse to the extent that they fit our conception of marriage, with its associated norms and expectations. For example, a couple who gets legally married just to avoid one of the partners being deported would be seen as a sham marriage by most people in our society. On the other hand, we also evaluate the institution of marriage itself and modify it or rethink it if it fails to live up to our beliefs and values. For example, a couple of hundred years ago, marriage was viewed primarily as a relationship based on property and inheritance rather than on love. Women were not allowed to own property, marriages were largely arranged, and the traditional marriage vows included a promise of the woman to obey her husband. Today, most people in Western industrialized societies see marriage differently, and so our conception of marriage, along with the institutional practices, has changed. Now it is generally seen as an equal partnership of two people who freely decide to commit to each other out of love.

NNL theorists claim that the only way to defend same-sex marriage is by appeal to the real essence of marriage. The argument, they insist, should be settled by answering the question, What *is* marriage? The only alternative to there being a real essence of marriage is anything-goes relativism, where marriage could be about anything, even tennis. This is obviously a false dichotomy. Rejecting realism about marriage does not commit us to anything-goes relativism. The meaning of "marriage" is constrained, not by some objectively real essence of marriage, but by linguistic meaning and social convention. We can and should ask, What *is* marriage? But we also can and should ask, What *should* marriage *be*? I suspect that the institution of marriage as conceived of by most people in our society is loose enough to include some same-sex relations. But even if it were not, the question would be whether we should rethink how we conceive of marriage.

The question of what marriage should be is a tricky one because there could be many ways to try to answer it. One way is to ask which conception of marriage would be better for society as a whole. That question will have to wait until chapter 9. Another way to answer this question is to ask what form of marriage would be better for the individuals in the marriage. That is a highly personal question. What works best for some people might not work best for others. For me personally, the NNL theorists' Victorian notion of "conjugal" marriage sounds bleak and stifling. And their prudish conception of "marital" sex strikes me as joyless and alienating. I am very thankful that my marriage is not like that. My wife and I thrive as husband and wife, and as individuals, thanks in part to the fact that our marriage is *not* a conjugal one. There may be conservatives who would prefer to have a conjugal type of marriage. The good thing about the socially constructed meaning of marriage is that it is less specific than the NNL notion of conjugal marriage and so it allows for more individual variation. Thus, it can include nonconjugal relationships while not excluding couples from trying to make their marriage into a conjugal one if that is what they are into. For this reason, I think the modern conception of marriage is better for a greater number of individual married persons. It allows more couples to find fulfillment in the kind of marital relationship that works best for them.

CONCLUSION

As we have found in this chapter, the natural law arguments (SNL and NNL) fail. And they fail in two ways. The SNL argument claims that homosexuality is unnatural and also assumes that any behavior or practice that is unnatural is thereby morally wrong. But homosexuality is not unnatural in most senses of the term "unnatural." Even if it were, being unnatural does not automatically make something wrong or bad. Many things that are unnatural (in whatever way) are morally neutral or even morally good. The NNL argument is no better. It assumes a very implausible realism about social institutions. Even if there were a true essence of marriage, that would not automatically mean that "true" marriages would be better than other marriage-like relationships.

6

HOMOSEXUALITY AND MORALITY II— THE TELEOLOGICAL ARGUMENT AND MORAL INTUITIONISTISM

Another prominent argument against homosexuality, closely related to the Natural Law argument, involves the idea of *teleology*, or purposes, in nature. The argument is that homosexual relations violate the "proper function" or "purpose" of the sexual organs. The major claim of the argument goes something like this: The purpose or function of the genitals (and of sexual behavior) is reproduction, just as the purpose of the stomach (and of digestion) is to provide nutrition to the body. Since sex between two men or between two women cannot result in reproduction, gay sex involves using the sexual organs in ways other than their proper function. When gay people have sex, they are using their sex organs to give or receive pleasure, to express affection, to bond emotionally, or some combination of these reasons. The argument is that since giving or receiving pleasure, expressing affection, and fostering emotional intimacy are not proper functions of the sex organs, gay sex is morally wrong.[1]

Notice that this argument supports a very puritanical view of sex. If it were successful, the argument would demonstrate that a lot of heterosexual sex acts are morally wrong, too. Oral sex or "heavy petting" would be morally wrong, according to this line of reasoning. So would having sex while using birth control. It would also be morally wrong for postmenopausal women to have sex. None of these sexual activities can result in pregnancy, so they all involve using the sex organs for purposes other than reproduction.

This "proper function" argument makes two crucial assumptions. First, it assumes that natural objects and processes—including the sex organs—have inherent or built-in purposes. Second, it assumes that this purpose has *normative weight*. In other words, it assumes that to use a bodily organ or process for some purpose other than its proper function is morally wrong. This second assumption is usually unstated. But it is a crucial premise of the argument. Both of these assumptions are highly dubious.

TELEOLOGY IN NATURE

First, let's consider the claim that a natural object can have an innate purpose or function. What does it mean for any object, natural or otherwise, to have a purpose or a function? Artifacts certainly have purposes. A hammer, for example, is for driving nails, a chair is for sitting, a handgun is for robbing liquor stores, and so on. The reason that artifacts have a purpose is that they were designed to help the user achieve some particular goal. The first person to make a chair did so with the intention that people would sit on it. Having a goal in this sense seems to require a will. (By "will" I mean a capacity to choose a goal.) A rock or a tree stump is not the kind of thing that could have a function in this sense without someone assigning one to it. I could decide that the tree stump in my backyard is going to be used as a stool or a pedestal. But the tree stump in itself cannot have one purpose or another.

This leads to the first interpretation of natural objects having a purpose—the divine creation interpretation. Suppose that there is a God who created the entire universe out of nothing. Suppose also that this God did not simply bring matter into existence in a big bang and then just sit back and wait to see what came out of it. Instead this God carefully designed every natural object in the universe (i.e., everything that is not designed by his creatures). In that case, God would probably have some intention for each thing that He invented. This is one way that natural objects could have a purpose.

But there are two problems with using this notion of purpose as an argument against homosexuality. First, even if God designed everything with a purpose, it would not necessarily mean that there would be anything morally wrong with using things for purposes other than he intended them. It is not even obvious that God would disapprove. This seems to be true for artifacts. I doubt that Thomas Edison would be offended at our contemporary practice of decorating Christmas trees with lights, even though that is not what he had in mind when he

invented the lightbulb.[2] For all we know, God might admire the inge-
nuity of his creatures when they find new and interesting off-label uses
for the things he created. Suppose, however, that God would disapprove of our using natural objects for ways other than what they were
intended for. With this interpretation, the teleological argument is just
another version of the divine command theory of morality. We have
already seen in chapter 3 why that theory must be rejected.

Another way that we can think of natural objects, such as human
organs, as having a proper purpose is through the idea of *telos*. This is
an idea that is very prominent in Aristotle's theory of nature. A natural
telos is a goal that a natural object of a given kind has an innate impulse
to strive toward. In the natural teleology view, all natural objects have a
goal or purpose, and these goals and purposes help to explain how
natural objects behave. It is this explanatory function of the telos that
makes it different from the divine command conception of purposes in
nature. We can determine the natural purpose of an object by observing
how that type of object typically behaves. We do not need to speculate
about the intentions of an infinite creator. This theory of natural teleology does not require a creator at all. Natural objects have their telos
independently of any intelligent being; they do not require any will to
assign them a purpose.

This idea of a natural telos is highly problematic. The notion that
natural objects can have goals or functions on their own (independently
of being assigned a purpose by us) conflicts with our best scientific
understanding. One problem with teleological explanation in nature is
that it seems to require backward causation. In other words, it requires
that some future state or event has a causal influence on some earlier
event. A goal is something that occurs in the future, but in the teleological view, this future goal somehow determines what happens now. It
influences the behavior of the object by drawing it forward, pulling it
toward its destiny. Our scientific understanding of nature, however,
requires that the cause occur before the effect (or at least contempora-
neously with the effect).

A defender of natural teleology might point out that goals and purposes can direct the behavior of sentient beings. For example, I go to
the kitchen and rummage through the refrigerator with the goal of
getting something to eat. But does the goal—the future event of my
eating—really cause my behavior? For the most part, no. It is not the
goal itself, occurring in the possible future, that draws me toward it. As
a sentient being, I can form a representation of, and desire for, that
future goal or purpose. Those mental states—intentions, plans, desires—can cause behavior because they already exist before the actions
or choices that they subsequently cause. But nonsentient natural ob-

jects (like rocks, trees, and bodily organs) cannot represent any future goals in the present.

Progress in the sciences over the last two hundred years or so is due in large part to eliminating any appeal to goals and purposes in our scientific explanations. This has been especially important in scientific explanations of biology since it is in biology that we are most tempted to posit goals and purposes. Modern biology has reduced the goals and purposes in biological systems to mechanistic causation. For example, we can explain what the heart does entirely in terms of the muscle tissues of which it is comprised, the nervous system to which it is connected, and the chemical and electrical processes that cause it to beat in rhythm. Still, there is a legitimate question of *why* the heart exists and *why* it beats. It seems natural to try to answer this by saying that its purpose is to circulate blood. The theory of evolution, however, allows us to say something like this without positing purposes in nature.

The beauty of Darwin's theory of natural selection is that it allows us to answer the question of why the heart exists, and why it does the things it does, without appealing to teleological causes. Instead of saying that an organ exists *in order to* perform some function, we can now say that the organ is the result of random mutation plus natural selection and exists (generally, throughout a population) *because it happens to* provide some useful benefit to the individuals within that population. Biologists might still talk in terms of an organ's purpose, as a metaphor or as a shorthand way to refer to the result of the evolutionary process. But to believe that natural organs literally have a "purpose" requires adopting a pre-scientific Aristotelian view of the universe.

Modern biology and evolutionary theory do allow for teleology in some sense. There is a meaningful sense in which we can say, for example, that the *purpose* of the large intestine is to expel solid waste from the digestive tract after absorbing any remaining water but that its purpose is not to smuggle contraband (even though it can be very successfully used for either purpose). Here is a rough account of the modern, scientifically informed way that an organ of the body can have a purpose: a particular organ has the purpose of bringing about some goal if that organ would not have evolved in the way it did (with all the specific features that it has) unless it tended to promote achievement of that goal.[3]

The large intestine would not have come to exist unless it absorbed water and moved bowels. However, the large intestine would still exist even if it was not useful for hiding contraband. Thus we can say that the purpose of the large intestine is to absorb water and pass waste and not to smuggle. The large intestine seems to have only one essential or proper function, a digestive one. In other words, only one of the things it can do explains why it exists and why it has evolved through natural selection.

Other organs seem, by this criterion, to have multiple purposes. The liver, for example, removes toxins from the bloodstream, synthesizes plasma proteins, produces hormones, decomposes red blood cells, and produces enzymes such as bile that are used in digestion. All of these processes are necessary for our health and are not performed by any other organs. Thus, we can say that the liver would not exist unless it did all these various things. If it only performed some of these functions—that is, had we evolved differently and some of these functions were performed by another organ—then it would not be a liver as we know it.

PURPOSE OF THE HUMAN GENITALS

Now let us consider the human genitals—what they do and how they work. Obviously, they would not exist were it not for their direct involvement in reproduction. Thus, we can say that at least one of the essential purposes of the genitals is reproduction. But human genitals are also the source of a distinct kind of pleasure, specifically *sexual* pleasure, and their stimulation satisfies a distinct kind of desire, specifically *sexual* desire. Genitals could of course exist without this function of producing intense pleasure. But the question is whether *human* genitals, with all those features they actually have, would exist unless they were the source of a distinct kind of satisfaction.

Before answering this question, let us consider a different kind of animal with rather different genitals, the rat. Sexual intercourse probably produces no pleasure in rats. I think it is safe to say that, unlike with humans, the anticipation of pleasure is not a motivation for a rat's sexual behavior. Rat sex is the result of a deep instinctual drive resulting in mostly automatic behaviors and has little or nothing to do with seeking gratification (and is certainly not a conscious desire to have pups). Female rats in heat engage in an instinctive, automatic behavior known as *lordosis*: shoulders to the ground, butt in the air, tail to the side, ready to receive the male rat's penis. Rats are driven to copulation by an instinct that controls their behavior. Copulatory behavior in rats (and many other animals) is easy to induce. Just give a female rat a dose of estradiol hormone and put a male in her cage, or touch her flanks, and she will assume the position.[4] Thus, even if it were the case that rats enjoy sex, this pleasure would be incidental, a mere side effect. They do not need pleasure to reproduce and any pleasure they happen to get from sex would have played little or no role in the evolution of their genitals or their sexual behavior.

By contrast, when human females ovulate, they do not go into heat. Nor do they have the instinctual lordosis behavior. The sight (or smell) of an ovulating human woman, even a sexually receptive one, does not automatically trigger copulatory behavior in (heterosexual) human men. So now the question is how our human sex organs and our human sexual behaviors evolved. Did pleasure play any crucial role in that evolution?

I think the answer to that question is almost certainly yes. Imagine what would have happened if our pre-human ancestors (*Australopithecus africanus*, perhaps) did not get pleasure from sex. Lacking the kinds of mechanisms that cause rats to engage in automatic sexual behavior— going into heat, pheromones, and automatic behavior like lordosis— they probably would not have had sex very often, if at all. They would have had few, if any, children and would have quickly gone extinct.

Evolutionary theory allows us to tell a very simple story of how the human sex organs became the source of powerful sensations of pleasure. Suppose there were two cavemen brothers, call them "Oop" and "Tunk." Due to some random genetic difference, Oop's genitals are the source of intense pleasure while Tunk gets little or no pleasure from genital stimulation. Oop will most likely seek out many opportunities for sex. Tunk, however, will not. Lacking any instinct to override his decision making, and ignorant of the fact that sex is how babies are made, Tunk is not likely to engage in sex very often. The result is that Oop has many children who will most likely inherit his genes for pleasure-inducing genitals. Since Tunk, on the other hand, does not sire any children, he does not pass on his genes for genitals that do not produce pleasure. Thus, if there were proto-human genitals that were not the source of intense pleasure, they would be selected against and quickly eliminated from the population. It is very likely, then, that our human genitals evolved the way they are in part because they are the source of a distinctive kind of pleasure. And so producing pleasure *is* one of the purposes of the human sex organs.

One could make a similar case for the claim that expression of affection is yet another purpose of the human genitals—not just any kind of affection, of course, but the unique sort of love that exists between two people in a committed romantic relationship. This is part of our biology, part of how our sex organs evolved. When a human being has an orgasm, the body releases hormones such as oxytocin and vasopressin. These substances also act as neurotransmitters in the brain. There they give rise to feelings of emotional closeness, foster trust, and facilitate pair-bonding. Humans are not the only animals that get a release of oxytocin and vasopressin upon orgasm. Some other mammals also do. Those animals, like wolves and dogs, whose bodies release these substances upon orgasm tend to be monogamous. Animals that don't get a rush of oxytocin and vasopressin upon orgasm, such as cats, tend to be more promiscuous and do not form couples.[5]

Pair-bonding is crucial for humans because human babies are so helpless. A female cat can easily raise her kittens without help. They require only eight to ten weeks before they are ready to take care of themselves. But a lone cavewoman would have great difficulty raising her human baby, who takes over a year just to learn to walk. Proto-humans with sex organs that release neurotransmitters that facilitate pair-bonding will have children who are more likely to be raised by two parents and thus more likely to survive to adulthood. Cavemen and cavewomen with genitals that didn't promote bonding or mate attachment would have had children who were less likely to survive into adulthood (due to insufficient parental care) and so would have been much less likely to pass their genes on to future generations. Thus, the expression of love and the fostering of emotional intimacy and closeness are also part of the essential function of the human sex organs. They would not have evolved the way they did if they were not so good at emotionally uniting intimate couples.

It is important, however, not to jump to the conclusion that the *real* purpose of the human sex organs is to reproduce. This conclusion might be tempting because these evolutionary explanations for the functions of the human genitals ultimately rest on whether or not certain sexual organs (or copulatory processes) result in having more children. Sexual pleasure and the pair-bonding influence of orgasmic hormones lead to having more children, who then pass those genes on to future generations. Thus, we might be tempted to say that pleasure and pair-bonding are not really functions of the human genitals. They are only the *means* by which our genitals and our sexual behavior bring about the true goal of having more children. This line of reasoning fails. *Every* evolutionary explanation ultimately rests on how some bodily organ or biological process allows its possessor to have more children and thus pass its genes on to future generations. But it would be absurd to say that the purpose of every human organ and every biological process is therefore reproduction.

Consider, for example, the evolutionary explanation of our human sweat glands. We humans lack fur, and most of our sweat glands produce watery sweat. Furry animals, including our closest ape relatives, have sweat glands that mostly produce oily sweat. Our watery sweat allows us to walk or jog long distances across open landscapes without overheating. The evolutionary explanation goes like this: those proto-

humans whose sweat glands produced more watery sweat hunted successfully in the savannas of east Africa, while those proto-humans whose
glands produced more oily sweat got too hot and either quit hunting
(and went hungry) or kept hunting and died of heat exhaustion.[6] Either
way, those with watery sweat ultimately ate better and lived longer. This
allowed them to have more children, who inherited their genes for
making watery sweat. The evolutionary explanation comes back to having more children. But that does not mean that the proper purpose of
our human sweat glands is reproduction! As with any other trait, the
purpose of our sweat glands, in evolutionary terms, is determined by
those proximal effects that enhance fitness (in this case, keeping the
body cool), not by the remote effect of fitness itself (passing more of
one's genes on to the next generation).

IS IT WRONG TO USE AN ORGAN FOR SOMETHING OTHER THAN ITS PROPER PURPOSE?

Let us suppose, for the sake of argument, that the human sex organs
have only one innate, natural purpose, and that is procreation. I have
already shown that that is not reasonable, since the other functions of
pleasure and emotional bonding are crucial parts of their evolutionary
explanation. But now we want to consider the second part of the teleological argument against homosexuality—the claim that it is wrong to
use an organ for anything but its "proper" purpose. Call this the *teleological principle*. This principle turns out to be false. Thus, even if the
sex organs had only one proper purpose, it would still not be wrong to
use them for other purposes.

Consider the human foot. If the human foot has any proper purpose
it would be for walking and standing. The human foot is a very important feature of human anatomy and has an important role in human
evolution.[7] One very important, though not so obvious, anatomical difference between apes and humans is that we have flat feet that are well
suited for walking long distances. Chimps and other apes, by contrast,
have feet better suited for hanging from trees than for walking. That is
why early humans (*Homo erectus*) wandered to every corner of Europe
and Asia, while our chimpanzee cousins never strayed from tropical
Africa. Does that mean that soccer players or karate enthusiasts, who
also use their feet for kicking, are misusing their foot organs in ways that
are morally objectionable? That is absurd. Since kicking soccer balls, or
planks of wood, is obviously not morally wrong, the teleological principle fails.

One reply that defenders of the teleological argument might give is that kicking is included in the many different functions or purposes that the foot has. They might then claim that the proper purpose of the foot is standing and walking, *and* kicking. But this list would have to be extended indefinitely to include all the uses of the foot that are obviously not morally suspect. The proper purposes of the foot would include walking, standing, kicking, hopping, pedaling a bicycle, tap dancing, manipulating a wah pedal, crushing cockroaches, and so on.

But some of these allegedly proper functions are quite implausible. The foot could not have evolved for bike riding since the bicycle has only been around for about 150 years. Moreover, if the teleological view is to be meaningful, there must be *some* use of the foot that is not included in its repertoire of innate, natural functions. Suppose I learn to write or draw with my foot. The manipulation of writing tools is surely not included in the innate, proper function or purpose of the foot. (The human foot is not well suited for tool use and its selection had nothing to do with being useful for that purpose.) The teleological principle would imply that I am doing something *morally wrong* by writing with my foot. That is obviously unreasonable.

If the foot has more than one purpose, then there is good reason to think that the genitals also have more than one purpose. And if it is not morally wrong to use a foot for something other than its purpose, then the same should be true of the genitals. Defenders of the teleological argument against homosexuality could try to argue that the purpose of the foot has no moral significance, but the purpose of the genitals does. But that would be ad hoc, meaning that this distinction would be proposed only because it is convenient for those who are trying to argue that homosexuality is morally wrong and not for any independent reason. The only reason someone would say that it is wrong to misuse the genitals but not wrong to misuse other organs is that he has already decided that homosexuality is wrong and needs to find some argument to justify it.

Now let's consider oral sex. According to the teleological argument, to engage in oral sex is to misuse the genitals. But if oral sex is a misuse of the genitals, then it seems it must also be a misuse of the mouth. (It would not make sense that the purpose of the mouth could involve oral sex but that using the mouth in this proper way would involve misusing the genitals.) If oral sex involves a misuse of the mouth, then it would seem that kissing should also be a misuse of the mouth. Kissing is a part of sexual intercourse for most couples, along with various kinds of acts that serve as "foreplay" (including oral sex).[8] But none of this is strictly necessary for intercourse to result in pregnancy. According to the teleological argument, the sole proper function for sexual intercourse is reproduction, and it is wrong to engage in sex (or use the genitals) for any other purpose. Thus, kissing and any other kind of foreplay should be avoided if we follow the teleological argument to its natural conclusion. Surely there is nothing morally wrong with kissing, at least under the appropriate circumstances (no PDA, please!). Thus, there is nothing morally wrong with using the mouth to express love and affection. And there is no reason to think that the sex organs—or any other body part—are any different from the mouth in this regard.

NNL TELEOLOGY—MARITAL SEX AND "TWO-IN-ONE FLESH"

Just as some scholars have formulated a fancy version of the Natural Law argument against homosexuality and same-sex marriage (discussed at the end of the previous chapter), these same scholars have formulated a fancy version of the teleological argument. I will refer to this as "New Natural Law" (NNL) teleology. Instead of claiming that reproduction is the proper function of the sex organs, this argument claims that reproduction is the proper purpose of marriage and sex.

Most people, whether they support gay marriage or oppose it, agree that sexual intimacy is an important part of marriage. We expect married couples to have sex with each other (exclusively). We think that sex (at least between married people) can and should be a good thing and that physical intimacy makes a marriage stronger. According to NNL teleology, however, sex contributes to the good of marriage because of the basic biological facts of reproduction. Sexual intercourse creates a "bodily union" between two people, joining them in "one flesh."[9] NNL theorists claim that "for two individuals to unite organically and thus bodily, their bodies must be coordinated for some biological purpose of the whole." And this purpose is reproduction. "In coitus, but not in other forms of sexual contact, a man's body and a woman's body coordinate by way of their sexual organs for the common biological purpose of reproduction."[10] This is because sex is the first step in the process of reproduction. In creating offspring through procreation, their two bodies are united in the children, toward which sex is naturally, biologically aimed.

One obvious problem with this view of marriage and sex is that it goes way too far. If we should not allow same-sex couples to marry because they cannot procreate, then we should also not allow infertile opposite-sex couples to marry. That would obviously be unjust. NNL theorists reply to this objection by saying that infertile heterosexual couples can still engage in the right *kind* of sex (penis-in-the-vagina coitus), sex that *could* result in pregnancy *if* the couple were fertile. But now they are changing their argument. The claim was that sex is *biologically* connected with reproduction, not that sex is the same *kind* of activity as some *other* activity that is biologically connected with reproduction. It is no more biologically possible for an infertile heterosexual couple to reproduce sexually than it is for a same-sex couple to reproduce sexually. (That is true by definition. If an infertile couple manages to reproduce sexually, then they were *not* in fact infertile.) Furthermore, this NNL teleology would imply that we should not allow opposite-sex couples to marry if they are unable to perform penis-in-the-vagina coitus. That would mean that many paraplegics or men with severe erectile dysfunction should not be allowed to marry.[11]

There is, however, an even more fundamental flaw in this NNL account of the "proper" purpose of sex and marriage—that it is based on magical thinking about reproduction and ignorance of biology. It may be true, in some sense, that "organic unity" and "two-in-one flesh" occurs in reproduction, even if no biologist would describe it using those terms. This unity, however, occurs only in the event of conception, not in the act of sexual intercourse. The act of coitus involves a penis thrusting in and out of a vagina, followed (usually) by ejaculation, which deposits semen at the base of the cervix (unless the couple uses a condom or the withdrawal method). Nowhere is there any unity, except perhaps symbolically. But symbolic unity is not *biological* unity. There is no less unity, symbolically speaking, if we substitute one of the genitals with a mouth, hand, anus, or whatever. We could only insist that there is a unique kind of biological unity in heterosexual coitus if we assume that reproduction is the sole proper function of the human sex organs. But that claim has already been discredited in this chapter.

In the event of conception, a sperm cell from the man unites with an egg cell of the woman to form a new individual with approximately half of its genes from each parent. If anything is an "organic unity" of a man and a woman, it is the zygote, and the eventual child, that results from this biological event. What the NNL theorists do not seem to realize is that sexual intercourse is not necessary for conception. With ordinary "natural" reproduction, sexual intercourse is the first step of the procreative process. But many couples conceive using artificial insemination. In that case, the first step will involve the man masturbating into a cup (perhaps with some assistance from the mother-to-be). Artificial insemination is rather low-tech. It could be done using a turkey baster, without any assistance needed from medical experts. A more high-tech form of artificial reproduction is in vitro fertilization. With this method, the "unitive" event does not even happen in the human body; it takes place in a petri dish in a laboratory. With future technology in cloning, it might even be possible for two men or two women to unite their DNA into "one flesh" and conceive a child with approximately half of the genes of each.[12] (Of course, reproductive cloning is highly controversial, and in no way do I mean to condone it. My argument is simply that it is theoretically possible, so there is no necessary connection between coitus and human reproduction.)

Of course, NNL theorists might disapprove of in vitro fertilization or even artificial insemination—and, in fact, the Catholic Church opposes all artificial means or reproduction on exactly those grounds. But that does not matter. Their argument for *why* gay sex (as well as artificial methods of reproduction, oral sex, and masturbation) is wrong is that penis-in-the-vagina sexual intercourse is essentially connected with procreation and child bearing. That claim is simply false. It ignores scientific facts of human reproduction and is based on symbolic and magical thinking. Even with ordinary, natural reproduction through sexual intercourse, the "unitive event"—conception—does not take place during the sex act. It happens several days later, after the sperm cells have migrated into the uterus and up the fallopian tube.[13]

NNL teleologists claim that "two men or two women cannot achieve organic bodily union since there is no bodily good or function toward which their bodies can coordinate, reproduction being the only candidate."[14] This seems to ignore obvious purposes such as pleasure and the expression of mutual affection. One reason why NNL theorists think the purpose of sex cannot be pleasure is that, as they argue, the pleasure of the two partners cannot be one unified thing since pleasure is a private experience. They compare sex for pleasure to mutual masturbation. It is not obvious why NNL theorists think that the good of sex has to be one unified thing. Presumably it is because they think that the proper purpose of sex is to unite the (married) partners. If that is the case, then they are interpreting "unifying" far too literally. When I say that good sex helps to *unite* a couple, I mean that the sex helps them both feel a greater fondness or sense of commitment toward the other. Thus, a healthy sex life will keep them together *as a couple* (meaning two distinct people), not that they will somehow be fused together into one person, like conjoined twins.

At any rate, mutual pleasure in two people is very different from two people simultaneously experiencing parallel but unconnected pleasures. The comparison with mutual masturbation is apt only if each partner engages in sex for his or her own selfish pleasure. That is certainly not ideal (though I would hesitate to say that it is *morally wrong*, as long as it is mutually consensual and there is not deception). Ideally, sex involves each partner aiming to please the other and receiving added pleasure from his or her partner's pleasure. Under these circumstances, their goal is something more than simply two separate, private experiences. They aim to achieve a *shared* goal of mutual pleasure through reciprocity. In fact, it is the NNL claim that the "proper" purpose of sex is reproduction that promotes selfishness by discouraging sexual reciprocity. Some women are unable to achieve orgasm through coitus alone. According to the NNL view, it would be *morally wrong* for a woman's husband to give her oral pleasure, or even for her to touch herself during sex. The implication of the NNL teleology is that women should not seek orgasm, since it is not a necessary part of reproduction. They should, at most, hope for orgasm as an unintended side effect of trying to have a baby.

The other reason why NNL teleologists think that the proper purpose of sex cannot be pleasure is that they think that pleasure is not bodily. They say that to engage in sex for pleasure is wrong because doing so "instrumentalizes" sex, making the physical act a mere means to the experience of pleasure. There are many reasons to reject this argument. First, it falsely assumes that any bodily activity can have only a bodily state as its proper goal. To engage in some bodily activity for the purpose of an enjoyable experience, in their view, would be morally wrong. But that is an absurd claim. Compare sex to other bodily activities, such as eating or exercise. Surely it is not morally wrong to eat for pleasure, or to exercise because one enjoys it. Of course, eating very unhealthy food may be imprudent, but that does not mean that we must choose food *only* on the basis of nutrition and then just hope that we enjoy it. It is absurd to think that pleasurable taste experiences must be only a by-product of eating healthfully and never something that we should aim at directly, lest we sully the act of eating and "instrumentalize" it.[15]

Another problem with this argument is that it assumes an implausible substance dualism by denying that experiences are bodily. Modern biology and neuroscience provide strong evidence that pleasure *is* bodily. This should be especially obvious when we are talking about *physical* pleasure. It is rather implausible to think that a disembodied spirit (if such an entity were even possible) would be capable of experiencing orgasm.

INTUITIONISM AND MORAL KNOWLEDGE

My criticism of the Natural Law and teleological arguments are primarily skeptical arguments. For example, I have argued that there is no good reason for thinking that there is an objective essence of marriage or that there is a "proper" purpose of sexual activity. But defenders of NNL argument and NNL teleology have an explanation for why they think these things are true. They support their claim that marriage has a true essence and that sex has a proper function by appeal to moral intuition.

According to moral intuitionism, moral properties like right and wrong are real properties that really belong to certain actions, or kinds of actions, independently of anyone's approval or disapproval and independently of social customs, practices, or conventions. NNL theorists claim that *having-procreation-as-a-goal* is a real, mind-independent property of marriage and sex, and that deviating from such a built-in purpose is objectively wrong. Wrongness is thus an objective feature of certain practices like masturbation, oral sex, premarital sex, and same-sex sex.

One challenge faced by realism of this sort is the epistemic question. If rightness and wrongness (or inherent essences and purposes) are properties that certain practices have independently of our beliefs, attitudes, and values, and independently of custom and social convention, then how could we *know* that practices have these properties? This is not a problem for physical properties, such as size and shape. The epistemological question of how we know the size and shape of an object is a fairly easy one to answer. For most objects, we come to know their size and shape through the senses. I know that a particular basketball is round because I can see it with my eyes and feel it with my hands. I know it has an orange-brown color because I can see the color. Moral properties are not like that. They cannot be detected by visual, auditory, or tactile senses. For us to know moral properties, we would have to have a special faculty of moral intuition or immediate intellectual insight.

In ordinary language, "intuition" is often used to describe a vague, gut reaction or an inarticulate, inexplicable seeming. But in the philosophical sense, an intuition is a belief that is justified without being inferred from any other beliefs or acquired from sense perceptions. It is self-evident.[16] NNL theorists seem to accept something like an intuitionist account of moral knowledge. For example, they say,

> The practical insight that marriage . . . has its own intelligible point, and that marriage as a one-flesh communion of persons is consummated and actualized in the reproductive-type acts of spouses, cannot be attained by someone who has no idea of what these terms mean; nor can it be attained, except with strenuous efforts of imagi-

nation, by people who, due to personal or cultural circumstances, have little acquaintance with actual marriages thus understood.[17]

In other words, when pressed, they ultimately appeal to some special intuition that allows them to see the "true" purpose of sex and to discern what "real" marriage is—an intuition that the rest of us poor fools simply lack, due to some character flaw, conceptual ignorance, or lack of relevant experience. I agree that buying into the NNL theory of "real" marriage does indeed take a lot of strenuous imagination. It seems to me, however, that that is a mark *against* the theory. Things that are harder to imagine are generally *less* likely to be true than things that are easy to imagine. At bottom, the NNL theorists defend their views by claiming to have moral authority due to their superior insight to moral and metaphysical matters. They see it better than the rest of us do. And they give no argument to back up their elitist pretensions.[18]

So NNL theorists claim to intuit the wrongness of masturbation, oral sex, and homosexual acts, and claim to intuit the true essence of marriage as essentially aimed at procreation. The rest of us intuit no such thing. Some of us even intuit the opposite. I have the intuition that masturbation (in moderation) is a morally *good* thing and should be encouraged, as Dr. Ruth Westheimer did on her popular radio show in the 1980s. I have similar intuitions about sex for pleasure when done responsibly and oral sex when it is done willingly and enjoyed by both partners. So NNL theorists cannot simply appeal to their intuitions. They need to give us reasons why their intuitions are better than mine or why my intuitions might be suspect.

Compare the intuitionist realism of NNL to realism about physical properties. I know that the basketball is orange-brown because I can see it. But how do I know that it is *really* orange-brown? If the color of a physical object is a real property, then it has that property independently of my observing it. So what reason do I have to think that the color of the basketball is a property that it has independently of my seeing it? One reason is that when other people observe the same basketball, they too report observing that it is orange-brown. If other people said that the basketball was "beige" or "yellow," I would have reason to doubt my perception, unless I could provide evidence that those who perceive it differently are mistaken or confused. Maybe they are color-blind or wearing tinted glasses. Maybe they think the word "beige" means orange-brown.

The best evidence for realism about certain facts or properties is a convergence of belief among different people. When the beliefs of different people diverge significantly, there is reason to have doubts that there are objective facts of the matter.[19] For example, realism about matters of taste is implausible in part because there is so little agreement. Some people like mushrooms, others hate them; some people find wetlands beautiful, others think they are ugly. This is reason to doubt that deliciousness and beauty are real properties. Disagreement of opinion is a reason to think that whether something is delicious or beautiful is merely a subjective reaction, in the eye of the beholder and not an objective fact of the world.

The question ultimately comes down to the best explanation for why certain people are opposed to homosexual behavior and same-sex marriage. The explanation given by the NNL theorists is that the conservatives have access to some real properties through a kind of intuition that informs them of the true essence of marriage or the proper purpose of sex or the inherent wrongness of non-procreative sex—an insight that the rest of us are simply blind to. But there are good reasons to think that disapproval of homosexuality is not due to any immediate intellectual insight. There is independent evidence that disapproval of homosexuality is caused either by one's own repressed homosexual inclinations or by irrational feelings of disgust. We will examine the psychological causes of disapproval of homosexuality in the next chapter.

CONCLUSION

The teleological argument relies on two crucial claims. The first claim is that the purpose of the human genitals is procreation and not pleasure or the expression of affection. The second claim is that it is morally wrong to use any organ for anything other than its "proper" purpose. As with the Natural Law argument, neither of these claims is reasonable. This is because, to the extent that it makes sense to say that the human genitals have any purpose(s), its purposes must include pleasure and the expression of affection. They are well suited for these uses and would not have evolved the way they are if they were not so well suited. More importantly, the theoretical (moral) assumption behind this argument is false. There are many ways that we use parts of our bodies other than for their normal purposes—we use our feet to pedal bicycles, we use our lips for drinking with straws and kissing, we use our ears to hold a pencil or cigarette. None of these activities can reasonably be claimed to be morally wrong.

The NNL version of the teleological argument substitutes sex and marriage for the genitals as having the essential goal of procreation, and they try to polish it up with poetic phrases like "two-in-one flesh" (whatever that means). But as we have seen, they are polishing a turd. They make absurd assumptions such as that a bodily activity cannot have pleasure as its purpose and that the real essence of marriage is for procreation. These are absurd assumptions that have more absurd implications, such as that it is wrong to eat for pleasure or that infertile people should not be allowed to marry. When pushed to defend these wacky claims, they appeal to their own authority and wisdom. But they have no evidence to support their claims to superior intellectual vision.

7

DEBUNKING PSYCHOLOGICAL EXPLANATIONS FOR DISAPPROVAL OF HOMOSEXUALITY

Those who are morally opposed to homosexuality claim to have some legitimate reason (or reasons) for their opposition. Some of them give arguments for why they think it is wrong. For example, they think that it is forbidden by God or that it involves a misuse of the genitals. Some claim to directly perceive the wrongness of homosexuality or same-sex marriage. The arguments people give for why they think homosexuality is wrong are not necessarily *good* arguments. And there are good reasons to doubt the intuitions that some people claim to have that homosexuality is wrong or that only "conjugal" marriages can be genuine marriages. Given the fact that most people have very different intuitions, it is unlikely that gay rights opponents are *actually* perceiving any *real* moral properties of homosexuality or marriage.

Nevertheless, we tend to assume that the arguments gay rights opponents give should explain why they disapprove of homosexuality and same-sex marriage. Even if the opponents of same-sex marriage are wrong when they say that only "conjugal" marriages can be true marriages, we assume that their belief in that claim is what causes them to oppose same-sex marriage. If conservatives claim to have direct perception of the wrongness of homosexuality, then these intuitions should explain why they disapprove, even if those perceptions are illusory.

There are, however, reasons to doubt that that is the case. The arguments and alleged intuitions might have little or nothing to do with why certain people actually disapprove of homosexuality. Many people who disapprove of homosexuality do so for other reasons, reasons that they themselves might not be conscious of. The moral arguments they cite (for example, that homosexuality is unnatural or involves a misuse of the genitals) are merely pseudo-arguments, concocted as post hoc rationalizations of their disapproval. And what some people think is a direct perception of the wrongness of homosexuality might really just be a subjective emotional reaction that they project onto homosexuals and their practices or lifestyles. This projection is then mistaken for a perception of some objective feature of wrongness.

Empirical studies have found that many people who disapprove of homosexuality do so for reasons other than the ones they explicitly give. More importantly, these real causes of their disapproval have no moral relevancy to whether homosexuality is morally wrong or whether we should recognize same-sex marriages. The real reason for their disapproval is one that they themselves would not accept as morally relevant. If this is true, then we have a *debunking* explanation for the belief that homosexuality is morally wrong.

DEBUNKING EXPLANATIONS

A debunking explanation for why an individual has a particular belief is an explanation that has nothing to do with the truth of what is believed. If your reason for believing something has nothing to do with the truth of what you believe, then you have no reason to believe it. That is because you would still believe it even if it were not true. A debunking explanation of why you hold some particular belief is an explanation that would show that your belief, or your belief-forming process, does not track the truth. If you have reason to suspect that your belief does not track the truth, then you have reason to doubt that belief and should stop believing it. That would not give you reason to think that the belief is *false*. But it would show that you have no reason to think that it is true. In light of a debunking explanation of your belief, you should suspend judgment, at least until acquiring further confirmation or disconfirmation.

Here is an illustration. I believe that the Denver Broncos lost Super Bowl XLVIII, rather embarrassingly. My reason for believing this is that I watched the game on television. Having watched the game is very good evidence for my belief that the Broncos lost. The fact that they lost the game is part of the explanation for why I believe they lost. If they had not lost, then the game I watched on television would have been different, and I would not have come to believe that they lost. My belief tracks the truth. I remember watching the game alone, and, as a lifelong Broncos fan, I avoided all news stories or discussion about the game afterward. So, for the first week or so after that abysmal game, my memory of having watched it was the *only* evidence I had. But even though it was the only evidence, it was good enough evidence for me to be relatively certain about it.

Now suppose a week or two later, I discovered that the *real* reason why I believed the Broncos lost Super Bowl XLVIII is *not* because I watched the game. Suppose I discovered that I had been hypnotized to believe that the Broncos lost. How would I discover this? Perhaps I found a charge on my credit card for a hypnosis session. Upon seeing this, I remember going to a hypnotist around the time of the Super Bowl. I ask my wife and she corroborates. She even has a video tape of the session. I watch the tape and see the hypnotist inducing each memory I have of the game. "Picture Payton Manning in the shotgun on the first play of the game," he says. "The center snaps the ball early, and it sails over Manning's shoulder. . . ."

Now I have overwhelming evidence that my reason for believing that the Broncos lost is not because I watched the game but because I have been hypnotized and have had false memories of watching the game implanted in my mind. This explanation for my belief that the Broncos lost Super Bowl XLVIII is a debunking explanation. The reason why I believe it—viz, that I have been hypnotized to remember watching the game—has no connection to the truth, no connection to the actual game that took place in MetLife Stadium on February 2, 2014. If they had won, I would still believe that they lost.

Once I discover that the only reason for my belief is that I have been hypnotized, the rational thing to do is suspend judgment. I have no reason to think they lost, but I have no reason to think they won, either. It is possible that my hypnosis session was the day after the game, and all the false memories implanted in my mind are "memories" of what really happened in the game. (They would still be false memories in that they would be memories *of my watching the game*, which did not happen.) Until I get more information, I should believe neither that they lost nor that they won.

Those who think that homosexuality is morally wrong should also suspend their disapproval when confronted with evidence that the reasons for their disapproval are not (or might not be) connected to the rightness or wrongness of homosexuality. If the actual cause of their disapproval is irrelevant to any legitimate moral considerations, then they should suspend judgment on the issue. As it turns out, there is good evidence that people who disapprove of homosexuality do so for reasons that are morally irrelevant. In particular, some people disapprove of homosexuality because they are repressing their own homosexual tendencies. That a person is repressing his or her own homosexual tendencies, however, is obviously not a good reason for that person (or anyone) to think that homosexuality is morally wrong. Others disapprove of homosexuality due to visceral feelings of disgust. Given that disgust is a highly subjective matter, the fact that I find something disgusting is no reason why others should avoid doing it.

Of course, it would be difficult, if not impossible, to show that *each and every* person who disapproves of homosexuality does so for one of these reasons. But if we can show that many of the people who disapprove of homosexuality do so for one or both of these bogus reasons, then everyone who thinks homosexuality is wrong should doubt that belief until they can rule out the possibility that they are among those people who disapprove for one of these bogus reasons. By analogy, suppose that instead of discovering that I have been hypnotized into believing the Broncos lost the Super Bowl, I discover that many of my friends and neighbors who think they watched the game were really just hypnotized into thinking they watched it. I would then have reason to doubt *my* beliefs about the Super Bowl because I could not be sure that I had not also been hypnotized.

WHAT ABOUT THE ARGUMENTS AGAINST HOMOSEXUALITY?

Suppose that many people who disapprove of homosexuality are either repressing their own homosexual inclinations or have a subjective, visceral reaction of disgust when contemplating homosexual acts. (I will give evidence that these claims are true below. For now, let us just assume, for the sake of argument, that they are true.) What reasons are there to think that it is the repressed homosexuality or the reaction of disgust that explains their opposition? Why think that the arguments are nothing more than post hoc rationalization of their emotionally driven moral attitudes and not genuine reasons for their disapproval? The answer to that question comes from facts about human psychology. There is good evidence that many, or even most, people form their moral judgments on the basis of emotional reactions and then fabricate bogus arguments to support those reactions.

Social psychologist Jonathan Haidt has conducted several experiments indicating that moral judgments are emotionally driven gut reactions. In one experiment, half of the test subjects were hypnotized to feel disgust upon hearing a particular neutral word (such as the word "often").[1] The subjects then read vignettes involving actions that are borderline morally wrong, such as driving to work when one could just as easily walk or marriage between first cousins. The story contained the trigger word, so when the hypnotized subjects read it, they felt disgust. The control group felt no such disgust. Those in the hypnotized group expressed significantly greater disapproval of the actions.

What is especially surprising is that one-third of the hypnotized subjects even disapproved of actions that are clearly *not* morally wrong. One of the vignettes involved a college student in charge of selecting topics for a series of lectures. When told that the student "often" chooses discussion topics that would be of interest to both students and faculty, many disgust-primed subjects disapproved of the student's behavior. When questioned why they thought the student was acting wrongly, they concocted absurd reasons. For example, some said that he is being sneaky or that he is a vain popularity seeker. It is obvious that the real reason they disapproved is that they were hypnotized to feel disgust. Their stated reasons were clearly fabricated, though the subjects falsely believed that their disapproval was based on these bogus reasons.

On the basis of experiments like this, Haidt has proposed what he calls the "Social-Intuitionist Model" of moral judgment (SIM). According to SIM, reasoning one's way to a moral judgment is possible, but rarely occurs. Moral judgments are mostly the result of automatic, emotionally driven reactions. Moral discussion, debate, and argument are post hoc rationalizations that are aimed primarily at influencing others. We engage in moral deliberation to influence others' beliefs, control our reputation, and form alliances. According to SIM, moral reasoning is not like a judge or a scientist who impartially weighs the evidence and comes to a conclusion. Instead, moral reasoning is more like a lawyer, presenting only the evidence that supports the client's position, or like a press secretary who spins things in ways most favorable to the person represented. This theory explains why moral debate is often so frustrating and fruitless. It also might show why some of the arguments people give against homosexuality are so weak and unconvincing.

Haidt goes on to endorse a kind of sentimentalist theory of moral judgment. He thinks that automatic emotional responses are, and should be, the source of our moral judgments. Reason should be used, not to form moral judgments, but to convince others and foster agreement. That is because he thinks the purpose of morality is to bind together members of a community. I disagree. I would argue that emotionally driven reactions lead to pernicious moral judgments and attitudes, including disdain for out-group members, blind obedience to authority, violent thirst for revenge, and subjugation of certain members of society, especially women and minorities. This is a debate, however, that need not be resolved here. What is important is that there is good evidence that—whether or not they should—most people, most of the time, do in fact come to moral judgments on the basis of automatic emotional reactions and then concoct pseudo-arguments as post hoc rationalizations for those reactions. That means that when social conservatives have strong emotional reactions to the idea of homosexuality (emotions such as fear, shame, or disgust) and also present arguments against homosexuality, it is highly likely that it is the emotional reactions, and not the arguments they give, that are driving the disapproval. This is especially so if the arguments are weak and would not convince those who are not already opposed to homosexuality.

REPRESSED HOMOSEXUALITY

Some of the most vocal opponents of gay rights have turned out to be secretly gay. Evangelical preacher Ted Haggard, for example, was a strident anti-gay activist. He preached that homosexuality is a sin and was a loud supporter of a proposed amendment to the Colorado state constitution that would have banned same-sex marriage. That was until 2006, when it was discovered that he had been a regular customer of a gay male prostitute for over three years. Then there was Larry Craig, the former Republican senator from Idaho. He opposed gay marriage and opposed legislation that would make violence against homosexuals a hate crime. In 2008 he was arrested for trying to solicit anonymous gay sex in an airport bathroom. George Rekers is another one of these secretly gay opponents of gay rights. He was a psychologist and Baptist minister who performed "conversion therapy" aimed at turning gay men straight. He was also the head of an organization that lobbied against gay marriage, adoption of children by same-sex couples, and allowing openly gay members in the Boy Scouts. In 2010 he was caught at an airport, returning from a two-week vacation with a gay male prostitute. These high-profile cases are just a small sample of gay rights opponents who have been discovered to be secretly gay. There are many more publically known cases.[2] Who knows how many more secretly gay opponents of homosexuality there may be who have managed to keep their homosexuality a secret thus far?

These highly publicized news stories illustrate the phenomenon, but they are merely anecdotal. They might represent only a tiny fraction of people who are morally opposed to homosexuality. That is why we need good scientific studies, not just well-publicized examples. Fortunately, there have been studies, and the results indicate that a large portion of people who disapprove of homosexuality are in fact repressing their own homosexual urges.

In the first study, self-identified heterosexual men were divided into two groups based on their scores from the Index of Homophobia (IHP).[3] The IHP is a widely used measure of disapproval of homosexuality, discomfort around homosexuals, and opposition to gay rights. Score on the index ranges from zero (perfectly tolerant of homosexuality and comfortable around gay people) to one hundred (highly intolerant and deeply hostile to gay people). There were thirty-five men in the group who scored high on homophobia (51–100) and twenty-nine men in the group that scored low on homophobia (0–50).[4] The men were then shown various pornographic movies, some heterosexual pornography with men and women, some films with women only, and some gay-male pornographic films of men having sex with other men. While watching the movies, the men wore a device on their penis to measure sexual arousal. The homophobic group showed significant sexual arousal while watching the gay pornography, whereas the men who scored low on the IHP test did not. Fifty-four percent of the homophobic men demonstrated "definite tumescence" in response to the gay pornography. (A few of the straight men were also physically aroused by the gay porn, but the extent of heterosexual arousal was not statistically significant.)

This indicates that some men who have a problem with homosexuality—as many as half of them—have homosexual tendencies that they deny or repress. But there is another possible interpretation of the results. It could be that the physical arousal of the homophobic men in response to the gay pornography was caused by anxiety, not sexual desire. There are other studies, however, that make this alternative interpretation unlikely.

One series of studies in particular shows that homophobic men unconsciously (and maybe also consciously, but secretly) identify themselves with homosexual words and images.[5] Test subjects were asked to rate their sexual orientation on a scale of one to ten—one being totally straight, five being equally attracted to men and women, and ten being completely homosexual. This self-report indicates the individual's conscious, explicit sexual orientation. Subjects then took a test to measure their implicit sexual orientation. This computer-administrated test works by showing a series of images and words on a screen. Some of the words and images represent homosexuality (for example the word "gay," a picture of a same-sex couple, or the image of a rainbow flag) while other pictures represent heterosexuality (such as an opposite-sex couple, or the word "straight"). Subjects are asked to put the words and images into the proper category—gay or straight—as fast as they can, and the computer measures reaction times. Just before each image appears, however, the word "me" or the word "other" is flashed for 35 milliseconds. This is too quick for most people to notice consciously, but long enough for the brain to process unconsciously.

A heterosexual person should have a quicker reaction time, on average, when the word "me" is matched with a straight image and when "other" is matched with a gay image. Their reaction times should be slower when there is a mismatch of "me"-gay or "other"-straight. The reverse is true of gay people. They will react more quickly with "me"-gay and "other"-straight combinations, and more slowly with "me"-straight and "other"-gay combos. These studies revealed that about 20 percent of the people who self-identify as strongly heterosexual are in fact implicitly homosexual. Their reaction times improve when the word "me" is paired with gay words and images and slow down when "me" comes just before straight imagery. The individuals who showed this discrepancy between their explicit and implicit sexual orientation—in other words, those who were secretly gay, in denial about their homosexuality, or repressing homosexual tendencies—were significantly more likely to support anti-gay public policies and expressed greater hostility toward gay people than those who showed no such discrepancy.

These two pieces of evidence make a convincing case that at least some people who disapprove of homosexuality do so because they are repressing their own homosexuality. Researchers are quick to point out that this does not mean that *all* people who disapprove of homosexuality are secretly gay. The studies do not prove that. What the research shows is that many people (and possibly even *most* people) who are strongly opposed to homosexuality and gay rights are secretly gay or repressing their homosexuality. At any rate, those who disapprove of homosexuality should reflect carefully on their own sexual preferences. They need to consider the possibility that the real reason they disapprove of homosexuality is not that they think that God forbids it or that it is unnatural or that it involves misuse of the sexual organs. It might have nothing to do with the reasons they explicitly cite in support of their anti-gay views.

One might reasonably question whether this explanation is really a debunking explanation. After all, why would they repress their gay urges, unless they thought that there was something morally wrong with homosexuality? It could be argued that they already disapprove of homosexuality, and that explains the repression. If it is their moral disapproval that explains why they repress their gay desires, then the repression cannot also explain their disapproval. That would be a circular explanation. On the other hand, we cannot simply accept as legitimate the initial disapproval of homosexuality that motivates these people to repress their homosexual urges. It depends on what motivated that original disapproval. So let us think about what might cause people to repress their homosexual tendencies.

It is extremely rare for an individual to go back into the closet. People do not generally go from being openly gay to repressing their homosexuality. Most repressed and latent homosexuals have been that way at least since the initial awakening of their same-sex desires around puberty, if not earlier. Prepubescent children do not typically have well-thought-out moral judgments that they have adopted on the basis of careful, rational deliberation. More often, their moral views are influenced by their parents, their peers, and the culture they have grown up in.

Empirical studies show that having parents who are controlling, disapproving, and biased against homosexuality is the best predictor for repressed homosexuality.[6] Thus, what motivates people to repress their homosexual desires is not the conscious, rational judgment that homosexuality is morally wrong but, rather, fear of rejection by parents, peers, or the community at large. The threat of rejection by one's parents, or of exclusion from society, might be a *practical* reason to hide one's sexual orientation, but it is not a good reason to think that that orientation is morally wrong. Disapproval of homosexuality that is caused by repressing one's own sexuality is a debunking explanation because this reason for disapproval does not track morally relevant facts. If these people did not have homosexual tendencies, or if they had more accepting parents, then they would not think homosexuality is morally wrong. Obviously, whether you have homosexual tendencies, or whether you have accepting parents, is not relevant to whether homosexuality is morally wrong.

Moral reasons are reasons to act. They are reasons that are supposed to apply to everyone. To say homosexuality is wrong is to say that everyone, including homosexuals, should not engage in homosexual activities. This is why repressing one's own homosexuality is not a legitimate reason to morally disapprove of the homosexuality of others. One person's shame, caused by his stern, homophobic parents, is no reason for *another* person, who had more tolerant and accepting parents, not to act on his or her sexual preferences, as long as he or she acts on these tendencies in responsible ways.

HOMOPHOBIA AND DISGUST

Empirical work in social psychology and neuroscience has also found a strong link between disapproval of homosexuality and disgust.[7] Some people are more prone than others to being disgusted. They feel disgust more easily, more often, and more intensely than other people. This disgust sensitivity can be more or less measured by questionnaires. People who score high on disgust sensitivity tests also tend to demonstrate implicit disapproval of homosexuality, as measured by implicit association tests.[8] The research focuses on implicit disapproval of homosexuality because of the social pressure these days to give lip service to tolerance of homosexuality, especially among the young college students who make up the bulk of the test subjects in psychology experiments. This social pressure makes self-reported attitudes toward homosexuality untrustworthy. (Of course, someone who explicitly disapproves of homosexuality will almost certainly also have an implicit disapproval of homosexuality.)

Given the solid empirical evidence that disapproval of homosexuality is, at least in some people, caused by visceral feelings of disgust, it is not surprising that much of the anti-gay propaganda is often loaded with language aimed at eliciting disgust in others. A paradigm example of this is found in the pamphlets of Paul Cameron, founder of the Family Research Institute, a hyper-conservative anti-gay lobbying organization and "think" tank. These pamphlets are filled with rather graphic descriptions of tongues in anuses, semen mixing with fecal matter, and the ingesting of various bodily fluids such as semen or urine. The goal of this rhetoric is to elicit disgust in the reader, with the hope that the reader will then project that disgust onto gay people.

The strategy succeeds because most people are naturally disgusted by bodily fluids like fecal matter, urine, and semen, and because feelings of disgust tend to drive intuitive attitudes of moral disapproval. But just because the strategy works to persuade many people to feel that there is something wrong with homosexuality, does that mean that these feelings of disgust give them any legitimate reason to think that homosexuality is wrong? Assessing the legitimacy of disgust-based disapproval requires asking two questions. First, should heterosexual people be disgusted by homosexual acts? That might seem like an odd question, since disgust is largely a subjective matter. But even a subjective reaction can be illegitimate if it is based on false beliefs, irrational biases, or magical thinking. The second, more important question, is whether the feeling of disgust is a reasonable basis for moral judgments or social policies.

WHAT IS DISGUST, AND HOW DOES IT INFLUENCE MORAL JUDGMENT?

Disgust is an aversion or discomfort directed at certain specific things.[9] The "primary objects" of disgust tend to be reminders of our animal nature and our mortality, especially things that are associated with death and decay. The disgust response is probably an evolutionary adaptation selected for because it helped our prehistoric ancestors avoid eating contaminated foods or contracting contagious diseases. Virtually all people, across different cultures, find the same primary objects disgusting. These include bodily fluids such as blood, semen, urine, mucus, and menstrual blood. Other primary objects of disgust are rotting meat, corpses, maggots, open wounds, and swarming insects.

When we are disgusted by another person, the typical response is avoidance or shunning. This is different from the typical response to moral disapproval of others. Moral disapproval typically elicits emotions of anger or resentment, which in turn motivate behaviors aimed at punishing the transgressors. When disgust is directed at oneself, the emotion that is normally felt is that of shame, which motivates hiding or withdrawing from social interaction. When we think we have violated moral norms, by contrast, we tend to feel guilt, which motivates self-punishment or restitution.

Because the capacity to feel disgust has evolved to prevent contact with disease and the ingesting of tainted food, our disgust reactions are highly sensitive to physical contact with disgusting things. Disgust reactions are especially elicited to protect the borders of the body—keeping disgusting things out of our mouths, nostrils, or eyes, for example. The central ideas surrounding disgust are notions of contamination, infection, and defilement. The feelings of disgust are primarily visceral. These feelings are often immune to explicit belief and thus irrational. For example, people are very reluctant to eat chocolate that is made to resemble dog feces, even though they know it is perfectly edible and even delicious.

The feeling of disgust has a strong influence on negative moral evaluations. When people feel disgust, they are more likely to judge an action to be morally wrong, and tend to judge wrong actions more harshly, than people who do not feel disgust. This influence of disgust on moral judgment is not based on the disgustingness of the action itself; the feeling can be entirely incidental to what is being judged and still influence moral attitudes. In other words, disgust need not have any connection to an action for us to judge the action as morally wrong. Haidt's hypnosis experiments show this. Another study illustrating the influence of disgust on moral judgment involved the same sorts of morally ambiguous actions or situations that were used in the hypnosis study. During the experiment, half of the subjects were exposed to a foul odor (induced by a commercially available "fart spray"). Those who were subjected to the smell, and who were thus primed to feel disgust, tended to express greater moral disapproval than those who were not.[10]

Although disgust has a general influence on negative moral judgments, we normally do not feel disgusted by paradigm instances of wrongdoing. The emotion that is normally associated with the wrongdoing of others is anger or resentment. If your house was burglarized or your car vandalized, you would probably not feel *disgusted* by the perpetrators. You would more likely feel anger or resentment. And when we judge ourselves to have acted wrongly we tend to feel guilt, not shame. We tend to think that we need to be punished or to make amends, not to hide or be shunned.

THREE KINDS OF "MORAL" JUDGMENTS—THE CAD THEORY

Social psychologists have identified three fundamentally different kinds of moral (or pseudo-moral) norms that they label "autonomy," "community," and "divinity."[11] *Autonomy* judgments include all those moral judgments that concern individual rights, individual well-being, and fairness. These are what most of us, at least in the West, would consider paradigmatic instances of moral norms. These would include duties to keep promises, not to steal or kill, to help those in need, and so on. Violations of autonomy norms cause us to feel anger or resentment when others transgress and cause guilt when we ourselves transgress. *Community*-based moral judgments, by contrast, focus on duties inherent in social roles, obligations to obey and respect authority, and loyalty to family, friends, or community. We tend to feel contempt toward others who violate these duties. Finally, the *divinity* judgments involve notions of what is natural or unnatural, sacred or profane, and clean or unclean (in either body or soul), as well as sin or moral taint.[12] These norms are guided by feelings of disgust and shame.

Part of my general strategy for defending the morality of homosexuality is to argue that only the so-called autonomy norms involve legitimate moral concerns. The community norms might also include some legitimate moral rules, but I suspect that those legitimate community norms are ones that can be derived from autonomy norms. For example, I owe obligations of loyalty to my family. As a community norm, this would be a basic rule: Honor thy Mother and Father. But I think the duty of family loyalty is better thought of as a duty of gratitude—I should take care of my parents because they raised and nurtured me as a child and continued to support me (financially and emotionally) well into adulthood.[13] Gratitude is demanded by fairness, which is an autonomy norm. Familial duties, on my account, are not basic. If my parents had abused and neglected me, then I would have no special duty to honor them or to care for them in their old age. (I might still have *some* moral obligations to them—for example, it would be wrong from me to run them over with my car when they are crossing the street. But I would have no *special* duties to my parents if they were abusive or neglectful; I would owe them nothing more than I would two elderly strangers.)

More importantly, I argue that *divinity* norms have no place in a legitimate moral code. They are not basic duties, nor can they be derived from legitimate autonomy-type duties. Divinity norms—also called "sanctity" or "purity" norms—include various kosher laws, rules that say men must avoid all contact with menstruating women, and that caste members should not accept boiled food from an untouchable. There are good reasons to reject these divinity norms, at least as *moral* norms. They might involve reasonable considerations for prudential judgments. For example, Judaism has rules for washing before a meal. It is pretty good advice to wash your hands before eating, but it would be weird to claim that it is a *moral* duty. Divinity norms might also work fine for special rules that apply to group members in a religion or other community. (See chapter 2 for a discussion of the difference between religious rules, such as requiring circumcision or forbidding cotton-wool blends, and moral rules, such as rules against stealing or killing.)

I am not simply claiming that these divinity norms are *false*. I am arguing that they are not *moral* norms at all. They are simply irrational superstitions, or thinly veiled prejudices, codified as taboo. Concepts such as "unclean," "sinful," and "profane" are fictitious and do not refer to any real properties of agents or actions (though they might be employed in ways that happen to supervene on real, natural facts and properties). Disagreement on the legitimacy of divinity norms can be explained away through differences in beliefs about the nature of reality and the existence of certain supernatural properties. For example, take a Muslim in Thailand who believes that pigs are "unclean," and pork should not be eaten for that reason. I disagree.[14] The debate need not end here. Suppose the Thai Muslim believes that pigs are *haram* in part because they were created by Satan, fashioned out of elephant feces on Noah's ark.[15] This story is, of course, false. It is a myth. Pigs were not created on a boat through an act of diabolical magic. They were domesticated from the wild boar in Central Asia about ten thousand years ago.

When we come to know the facts about the origin and nature of pigs, it is no longer rational to see them as inherently disgusting or "unclean" in some supernatural way.

IS THERE ANYTHING DISGUSTING ABOUT HOMOSEXUAL ACTS?

Since disgust is a subjective reaction, it seems unreasonable to claim that anything is *inherently* disgusting. The disgust I feel in response to a close encounter with rotting food, for example, is in my mind (or my brain) and not in the food itself. We naturally project our disgust onto the objects that trigger it. On reflection, however, it is unreasonable to think that disgustingness is a real feature of the object itself, a feature it has independently of our tendency to be disgusted by it.

On the other hand, our capacity to feel disgust has evolved to respond to certain kinds of things, especially human or animal waste and decaying flesh. Thus, even if the feeling of disgust is not literally in the object, there is a sense in which certain things are naturally disgusting to us; they are appropriate objects of disgust. By analogy, the sweetness of sugar is in our minds (or brains) not in the sugar itself. But since our taste receptors for sweetness have evolved to respond to foods that are high in sugar, it makes sense to say that sugar *really is* sweet, even if the sweetness we taste is not an inherent property of the sugar. So we can say that certain substances—blood, sweat, semen, and saliva—are disgusting, even though the disgust we feel is a matter of how these substances generally affect us. Disgustingness thus cannot be an *inherent* property of gay sex, but gay sex might be naturally disgusting in the way that rotting meat or fecal matter is. So the question, then, is whether gay sex is naturally disgusting.

It is true that gay sex involves contact with bodily fluids. But so does heterosexual sex. Engaging in heterosexual sex involves exposure to saliva, semen, sweat, vaginal secretions, and sometimes menstrual fluids. These are substances that most people, under normal circumstances, find disgusting. Given all the bodily fluids involved in sex—gay *or* straight—it is a wonder that any of us engage in any kind of sex at all. Fortunately, there seems to be a natural mechanism in the human brain to reduce our disgust sensitivity when we are sexually aroused.[16] Studies have shown that women who are sexually aroused report being less disgusted by gross things than women who are not sexually aroused. They were shown to be more willing to engage in activities that are normally considered disgusting, such as handling a frog or drinking a cup of juice with an insect (sterilized) in it. This phenomenon is not unique to women.[17] (This particular study focused on women because they are generally more disgust-sensitive than men.)

There is no reason to think that heterosexual sex is naturally or inherently any less disgusting than gay or lesbian sex. Disgust at the thought of homosexual activity—or any particular sexual activity such as fellatio, cunnilingus, anal sex, and so on—is a purely subjective matter. Maybe *some* of these acts are disgusting to you; but a case could be made that they are *all* disgusting in some way, under some circumstances.

IS DISGUST A REASONABLE BASIS FOR MORAL JUDGMENT?

Perhaps some of the people who say that homosexuality is morally wrong are simply expressing their personal feelings of disgust. The thought of homosexual behavior fills them with revulsion, just as the thought of certain unusual foodstuffs fill some people with revulsion. They express this disgust by saying that it is "wrong." This would be an emotive usage of moral language. (See chapter 2 for a discussion of emotivism.) When they say "Homosexuality is wrong," what they really mean is something like "Yuck, homosexuality!" If that were the case, then there would be little else to say about the issue. It would be the same as when I say, "Yuck, eggplant!" This signifies to others not to serve me eggplant, or maybe even not to eat it in front of me, if I shout "yuck!" loud enough. But nothing about expressing my subjective attitudes should stop them from enjoying eggplant, if that is what they are into.

Most people who disapprove of homosexuality, however, do not intend merely to express their own subjective attitudes. When they say that it is wrong, they mean that other people have a reason not to do it—even if those others want to do it, enjoy doing it, and approve of doing it, and even if they only do it in the privacy of their own homes. When I say that stealing is wrong, I am not just expressing my distaste for stealing; I am saying that *people should not steal*, whether or not they share my attitudes toward theft. Let us assume that people who say that homosexuality is morally wrong are expressing genuine moral judgments—in other words, they are claiming that there are reasons why even gay people should not engage in gay sex. If these genuine moral judgments are based on disgust, should we take them seriously? The answer to that question depends on whether there are any reasons to

think that disgust-based moral judgments have any connection to legitimate moral reasons. In order for disgust-driven disapproval to have any
legitimacy, either the disgust feelings that lead to the attitude are themselves moral reasons, or they indicate the presence of morally relevant
considerations. There are reasons to be highly skeptical of either claim.

Let us consider another sort of disgust reaction that varies from
person to person: foods. Here are some foods that many people find
disgusting: lutefisk (a Norwegian dish of cod fish pickled in lye), uni
(sea urchin roe), durian (southeast Asian fruit that tastes sweet but
smells like rotting meat), braised chicken feet, haggis (Scottish dish of
various offal and oats stuffed into a sheep's stomach), lamb's brains,
blue cheese, oysters, "Rocky Mountain oysters" (fried bulls' testicles),
chitterlings (fried pork intestines), and eggplant. Although each of these
dishes elicits disgust in many people, each of them is also beloved by
some. Also, almost everyone would find at least one of these dishes
disgusting (except maybe Andrew Zimmern). And I'll bet almost everyone will find at least one of these dishes delicious. Given the wide
variation in reactions to these various foods, it is implausible to claim
that any of them are inherently—or naturally, or objectively, or properly—disgusting.

The same is true with various sexual practices. There is nothing
about gay sex that makes it naturally more disgusting than heterosexual
sex. I would not be surprised if some gay men find the idea of sex with a
woman disgusting. So if you are disgusted by one and not the other, that
reflects a purely subjective preference. Here is an illustration of how
disgust is especially subjective when it comes to sex. Imagine your parents having sex. Don't just think about it abstractly, try to visualize it in
your mind. The idea is probably so disgusting to you that you resist
imagining it.[18] But it would be absurd to think that sex between your
parents is inherently disgusting. Other people will probably not be disgusted by the idea of those same two people, who happen to be your
parents, having sex (or at least not nearly as much so). Presumably your
parents are not disgusted at the idea of having sex with each other (at
least I hope not). Surely there is nothing *morally wrong* with your
parents having sex with each other (assuming they have not divorced
and married other people).

Disgust often triggers moral judgments, but should we take these
subjective attitudes as legitimate grounds for moral judgments? Moral
concepts are about reasons to act. If something is morally wrong, then
there are reasons not to do it, and these reasons apply to everyone. If I
think that eggplant is disgusting, then certainly I have a reason not to
eat it. But that obviously does not mean that *everyone* has a reason not
to eat it and certainly not one that overrides reasons that they have in

favor of eating it. To say that homosexuality is wrong means that homosexuals should not engage in homosexual behavior. But one person's subjective reaction to a practice does not give others any reason not to do it, just as a Chinese person's disgust toward the idea of eating moldy, fermented, coagulated milk curds gives *me* no reason not to enjoy a good Roquefort. Likewise, if some conservatives find cunnilingus disgusting, that is no reason for a man who enjoys it not to give oral pleasure to his wife in the privacy of their own home. Some people are disgusted by the idea of sex between elderly couples, or obese people. Certainly that does not make it morally wrong for them to have sex.

REALISM ABOUT DISGUST AND DIVINITY NORMS

Some conservatives argue that disgust is a reliable warning of things to be avoided. For example, Leon Kass, physician and head of George W. Bush's President's Council on Bioethics, claims that "there is *wisdom* in disgust." When Kass tries to illustrate this "wisdom," however, he succeeds only in demonstrating how subjective and irrational disgust really is. In one place, he argues that it is morally wrong to eat ice cream cones in public because by licking the cone you are acting like a cat—and of course (!?) acting like a cat is disgusting.[19] (I shudder to think what his reaction might be to the Broadway musical *CATS*.) Mr. Kass's disgust response to catlike behavior is highly idiosyncratic, even though he takes it to be authoritative. I suppose he would be disgusted by Michelle Pfeiffer's performance as Catwoman in the 1992 film *Batman Returns*. I, however, had quite the opposite reaction (as I suspect did most other heterosexual men).

Not only are there commonsense reasons and anecdotal evidence for thinking that disgust is subjective and irrational, rather than wise and authoritative, but there is also good empirical evidence that disgust judgments suffer from various systematic irrationalities. In particular, our disgust reactions are subject to *sympathetic magic*. Sympathetic magic is a pattern of thinking whereby we implicitly think that one thing can influence another because of their similarity or that properties can be transferred from one object to another on the basis of mere contact, proximity, or even resemblance.[20] For example, we tend to think that a cup shaped like a toilet bowl is unsanitary simply because of it resembles something that is normally unsanitary, even if we know that it has never been used as a receptacle for waste. Similarly, we think that objects owned or used by evil people are somehow tainted. For example, people are disgusted by the prospect of wearing clothes that had belonged to a serial killer, though they would not object to wearing clothing that had belonged to someone else. Of course, rationally we know that having a similar shape to a toilet does not make the cup unsanitary. We know, rationally, that the serial killer's evil is not a property that can spread through his clothing. Magic is not real. So insofar as our disgust reactions are guided by magical thinking, they distort our judgments.

Of course, there may be *some* wisdom in disgust, when it is guided by primary objects such as corpses or rotting meat. If your milk smells foul or your meat looks slimy, then you should probably throw them out. But when these feelings of disgust are projected onto things or people that we merely *associate* with objects of disgust, we have serious reasons to doubt our resulting intuitions.

THE DARK SIDE OF DISGUST

Philosopher and legal scholar Martha Nussbaum has examined disgust-based norms extensively and disgust as a basis of anti-gay laws and public policies in particular.[21] She points out that, historically, dominant groups have a tendency to project their discomfort about their own human bodies onto vulnerable and subordinate groups, including women, foreigners, people of lower castes, the disabled, and Jews. This projection allows the dominant group to feel clean and pure. It also allows for the stigmatization of those in the lower group who are seen as "unclean" or "impure."

When we project our feeling of disgust onto certain individuals, it has a dehumanizing effect that desensitizes us and enables cruel and inhumane treatment of them. For example, when prisoners in the Nazi concentration camps of World War II were deprived of toilets or cleaning facilities, it became easier for the guards to think of them as animals rather than persons. The prisoners would even tend to see themselves this way. This dehumanization made it easier for the guards to torture and kill prisoners. And prisoners, stripped of their human dignity, would become more docile and resigned. Those prisoners who made an effort to maintain their sense of humanity by finding ways to bathe and to wash their clothes, even in dirty water, were less likely to be abused by guards and were more able to resist brutal treatment.[22]

This kind of evidence is historical and anecdotal. But there is also good scientific evidence that disgust reactions tend to cause a dehumanizing attitude toward people who are seen as disgusting. For one thing, we are less inclined to make inferences about mental states of people we find disgusting. In other words, if someone disgusts you, you are less likely to explain his behavior by ascribing thoughts, intentions, perceptions, or feelings to him.[23] The dehumanizing effect of disgust also shows up in brain-scanning studies.[24] Activation of an area of the brain known as the *medial prefrontal cortex* (mPFC) is necessary for social cognition. This area, however, is less active when disgust is high. In one study, people were shown images of various people from different social groups while in an fMRI machine. Photos of homeless people and drug addicts (two groups that tend to elicit disgust) were correlated with elevated activation in the anterior insula and anterior cingulate (a pattern associated with disgust reactions) and lower activation of the mPFC. Disgust sensitivity has also been linked to racism and xenophobia.[25]

Nussbaum advocates and defends what she calls a "politics of humanity," which involves mutual respect. In doing so, she appeals to the values embodied in the founding documents of the United States and the ideals and values of the founders, especially the idea that all persons have equal human dignity and equal natural rights.[26] This does not require us to approve of what others do. Many of the early Americans were religious fanatics who believed that practitioners of other faiths, even other Christian faiths, were sinful heretics on the road to perdition. What they believed in was the capacity of each individual to search for life's meaning and find their own values, and what they protected (at least in theory) was the right of each person to answer to his or her own conscience. A necessary condition for achieving this ideal is sympathizing, or at least having the capacity to sympathize, with others who are different from us. We need to be able to imagine the situations of people from different social groups and assess their practices from their perspective. Disgust makes sympathy impossible and encourages dehumanizing those others.

Not all laws that are based on disgust are unjust. Laws that prohibit people from defecating in public, for example, are based largely on disgust but are not thereby unjust. Laws may legitimately appeal to the disgust sensitivity of the average person when the object of disgust is one of those primary objects of disgust—things like feces, rotting corpses, or maggots, which our disgust mechanism has evolved to detect. Laws that are based on projective disgust, however, are unjust. This happens when our disgust reactions are redirected, by association or by sympathetic magic, and used to target individuals, usually members of lower status groups. It is this form of disgust that dehumanizes, enables brutal treatment of out-group members, and makes sympathy and respect impossible.

CONCLUSION

Empirical evidence indicates that many people who disapprove of homosexuality do so because they are repressing their own homosexual tendencies or because the idea of homosexual activity causes them to feel disgust, and that disgust in turn drives an intuitive, gut-level disapproval. Those who object to homosexuality for either of these reasons ought to reconsider their moral attitudes, even if they *think* they disapprove for other, legitimate reasons. One person's discomfort with his own sexual desires is no reason for other people not to act on their sexual desires. Moral judgments based solely on projective disgust should also be rejected. For one thing, disgust is highly subjective. For *any* sexual activity that anyone might perform—even ordinary, heterosexual, missionary-style sex between a married couple—there is someone in the world (such as the children or siblings of the sexual partners) who would probably be disgusted. Also, one person's subjective reaction at the thought of an action is no reason for others not to do it. Disgust is also a highly irrational emotion, subject to biases and irrational magic thinking. Thus, there is reason to think that disgust reactions do not track any legitimate moral considerations.

8

HOMOSEXUALITY, CONSEQUENCES, AND JUSTICE I—SLIPPERY SLOPE ARGUMENTS

So far we have examined arguments that make the case that homosexuality is morally wrong. But the explicit debate over homosexuality and gay rights is more about politics and law than it is about morality. Although many of those opposed to gay rights start with the assumption that homosexuality is morally wrong, what they explicitly oppose is gay marriage, adoption of children by gay parents, openly gay people serving in the military, and antidiscrimination laws protecting homosexuals. In other words, the public debate is more about the legal recognition of gay rights than it is about the morality of homosexuality per se. In the next two chapters, we will examine the political and legal arguments against the recognition of gay rights.

Moral questions of whether a certain activity is right or wrong and political questions about whether it should be legally allowed are distinct, even though they may be closely related. For one thing, something can be morally objectionable, yet there might be good reasons against criminalizing it. Adultery, for example, is a private matter and it would be unjust for the state to punish adultery as a crime. Nevertheless, cheating on one's spouse is, in most instances, morally wrong. So just because an action is morally wrong does not necessarily mean that it should be illegal. To justify outlawing an activity, it is not enough to argue simply that the activity itself is wrong. We must also give reasons for thinking that the act is pernicious enough to justify sanctions by the state.

Not only should some wrongful acts be legally permitted, but also sometimes we even have a *right* to do things that are morally wrong. That might sound paradoxical, but not if we carefully define what it means to say that someone "has a right to" do something. When I say that someone "has a right to X," I mean that it would be morally wrong for others to interfere in that person's partaking in X. For example, to say that you have a right to free speech means that it would be wrong for other people (or the state) to censor you, compel you say things against your will, or to punish you for voicing your opinion. Of course there are limits to free speech. But the limits usually involve proper venue (e.g., talking in a theater during a performance) or violating the rights of others (e.g., slander or inciting a riot). It might be morally wrong for me to say things that are offensive, but I still have a right to say them. It would be wrong for the state to punish me for voicing my opinions, even if those opinions are appalling or distasteful.

The moral arguments against homosexuality we have considered thus far—based on biblical commands or claims that it is unnatural or that it is a misuse of one's organs—provide only *moral* arguments against homosexuality. Even if they were successful, they would only give individuals reasons to avoid homosexual practices and lifestyles in their private decisions. That is not enough to justify forbidding or discouraging homosexuality in our laws and public policies. To support the legal and political case against homosexuality and gay rights, it needs to be shown why the coercive power of the state should be used to encourage or discourage certain kinds of personal relations or lifestyles or to favor certain kinds of personal relations and lifestyles over others.

One reason why certain activities are against the law is that they are seriously morally wrong. Or more accurately, sometimes the justification for making something illegal is the same as the reasons that it is morally wrong. Murder, for example, is morally wrong because it deprives the victim of his future life and because of the pain and suffering that it causes to the victim's friends and family as well as to the community as a whole. Those are the same reasons that murder is illegal. This works only for actions that are obviously very wrongful. While there may be some otherwise reasonable people who think that homosexuality is morally wrong, it would be unreasonable to claim that homosexuality is on a par with theft, murder, or rape.

Sometimes there are reasons to outlaw certain activities, reasons that have nothing to do with the activities being morally wrong. Consider seat belt laws. Although it may be imprudent to drive without a seat belt, it would be quite a stretch to claim that it is morally wrong. Still, there are good reasons for making it against the law to drive without buckling up. Seat belt laws require drivers and passengers to strap themselves in, in order to protect them from their own poor judgment and also to prevent unnecessary injuries that would waste scarce health-care resources.

Thus, the arguments against the legal recognition of gay rights are, for the most part, separable from the arguments that homosexuality is morally wrong. Most of these arguments that opponents of gay rights put forth claim that recognition of gay rights would have bad conse-quences, either to certain innocent third parties (such as children) or to society as a whole. Not only is this a different kind of argument from the moral arguments against homosexuality that we have examined so far, it is also a *better* kind of argument. The arguments people typically give for *moral* opposition to homosexuality assume very implausible moral theories, such as the divine command theory, Natural Law theory, and the teleological theory of "proper" use of one's organs. It is a different matter, however, with arguments that appeal to consequences of an action or practice. Good and bad consequences are obviously relevant to the morality or justice of an action, practice, or policy.

CONSEQUENCES AND PUBLIC POLICY

One of the most prominent moral theories today in professional philos-ophy, utilitarianism, bases the rightness and wrongness of an action entirely on its consequences. An action is morally right, in this view, if it has the best possible consequences for everyone who is affected, short term and long term. The consequences are all that matter. Although popular in philosophy, utilitarianism is a controversial view, for many reasons. But one need not adopt an orthodox utilitarian theory to accept arguments based on consequences. Even if consequences are not the *only* considerations that make an action, practice, or policy morally right or wrong, surely the consequences are *among* the morally relevant considerations. That an act would be harmful to innocent people or detrimental to society as a whole is certainly *some* reason to oppose it. (We will examine utilitarianism in more detail in chapter 10.)

Since it is uncontroversial that good and bad consequences are rele-vant to the morality of an action or the justice of a law, this chapter and the next will focus primarily on whether legal recognition of gay rights would have the dire consequences that opponents claim. We will, for the most part, not question the background assumption that conse-quences are morally relevant, though it is legitimate to ask whether the bad consequences of an action or practice are *enough* to justify crimi-nalizing it. We do not, for example, criminalize minor peccadilloes—

such as white lies, obnoxious pranks, or ingratitude—because the cost of enforcing such laws, and the inconvenience caused by such intrusive state intervention in trivial aspects of our lives, would far outweigh the benefits of discouraging those kinds of behavior.

PERFECTIONISM

Although most of the arguments against the legal recognition of gay rights appeal to consequences, there is one important exception that we need to consider first. Some of the arguments against gay rights start by claiming that homosexuality is morally wrong (usually on the basis of divine command, Natural Law, or teleology) and then claim that the state has a legitimate interest in promoting moral values and fostering moral virtues. The New Natural Law (NNL) theorists, for example, claim that the proper role of government is (at least in part) to promote and facilitate the achievement of "basic goods" and to discourage and inhibit whatever is detrimental to these basic goods.[1] These basic goods, according to NNL, are not happiness, pleasure, or fulfillment of one's desires. The good for humans, they claim, consists of those things that fully develop our human nature.

This view is called "perfectionism." In order to argue that same-sex marriages ought not to be recognized legally *because* homosexuality does not contribute to "the human good," or *because* homosexual marriages are not "true" marriages, social conservatives must argue, or at least assume, that the state has a legitimate role in molding the values and character traits of its citizens and in encouraging certain kinds of relations, habits, and lifestyles while discouraging others. This kind of Natural Law Perfectionism (NLP) starts with the claim that there are certain qualities or activities that constitute the good life for a human being in that they contribute to human "flourishing," even if that person does not want those qualities or activities and takes no pleasure in them. NLP adds to this the controversial claim that these features of human flourishing include marriage, family life, and the "two-in-one flesh" union of procreative sex. Conversely, other activities—including any non-procreative sex—are objectively bad for us, no matter how much we value them and enjoy them. Finally, they go on to claim that the state has a legitimate role in encouraging certain lifestyles over others. Specifically, the state should encourage those lifestyles that embody these objective goods—the lifestyle that prudish conservatives refer to with the euphemistic term "family values"—and should discourage other lifestyles, even if many people prefer them.

There are two main arguments against NLP. One argument is that we should reject the particular ideals and values that the perfectionist state of this sort would intend to promote. We might do this by rejecting the particular values, in this case, the conservative "family values," and claim that this lifestyle is not good. Alternatively, we might argue that, given the widespread disagreement in beliefs and values, we have reason to doubt that these values represent the ideal lifestyle for everyone.

Many philosophers reject the idea that there are objective values that constitute human flourishing for every individual, regardless of his or her personal preferences or values. Instead, what constitutes the good life for any individual will depend, at least in part, on that individual's beliefs, preferences, and goals. What constitutes a good life for you might not be a good life for me. This is a subjectivist view of well-being. Note that according to this subjectivist theory, we can still say that some people are wrong when they claim that certain things are good for them. They might be mistaken about what constitutes their own well-being if, for example, their desires and goals are based on ignorance or false beliefs. For example, suppose I want to be a surgeon because I think I will be good at it, but in fact, I get nauseated at the sight of blood. Pursuing medical school will not be good for me, even though I mistakenly believe that it would be. Pursuing med school would be a bad idea for me *based on my own desire* to pursue something that I could be good at.

Some political philosophers, however, argue that perfectionism would still be unjust—in a diverse democratic society like ours—even if there were objective facts about what constitutes human well-being. These philosophers claim that justice requires *state neutrality*.[2] The principle of state neutrality is the claim that government should not promote certain virtues, values, or lifestyles and should not base laws or public policy decisions on some narrow conception of the good life, at least not if there is reasonable disagreement among the governed about what sort of life would be best. It might be legitimate for the state to promote certain goods, such as health, autonomy, leisure time, self-respect, opportunity, and wealth. But that is because these goods are nearly universally valued by members of society. Also, these goods are themselves relatively neutral. You can use your liberty, leisure time, and wealth to pursue a variety of different pursuits and lifestyles, depending on your particular values. For example, if your religious faith is important to you, you can use your leisure time to pray and your wealth to donate to the church. If, instead, you value the arts, you can use your leisure time painting or visiting art museums, and you can spend your wealth on art supplies or opera tickets. What state neutrality forbids is government promotion of specific lifestyles or values. When we, as a society, try to curtail tobacco or alcohol use through steep taxes, this is not perfectionism. Although they may be called "sin taxes," the justification is not that the state should promote the virtues of sobriety or self-control. These laws are justified in terms of public health, not moral values, religious beliefs, or a preference for a certain sort of lifestyle.

There are, however, reasonable people who reject state neutrality and defend perfectionism, at least in some form.[3] Some argue that perfectionism is not unjust as long as it is pluralistic. According to *pluralist perfectionism*, the state should encourage and enable several different and even incompatible conceptions of the good life. For example, the state might support and encourage religious and secular values, conservative and liberal virtues, scientific and artistic pursuits. Individuals would then be free to choose among different goods and different lifestyles, and the state would enable these choices. This is consistent with acknowledging diversity, respecting individual choice, and recognizing that reasonable people disagree on their conception of human well-being. This form of perfectionism, however, is perfectly consistent with, and might even require, legal recognition of gay rights. The state could legitimately promote marriage and married life without promoting one narrow conception of what a marriage is supposed to be. Individuals would be free to define, within limits, the meaning of their own marriage, whether as a union aimed at procreation or as an equal partnership based on mutual love. NLP, however, is not pluralist. This form of perfectionism insists that the state should promote a very narrow conception of the good life and a very narrow conception of what marriage and married life are supposed to be.

Whether or not perfectionism is a just form of government is a theoretical question that we will be unlikely to settle here. But we are concerned with specific practical issues—homosexuality, gay rights, and especially same-sex marriage. We do not need to settle the theoretical question. It does not matter whether perfectionism, in some form or other, could be just. We only need to ask whether the kind of perfectionism that is argued to support a ban on same-sex marriage and the denial of gay rights—in other words, NLP—is just.

Perfectionism comes in varying kinds and degrees—some extreme forms are obviously oppressive and unjust while others might be defensible. On the extreme end is the Taliban style of perfectionism, which attempts to control every aspect of an individual's life. The Taliban, for example, bans women from working outside the home or even leaving the house unescorted by a close male relative. Women are also forbidden to study or receive an education and must cover themselves from head to toe in public places. Women are not allowed to laugh or talk loudly enough for their voices to be heard by strangers; they are banned from playing sports, riding bicycles, or driving cars. Men and women both are forbidden to listen to music, watch movies or television, fly kites, or play cards or chess. Males are required to have their hair cut and wear turbans and are forbidden to shave or trim their beards. And everyone—man, woman, and child—must attend prayers five times every day at the mosque.

One thing that makes the Taliban-style perfectionism obviously evil is the content of the values and lifestyles that are encouraged and the brutality of the coercion used to enforce them. But another thing that makes it unjust is the sheer *extent* of the rules. Any kind of perfectionism that is this pervasive and intrusive would be unjust, even if the content of the rules themselves and the method of their enforcement were not objectionable. Suppose we were to replace the Taliban-style rules with a set of rules that we all agree with and enforced them with very mild sanctions (such as small fines). For example, suppose the state tried to encourage tolerance, equality, education, and health by extensive public policies aimed at getting every citizen to eat three portions of vegetables every day, brush their teeth every night, exercise for twenty minutes three times a week, go to school, avoid tobacco, read the newspaper regularly, and always invite a diverse group of people to their private parties. This sort of micromanaging of the lives of citizens would still be oppressive, no matter how well-meaning. It would be excessively intrusive, even though we might agree that these things are good for us individually as well as for society.

Weaker forms of perfectionism that more gently promote worthy values and good character traits, without significantly curtailing liberty and autonomy, might be justifiable, or at least not obviously unjust. The questions are: 1) To what extent can the state justly practice perfectionism? and 2) Would promoting the conservative "conjugal" conception of marriage go beyond the limits of legitimate state intervention in the lives of its citizens? To answer this question, we need a criterion to distinguish excessive, Taliban-level perfectionism from weaker, more acceptable forms of perfectionism. Here are two criteria that seem reasonable for determining the limits of acceptable perfectionism. 1) The state has a legitimate interest in promoting only uncontroversial goods (ones that are nearly universally valued) or those traits that citizens must have for a stable, well-functioning society. Candidates for uncontroversial goods might include health, education, basic liberties, and opportunities. Examples of traits necessary for a functioning society might include tolerance, civic education, and some minimal respect for the law. 2) The promotion of these goods and traits must not be overly intrusive and must not place undue burdens on citizens. Some might say that the attempt by New York City to limit soda consumption is excessively intrusive. On the other hand, defenders of the policy could point out that consumers can still drink as much soda as they please. Nothing prevents them from ordering two or more sodas at a restaurant or convenience store. How much burden or intrusiveness is too much? There is no way to draw a sharp line. But we need not do so in order to see that NLP would support what are clearly Taliban-level intrusions and limits on personal liberties.

It should be obvious that the NLP argument against gay marriage fails the first criterion of legitimate perfectionism in that it makes very controversial assumptions about which things are objectively good, especially when compared to obvious examples of universally desired goods. Conjugal marriage, procreation, and "two-in-one flesh" union are not nearly so obviously good as education, health, or liberty. If someone professes not to value his own health or his own liberty, most of us would question his sanity. People who choose not to have children, by contrast, do not warrant such incredulity or suspicion. We do not automatically suspect childless couples of being incompetent, insane, or wicked.

More importantly, even if NNL were correct about the importance of conjugal marriage and the claim that the only good sex is procreative sex, state promotion of these values would be highly invasive. The kinds of public policies that NLP would support include not only prohibiting gay marriage but also prohibiting (or at least discouraging) masturbation, contraception, and divorce. It would be unjust for the state to meddle in these highly personal choices and practices.

OUTLINE OF THE CONSEQUENCE-BASED ARGUMENTS AGAINST GAY RIGHTS

Gay rights is a broad category, and those who oppose some gay rights do not necessary oppose all gay rights. For example, the most recent public opinion polls in America show only slightly more than 50 percent of the population supports legal recognition of gay marriage, while more than 75 percent support allowing openly gay people to serve in the military.[4] That means that almost 25 percent of Americans (75 minus 50) think gay people should be allowed to serve in the military *but* also believe that they should *not* be allowed to marry their same-sex partners. Furthermore, even though most of the arguments against various gay rights appeal to the alleged negative consequences of recognizing those rights, opponents claim that different gay rights pose different threats to the social good. For example, opponents of openly gay military service argue that it would compromise our national defense, while opponents of gay marriage argue that it would weaken the bonds of matrimony, leading to various domestic social ills.

Gay military service is no longer much of an issue. 75 percent approve of openly gay people being allowed to serve in the military, and an additional 8 percent approve of gays in the military as long as they are not openly gay. That adds up to 83 percent total approval of gay military service. That is almost as high as the approval of interracial marriage, which was only 86 percent in 2011.[5] It would be absurd to debate anti-miscegenation laws, so I will not discuss gay military service either. Instead, I will focus on gay marriage, adoption of children by gay parents, and antidiscrimination laws, since those are still live issues in the public eye.

Anti-gay conservatives argue that allowing same-sex couples to participate in the institution of marriage would require redefining marriage—abandoning the traditional "conjugal" view. They offer three main arguments why this would be detrimental to society: 1) it would weaken the institution of marriage, 2) it would be bad for children, and 3) it would violate the religious freedoms of those who oppose homosexuality on religious grounds. We will look more closely at these arguments in the next chapter.

In this chapter we will focus on a different kind of consequence-based argument against gay rights—one that appeals not to the *actual* consequences of homosexuality or gay-tolerant public policies but to the *logical* consequences. The idea is that, even if the legal recognition of gay marriage would not itself be detrimental, it would establish a precedent that would inevitably lead to the legalization of other kinds of marriages that would be bad for society. Specifically, they argue that only the conjugal view of marriage (with its essential connection to reproduction and parenting) can justify limiting marriage to two people and to human beings. If our society were to adopt a view of marriage that is not essentially tied to procreation, then "we would still . . . be discriminating against those seeking open, temporary polygamous, polyandrous, polyamorous, incestuous, or bestial unions."[6] This sort of argument is so common among anti-gay activists that John Corvino refers to them collectively at the "PIB" argument: polygamy, incest, and bestiality.[7]

According to opponents of gay marriage, the conjugal (procreative) conception of marriage can justify limiting marital relations to two human beings because it takes exactly one female and one male of the same species to reproduce sexually. If marriage is not fundamentally oriented toward reproduction, and instead is based on love, then the state could not justify banning polygamous or bestial marriages.

PIB ARGUMENTS AND THE SLIPPERY SLOPE

These arguments, that allowing gay marriage would require allowing polygamous, incestuous, or bestial marriages, all take the form of a *slippery slope* argument. A slippery slope argument claims that, although a certain activity or policy may be reasonable in itself, engaging in the activity or adopting the policy will result in more extreme activities or policies as a consequence. These more extreme actions or policies are morally objectionable, so we must avoid the moderate actions or policies, lest we open the door for the extreme ones.

These sorts of arguments appeal to two distinct senses of "consequences" and, correspondingly, two distinct kinds of slippery slopes. The more familiar sense of "consequences" refers to *causal* consequences—the actual consequences that will result from engaging in the activity or adopting the policy. The argument that marijuana is a "gateway" drug is a prime example of the *causal* version of the slippery slope argument. The claim is that, even if marijuana itself is not especially harmful, those who smoke marijuana regularly will inevitably switch to more and more harmful drugs, like heroin, PCP, or crack. To prevent people from doing those more dangerous drugs, we should not allow them to do the relatively safer drug, marijuana. The moderate position, allowing marijuana but not allowing other narcotics, lies on a metaphorical "slope." The only way to avoid sliding down the slope to the undesirable situation at the bottom (crackheads running rampant in the streets) is to stake out a position at the opposite extreme, on the summit (a strict antidrug policy).

Slippery slope arguments against gay marriage, however, typically appeal to the *logical* consequences of extending the institution of marriage to same-sex couples. This *conceptual* form of the slippery slope starts with the claim that adopting a moderate policy (which may be harmless when considered on its own) commits us, on pain of contradiction, to adopting a more extreme policy that would be bad or harmful. This is because any reasons that could count in favor of the more moderate policy would count equally in favor for the more extreme policy. Any attempt to justify the more moderate policy while opposing the more extreme policy would require making an arbitrary cutoff.

An illustration of the conceptual slippery slope can be found in Genesis, where Abraham successfully employs a slippery slope argument against God (Genesis 18:22–33). When God tells him that he intends to destroy Sodom and Gomorrah, Abraham asks him if he would spare the city if it contained fifty decent men. Surely, he says, you would not destroy the righteous along with the wicked? When God agrees to save the town if it contains 50 good men, Abraham asks him if he would spare the town if it contained only forty-five decent men. God must agree because there is no significance difference between fifty good men and forty-five good men. But if he would save the town for forty-five good men, then why not save the town if it contained only forty good men? The argument continues until God must agree to save the town if it contained only one good man.[8] God could not reasonably insist that he would save the town if it had, say, seventeen good men but not if it had only sixteen good men. There is no way to justify that particular number. There is, however, a significant difference between one and zero. If there are zero good men, then he can destroy the town without harming any innocents.

Some slippery slope arguments can be formulated in either the causal form or the conceptual form. For example, we could formulate a conceptual version of the gateway argument against legalizing marijuana by claiming that allowing people to smoke marijuana but not hashish would be arbitrary. There is no significant difference between them, since hash is only slightly stronger than marijuana. So whatever reason you have for legalizing marijuana also applies to legalizing hashish. But then if we allow people to use hashish but not to use psilocybin, that would also be arbitrary and justified, since psilocybin is only slightly stronger than hashish. And so on.

Nevertheless, although we can often make conceptual analogs to causal slippery slope arguments, and vice versa, there is still an important difference between the two. The causal version appeals to the real-world consequences of practices and policies, so is best supported or refuted by empirical evidence. We might try to refute the gateway argument, for example, with facts about human psychology. There might be evidence that most people who try marijuana never move on to harsher drugs or that those who enjoy marijuana are not likely to enjoy crack.[9] The conceptual slippery slope argument, on the other hand, relies on logical consistency. If you approve of A, then you must approve of B because there is no relevant difference between A and B. This means that the conceptual slippery slope is defeated in a different way. Instead of looking for empirical evidence that certain consequences are unlikely to occur, we refute a conceptual slippery slope by presenting principled distinctions that justify adopting the moderate policy and rejecting the more extreme policy.

The slippery slope argument against gay marriage is a conceptual slippery slope. The claim is that if we allow same sex-marriage, then we will be logically committed to allowing for polygamous, incestuous, or bestial marriages. Any reasons given in support of same-sex marriage could also be used to support marriages between close relatives, marriages of human beings with animals, or marriages of three or more people. They all lie on a slope, and there is no way to justify gay marriage without justifying these other types of marriages.

THE LOGIC OF SLIPPERY SLOPES

The conceptual slippery slope argument style suffers from numerous flaws. For one thing, slippery slope arguments are usually straight-up invalid. In other words, they can generate false conclusion from true premises. Consider, for example, the following slippery slope argument applied to speed limit laws. If it is safe to drive at 55 mph, then it must be safe to drive at 56 mph, since there is no significant difference between driving at 55 mph and driving at 56 mph. But if it is safe to drive at 56 mph, then it must be safe to drive at 57 mph. One could proceed this way, from 57 mph to 58 mph, 58 mph to 59 mph, and so on. The conclusion would be that it must be safe to drive at 120 mph. But this conclusion does not follow. Although there is no significant difference in any of the individual steps, there is a huge difference between the first step, driving at 55 mph, and the last step, driving at 120 mph.

Another problem with slippery slope arguments is that they can usually be made in either direction. So for example, we could start with the claim that it is unsafe to drive at 120 mph. If it is unsafe to drive at 120 mph, then it is unsafe to drive at 119 mph, since there is no significant difference between driving at 120 mph and driving at 119 mph. And so on. Eventually, we could conclude that the speed limit should be zero. There are two different problems here. The first problem is that the slippery slope argument can lead to obviously false conclusions—that the speed limit should be infinite. One could bite the bullet and say, okay, the speed limit should be infinite. The second problem is even bigger. The very same kind of slippery slope argument, applied to the same issue can be used to derive contradictory conclusions. The same argument form can prove *both* that the speed limit should be infinite *and also* that it should be zero. If the same form of argument can derive contradictory conclusions, then there is something seriously wrong with that kind of argument.

Even if (conceptual) slippery slope arguments were valid, there would still be problems with applying this argumentative form to issues like gay marriage. The argument only works when the difference between the moderate position and the extreme position is a matter of degree, lying on a smooth continuum. That is why drawing a nonarbitrary cutoff point is impossible. If God agrees that he should spare the town for the sake of fifty good men, he would have a hard time justifying destroying it if there were forty-five good men. But the slippery slope does not work when the difference is a difference in *kind*. If God agrees that he should save the town if it contains fifty good men, he would not thereby be committed to saving the town if it contained fifty good *horses*. God could make a principled distinction between human beings and horses.

The difference between gay marriage and polygamous, incestuous, or bestial marriages is not a matter of degree. They are qualitatively different, not just quantitatively different. It is not like a slope at all but more like a stairway. There are reasons in favor of same-sex marriage that do not count in favor of polygamous, incestuous, or bestial marriages. And there are reasons to oppose polyamorous, incestuous, and bestial marriage that are irrelevant to the gay marriage issue.

CRITIQUE OF THE PIB ARGUMENT I—BESTIALITY

There are *many* good and very obvious reasons for refusing legal recognition of polygamous, incestuous, or bestial unions—much better reasons than the fact that the partners in these unions cannot reproduce sexually. Let us start with bestiality.

One reason that a marriage between a human being and a nonhuman animal should not, and cannot, be legally recognized is that the animal cannot meaningfully consent to the marriage contract. Even if a bird could be trained to say "I do" at the appropriate time in the ceremony, it would obviously have no clue what it was agreeing to. All marriages should require voluntary informed consent by both parties. Even New Natural Law theorists who make the bestiality argument admit that marriage must be consensual.[10] Yet somehow they fail to see that this would also disallow bestial marriages. It is impossible for creatures lacking the necessary conceptual and linguistic capacities to consent to marriage. (Lest anyone accuse me of making an ethnocentric assumption that arranged marriages are morally wrong, I should point out that there is a significant difference between an arranged marriage and a *forced* marriage. Forced marriages are unjust. But there are people who voluntarily accept their traditional customs and who prefer to have their marriages arranged.[11] Nothing I said commits to disapproving of that.)

The consent requirement is a reason for banning bestial marriages, but it obviously does not apply to same-sex marriage. Two normal adult humans of the same sex can voluntarily consent to all of the obligations that, in our society, constitute the marriage contract. They can agree to love, honor, and cherish, for richer or poorer, in sickness and in health, and so on for as long as they both shall live. Furthermore, this simple explanation for why humans cannot legitimately marry other animals has the added benefit that—unlike the Natural Law argument that the purpose of marriage is reproduction—it does not require any ad hoc gerrymandered explanation for why two infertile humans of the opposite sex should be allowed to marry.

Opponents of gay marriage might object that if we base the ban on bestiality on consent, we could not ban all cross-species marriages. It would not ban marriages between human beings and other intelligent life-forms. But that is an implication I am willing to accept. If elves or Vulcans or Na'vi actually existed, then perhaps humans should be legally allowed to marry them.

CRITIQUE OF THE PIB ARGUMENT 2—POLYGAMY

The polygamy version of the slippery slope argument against gay marriage claims that adopting a conception of marriage that is based on love and not procreation will not justify limiting marriages to two people. Our emotional attachments are not exclusive—it is possible to be in love with more than one person at one time. If the institution of marriage is seen as based primarily on love, then it is unclear why we should expect marriage to be monogamous or why we should expect sexual fidelity in marriage partners. Seeing marriage as an institution aimed at reproduction and child rearing explains these norms of fidelity, exclusivity, and—most importantly—monogamy.

However, there are many other, and better, reasons to refuse legal recognition of polygamous relationships—reasons which would not apply to same-sex marriages. For one thing, a ban on polygamy, unlike the ban on gay marriage, does not restrict *the kind* of person an individual may marry; it only restricts *how many* persons an individual may marry. Thus it is only a *rationing* of marriage partners. Restricting marriage partners to one spouse per person (at one time) is no more unjust than restricting voting to one vote per person.

This limit, of only one spouse per person, can thus be justified in terms of an analogue to the Lockean proviso for property acquisition—viz, that one must leave "enough and as good" for everyone else.[12] According to the proviso, acquisition of property is unjust if some people will not have enough because greedy hoarders have taken far more than they need. Of course, this is not to imply that spouses are property. But it seems at least prima facie reasonable that we might want to extend the proviso to some institutions besides property, especially ones that involve the distribution of scarce resources. On the basis of the Lockean proviso, we can say that it was unjust for King Solomon to take seven hundred wives (regardless of what the writers of the Old Testament might have intended) in part because doing so did not leave enough available wives for other men. Given that the proportion of males and females in any human society will generally be about fifty-fifty, whenever a man takes more than one wife some other man will have to go without a wife. This is a serious problem for those fundamentalist Mormon societies that continue to practice polygamy. A certain number of young men must be continuously expelled, cast out to fend for themselves in mainstream society where they are ill prepared to cope.[13] (The same reasoning would make it unjust for a woman to take more than one husband.)

This justification for the ban on polygamy does not apply *directly* to same-sex unions. If a gay King Solomon married half of the gay men in the community, the remaining gay men could still pair off. But this justification of rationing opposite-sex marriages partners can justify the rationing of same-sex marriages *indirectly* on grounds of equality. Equal status under the law is one of the major arguments in favor of same-sex marriages. And this equal application of the law must apply to benefits as well as to responsibilities, to equal liberties as well as to equal constraints. To put it simply, if straight people are legally limited to having only one spouse, and the law must apply equally to everyone, then gay people also should also be limited to one spouse.

There is another reason to refuse legal recognition of polyamorous marriages, one that applies more directly to same-sex relations. The state has a compelling interest in refusing to recognize marriages that are (or are likely to be) unfair, unequal, or exploitative. If a man has two wives, his relationship with his wives will be asymmetrical and unequal. He has two spouses while each wife has only one spouse (or, more accurately, each has only half of a spouse). Of course, this inequality is due in part to the fact that the two wives are not also married to each other. So the gay marriage opponents could try to argue that basing marriage on love and not procreation would not justify forbidding marriages in which three or more people are all married to each other. But this sort of relationship is highly unrealistic. While we can point to real examples of polygamous marriages in certain Arab and Mormon communities, I know of no such round-robin polyamorous practices. The virtual nonexistence of such practices in human societies is not because all members of a group marriage cannot participate in one and the same reproductive act. It is most likely due to features of human psychology rather than features of human biology. We might be able to envision—with strenuous effort of imagination—group marriages that are stable and in which all members love and care for each other equally. But we also know that in the real world this is almost never going to be stable.

Polygamous marriage exists only in societies in which women have significantly lower status and less power than men. In these sorts of societies, when a man decides to take a second wife, there is little or nothing that his first wife can do about it. But rarely if ever do wives willingly give consent for their husbands to add additional wives to the household. The recent case of a Kuwaiti woman convicted of setting fire to her husband's wedding tent out of revenge for his decision to take a second wife (and killing fifty-seven people in the process) is a striking example of the potentially devastating force of human jealously.

This is not just anecdotal. There is considerable empirical evidence that spouses in polygamous marriages are prone to jealousy, conflict, tension, emotional stress, insecurity, and anxiety[14] and that the jealousies between competing wives often result in serious emotional problems for the children.[15] In light of the conservative argument for traditional marriage on the basis of procreation, it is ironic that infertility was the number one reason that women submit when their husbands plan to take a second wife. Infertile women often feel that letting their husband take a second wife, who can provide an heir, is necessary to preserve the marriage and to prevent their husbands from leaving them.[16]

Conservatives claim that marriage involves, or should ideally involve, a complete and comprehensive sharing of lives together. That is a nice ideal that most reasonable people, progressive or conservative, would accept. The mistake is assuming that this ideal is explained by marriage having the sole or primary goal of procreation and child rearing. Instead, the nature of marriage as a comprehensive union is better explained and justified by the nearly universal desire that human beings have for this kind of relationship—unlike, say, lions, chickens, or horses, which are instinctually polygamous. It is this need to be the most important person in someone else's life that explains why polygamous marriages are inevitably unstable, unequal, or exploitive. You cannot share yourself completely with more than one person. And two people cannot both be the most important person in someone's life.

There is also empirical evidence that human beings are, for the most part, naturally monogamous. First, most societies throughout the world forbid, or at least discourage, polygamy.[17] And even in societies in which polygamy is allowed, it is still quite rare, existing only among the wealthy and powerful few.[18] Even adultery is unusual in our society. In the United States only 10–15 percent of women and 20–25 percent of men have extramarital affairs.[19]

Some conservatives try to support their slippery slope claims by citing several defenders of gay marriage who express a hope that legal recognition of same-sex unions will result in the further expansion of marriage to include polyamorous and/or nonromantic relations. They refer to Elizabeth Brake, who "supports legal recognition of any size, gender composition, and allocation of responsibilities."[20] Another example they cite is Judith Stacey, who hopes that the triumph of the more open view of marriage would give it "varied, creative, and adaptive contours," contours that would include "small group marriages."[21] They go on to cite other "scholars" such as E. J. Graff, Victoria Brownworth, Ellen Willis, and Michelangelo Signorile. Certain NNL theorists go out of their way to insist that Stacey "is in no way regarded by her academic colleagues as a fringe figure."[22]

Of course, "fringe" is a relative term. Regardless of how Ms. Stacey's colleagues view her work, I have never heard of her—or any of these other writers, with the exception of Brake.[23] It is quite surprising that conservatives cite these relatively obscure writers and yet never mention the work of such important mainstream philosophers as Ronald Dworkin, Joel Feinberg, Martha Nussbaum, Ralph Wedgwood, and John Corvino or more influential journalists such as Andrew Sullivan—all of whom advocate expansion of the modern institution of marriage to include same-sex couples without advocating radical relativism with regard to the institution of marriage.

The conservatives ignore prominent scholars with good arguments and instead cite only comparatively obscure writers, carefully selected for their radical views. These lesser known radicals are cited as representative of defenders of same-sex marriage generally. This is a selective form of the *straw man fallacy*, which is known as the "weak man" fallacy. The weak man fallacy involves "selecting the weakest argument or position when a stronger argument or position is known to be available."[24] Conservatives critique weak arguments and radical, fringy versions of the pro–gay marriage position and then claim to have defeated the overall pro–gay marriage position.

CRITIQUE OF THE PIB ARGUMENT 3—INCEST

The traditional conception of marriage, centered on reproduction, has more difficulty explaining why we should disapprove of incestuous marriages, since close blood relatives (of the opposite sex) can reproduce. Conservatives could simply define "conjugal marriage" as being between one man and one married woman *who are not close blood relatives*. In that case, conjugal marriage would exclude incestuous unions. The problem is that the definition would be merely stipulative. There is no explanation as to *why* conjugal marriage should exclude blood relatives. By appealing to this definition, the conservative would be merely *asserting that* incestuous marriages should not be legally recognized. But they would not be giving any reason why.

Some might argue that when blood relatives mate, they have an increased chance of birth defects. Thus, if marriage is aimed at procreation, it should exclude incestuous unions. But older men and women also have an increased chance of having children with birth defects. Yet it would be absurd to claim, for that reason, that we should not allow middle-aged couples to marry or to stay married. Furthermore, if increased chance of birth defects were the *only* reason against incestuous marriages, then there would be nothing wrong with brothers and sisters marrying if they are not blood relatives. We would have to allow adopted siblings who were raised as brother and sister to marry. We would even have to allow parents to marry their adopted children. I think most people, however, would agree that there is something morally objectionable about incestuous relations between adopted family members. That is why there was so much outrage when Woody Allen married Mia Farrow's adopted daughter Soon-Yi.[25]

As with bestial and polyamorous relations, there are better explanations for why we should disapprove of incestuous relationships. For one thing, they are likely to be exploitative, especially when it is between parent and child. Parents and children are not equals. Parents have authority over their children, and children depend on their parents for nurturing and support. This authority and dependence makes the parent-children relationship highly asymmetrical, and this asymmetry does not suddenly end the moment the child becomes an adult. Thus, even incest between parents and their adult children is likely to be exploitative, psychologically damaging, or the result of a dysfunctional attempt to resolve already existing psychological problems. Sibling relations are also not usually equal (with the possible exception of twins), since older siblings have certain advantages over younger siblings while they are growing up.

Incest also destroys already existing family relations.[26] If a man marries his daughter, his son becomes his brother-in-law; if an aunt marries her nephew, her brother becomes her father-in-law. Roles in the family become confused and the family structure is distorted. Incest also causes strife and conflict in the family, since other family members are likely to be appalled by the relationship. A revealing view of the many harms caused by incest is presented in *The Kiss*, a memoir of a prominent author who had a four-year-long incestuous relationship with her father.[27] Even though she barely knew her father until she was twenty years old, the relationship was devastating to her and to the rest of her family. None of that is a problem in the case of gay marriage. When two unrelated individuals of the same sex marry, they are forming a new family, not destroying an already existing one.

Another important difference between incestuous relationships and same-sex relationships is that banning incest only forbids a person from marrying a few particular individuals. If a man is not allowed to marry his daughter, he can still hope to find another woman just like his daughter whom he can marry. But banning gay marriage would mean that homosexuals would not be allowed to marry any suitable partner whatsoever.

CONCLUSION

It is a common argument against same-sex marriage that allowing legal recognition of such relationships would open the door to all manner of undesirable relationships—in particular, marriage of humans to nonhuman animals, polygamous or polyamorous marriages, and incestuous marriages. We have seen that such arguments fail on many levels. First, they rely on fallacious slippery slope argumentative structure. Second, there are many good reasons for denying these other kinds of relationships. Animals cannot consent to marriage; polyamorous relationships tend to be unfair and exploitive; incestuous relationships destroy families. None of these considerations apply to same-sex marriage.

9

HOMOSEXUALITY, CONSEQUENCES, AND JUSTICE II: ALLEGED BAD CONSEQUENCES OF GAY-TOLERANT PUBLIC POLICIES

Not all of the objections to the legal recognition of gay rights take the form of slippery slope arguments. Some of the objections appeal to the actual consequences that would result directly from the relatively moderate policies themselves (such as gay marriage), rather than on the claim that logical consequences and precedent will compel us to accept more radical policies (such as bestial or polygamous marriages). Rather than relying on gradual, incremental links in a conceptual (or causal) chain, these arguments make empirical claims about the detrimental effect of homosexual acts, homosexual lifestyles, or gay-tolerant laws and policies. Different versions of these arguments appeal to different *kinds* of harm and to harms to different *people*. First we will consider various arguments that homosexuality is harmful to homosexuals themselves. Then we will consider several arguments that homosexuality is harmful to certain third parties or to society at large.

There are three prominent versions of this second kind of argument. First, conservatives claim that legalizing gay marriage weakens the institution of marriage and threatens the marriages of heterosexual couples. Second, they claim that homosexuals are a threat to children, especially (but not only) the children of openly gay parents or same-sex couples. And finally, some conservatives claim that legal recognition of gay marriage or other gay rights threatens the religious freedom of those who are opposed to homosexuality on religious grounds.

PATERNALISTIC ARGUMENTS AGAINST GAY RIGHTS

There are many ways in which opponents of gay rights claim that homosexuality is harmful to homosexuals themselves. We will look at several of these claims individually. What they all have in common is that whenever they are used as an argument against gay rights or liberties, the result is a form of *paternalism*. Paternalistic laws, policies, or practices are those that limit individual freedom in some way in order to prevent people from harming themselves. Moral philosophers and legal scholars disagree on the extent to which paternalism is justified, as well as on the criteria with which to determine how much paternalism is acceptable. Insofar as we are limiting an individual's freedom and autonomy, there is a moral presumption against paternalism. On the other hand, insofar as we are doing it for the benefit of the individual whose liberties are being curtailed, there is some moral presumption in favor of it.

It is unlikely that any principle I could formulate for determining when paternalism is justified would be generally accepted by people on both sides of the debate.[1] But we can at least describe the factors that are relevant to determining whether, and under what conditions, paternalism might be acceptable. One of these factors is the capacity of the individual to make rational, informed choices that could significantly impact his or her own welfare. We do not allow young children to make important life decisions, such as dropping out of school or having unnecessary cosmetic surgery. We also do not allow mentally disabled adults, people with advanced dementia, or the insane to make certain important life decisions. That is because these individuals lack the capacity to make reasonable, informed decisions about important matters—not decent ones by our standards, but decent even by *their own* standards. For example, we would not allow eight-year-old Timmy to drop out of school, not because we disapprove, but because we are reasonably certain that Timmy himself would seriously regret that decision later in life when he finds himself shoveling shit for a living.

Other considerations relevant to the justification of paternalism are the seriousness of the decision and the potential consequences. These need to be weighed against the burdens of intervention and the importance, to the individuals in question, of the liberties they are being deprived of. For example, seat belt laws are justified, in part, because the harm that could be caused by not wearing a seat belt is potentially severe and irreversible. Also, the inconvenience of being required to buckle up is small, and few people take the freedom to decide to drive without a seat belt to be especially important (except maybe people in New Hampshire). Contrast this with dangerous hobbies like rock climbing or hang gliding. These practices are obviously riskier than driving around without a seat belt. Nevertheless, it would be unjust to outlaw them because rock climbing and hang gliding, unlike driving without a seat belt, are felt to be an important part of the self-identity and life plans of the people who engage in those practices.

Clearly the denial of gay rights and same-sex marriage impose a considerable burden on homosexual individuals. Being vulnerable to discrimination or being denied the legal right to marry any suitable partner can have drastic implications for an individual's life prospects. Thus, it is not enough to show that homosexuality or the gay lifestyle is harmful. The harms must be serious enough to warrant the considerable restriction of freedoms that the gay-intolerant policies impose. Most of the threats that homosexuality allegedly poses to gay people themselves are relatively insignificant. Even if the conservative opponents of gay rights were correct about these threats, they would not meet the burden necessary to justify denying equal rights to homosexuals.

Some paternalistic practices can be justified on the grounds that they are voluntarily accepted by those they apply to. For example, I might vote in favor of seat belt laws, even though they take away my own freedom, because I agree that I should wear my seat belt and want to have an added incentive to make me do it. But obviously most gay people do not agree with the conservatives who claim that their practices or lifestyles are harmful for them or that they would be better off without the same rights and liberties enjoyed by heterosexuals and opposite-sex couples.

Another important consideration is how well we can determine what is in the best interests of another person. John Stuart Mill argued against paternalism partly on the grounds that the individual is usually the best judge of what is in his or her own best interest.[2] This is not always the case, but it usually is, especially with informed, competent adults. Thus, those who would impose nonvoluntary paternalistic laws and policies on others have the burden of proof. They must show either that those whose liberties are to be limited are not competent to make their own decisions on these matters or that they know what is in the best interests of those individuals better than those individuals themselves. This burden is very unlikely to be met in the case of paternalistic grounds for denying gay rights, especially considering the extent to which most conservative homophobes are uninformed about the lives of gay people.

ALLEGED HARMS OF HOMOSEXUALITY TO HOMOSEXUALS THEMSELVES

One paternalistic argument some people give against gay rights is that homosexuality is forbidden by God. Since it is forbidden by God, those who live the gay lifestyle are risking eternal damnation. Refusing to recognize gay rights will discourage homosexuals from doing things that would preclude their salvation, thus rescuing them from spending eternity in a lake of fire (where they will eat naught but burning-hot coals and drink naught but burning-hot cola, where fiery demons will punch them in the back, where their tongues will be torn out by ravenous birds, where there will be wailing and gnashing of teeth).[3] Note that this is not a version of the DCT. The claim is not that homosexuality is wrong because God disapproves; it is simply the claim that God will punish gay people because he disapproves.

This kind of argument is obviously very weak. It makes highly controversial assumptions about the existence of a vindictive God, his commands, and the afterlife. Furthermore, if we were to accept this as an argument against gay rights, we would also have to accept the same sort of argument against freedom of religion and in favor of laws forbidding blasphemy, heresy, working on Saturdays, making graven images, usury, and so on. Most people who want to live an openly gay lifestyle do not believe that God will punish them for doing so. Since there is no convincing evidence to prove that they are wrong in that belief, these are not legitimate grounds for limiting their freedom.

Another paternalistic argument against homosexuality rests on the claim that homosexual activities are unhealthy. Since this argument rests on the claim that homosexuality causes damage to the physical body, rather than the eternal soul, it can be assessed in part by consulting objective, empirical evidence. One way that gay sex is supposed to be unhealthy is that it significantly increases one's chances of contracting AIDS. There are several problems with this argument, which were reviewed in chapter 5. One is that women who have sex with other women have a significantly *lower* risk of contracting AIDS or other STDs than do women who have sex with men. So this argument would actually *support* the lesbian lifestyle. More importantly, the higher risk of AIDS does not come from gay (male) sex but from unprotected sex with multiple partners (or more precisely, with partners who have had multiple partners). Unprotected sex with promiscuous partners increases your risk of AIDS and other STDs whether it is gay sex or straight sex.

Another alleged health risk of gay sex involves anal intercourse. For example, psychotherapist Jeffrey Satinover argues against gay rights by claiming:

> Anal intercourse, penile or otherwise, traumatizes the soft tissues of the rectal lining. These tissues . . . are nowhere near as sturdy as vaginal tissue. As a consequence, the lining of the rectum is almost always traumatized to some degree by any act of anal intercourse. Even in the absence of major trauma, minor or microscopic tears in the rectal lining allow for immediate contamination and the entry of germs into the bloodstream.[4]

Here is another example of this kind of warning given by conservatives.

> With repeated trauma, friction and stretching, the sphincter loses its tone and its ability to maintain a tight seal. Consequently, anal intercourse leads to leakage of fecal material that can easily become chronic.[5]

Sometimes these alleged health risks of anal sex are appealed to as part of an argument that gay sex is unnatural or involves misuse of the organs. The point of the unhealthiness claim is that the rectum, unlike the vagina, is not well suited for sexual intercourse. (We rejected these arguments in chapters 5 and 6.) But sometimes the alleged unhealthiness is used as direct support for anti-gay public policies, especially sodomy laws. The argument is that if we can enact statutes that discourage tobacco consumption on the grounds that it is unhealthy, then we can do the same for gay (anal) sex.

I do not have any firsthand experience with this sort of thing, but I assume that if these conservatives find that anal sex causes so much physical damage to the rectum, then they are probably not doing it right. Vaginal sex between a man and a woman can also be damaging if it is too rough. Just as there is a right way and a wrong way to have vaginal intercourse, I assume the same is true for anal intercourse. More importantly, not all male homosexuals engage in anal sex, while some heterosexual couples do. (And I suspect that very few lesbian couples do. Yet another argument *in favor* of lesbianism!) So this really has nothing to do with most gay rights, such as the legal recognition of same-sex marriage or antidiscrimination laws. The only laws this would justify are sodomy laws, and it would justify them equally for same-sex as well as opposite-sex couples.

So now the question is, assuming that anal sex is harmful in the ways alleged (even when done properly), would this justify paternalistic sodomy laws? It is hard to see how these harms would be significant enough to justify the intrusive burdens such laws would impose on the private lives of individuals. The contrast with tobacco helps to illustrate this. Cigarettes are estimated to kill about 480,000 per year in the United States.[6] No one dies from anal sex (except perhaps under *very* unusual circumstances). Furthermore, people have a right to take certain risks with their health, and even to purposely inflict minor damage to their own bodies, when pursing their personal vision of the good life. It would be unjust, for example, to outlaw soccer, even though repeated heading of the soccer ball can cause irreversible damage to the frontal lobes of the brain. Likewise, laws against body piercing and tattoos would be unjust, even though these forms of bodily mutilation are more irreversible than any damage caused by doing it up the butt.

Another of the alleged harms of homosexuality is that gay people are less happy or that they lead less fulfilling lives than straight people.[7] This is usually connected to, or supported by, claims that gay people (or at least gay men) tend to be more irresponsible and promiscuous than their straight counterparts. This may be a stereotype, but like many stereotypes, there may be some truth to it. People who make this argument often trot out empirical evidence that supposedly shows that gay people have higher incidences of depression, suicide, or substance-abuse problems. Even if that were true, however, it would not prove that their unhappiness is caused by their being gay. Another plausible explanation is that it is the stress and anxiety of social disapproval and discrimination that diminishes their happiness.

Philosopher Michael Levin argues against this alternative interpretation by claiming that other groups who have been persecuted have not suffered the same sorts of psychological issues as gay people.

> This prediction, that homosexuality being unnatural homosexuals will still find their behavior self-punishing, coheres with available evidence. It is consistent with the failure of other oppressed groups, such as American Negroes and European Jews, to become warped in the direction of "cruising," sado-masochism and other practices common in homosexual life.

There are obvious differences, however, in the nature of the discrimination against homosexuals and the discrimination faced by those other groups. Jews and African Americans, unlike homosexuals, are not routinely scorned or rejected by their own families for being Jewish or black.[8] Even under some of the worst oppression, Jews and African Americans were not forbidden from marrying suitable partners. When marriage is not an option, promiscuity should be expected, as well as loneliness, irresponsibility, and superficiality. If irresponsibility is a part of the gay lifestyle (which I doubt), it would be best explained by the fact that marriage has not been a viable option for gay people until recently. People become responsible by taking on responsibilities and meeting the challenges that come with them—including the challenges and responsibilities of marriage, parenthood, and family life.

Even if Levin were right and most gay people are doomed to a life that is less fulfilling than straight people's (which I also doubt), that would not mean that living a gay lifestyle would be less fulfilling *for those gay people* than the alternatives. Living a fulfilling heterosexual lifestyle is not a realistic option for most homosexuals. The only alternatives to living a gay lifestyle, for most homosexuals, is either 1) trying to live a straight, closeted lifestyle or 2) living a sexually repressed, celibate lifestyle. Neither of those would be as fulfilling, for most gay people, as living openly gay and married to a partner of the same sex. For these reasons, gay marriage and other gay rights will have good consequences for the gay people themselves as well as for society as a whole. The result, in the long run, will be that gay people will have the opportunity to live the most fulfilling lives they can.

NEGATIVE CONSEQUENCES OF GAY RIGHTS I: WEAKENING THE INSTITUTION OF MARRIAGE

It is hard not to doubt the sincerity of those who claim that their opposition to homosexuality and gay rights is motivated by concern for the well-being of the gay people themselves. Even if they are sincere, it is very unlikely that they know what is best for those people, especially given the fact that those who are most opposed to homosexuality tend to be those who are least acquainted with openly gay persons. Most of the consequence-based arguments against gay rights, however, involve alleged bad consequences for society as a whole or for individuals other than the gay people themselves.

One of the alleged negative consequences of the recognition of gay rights, and same-sex marriage in particular, is that it would weaken the institution of marriage and threaten the relationships of heterosexual couples. The argument goes like this. People are heavily influenced by cultural norms, which are shaped at least partly by law. Changing our traditional conception of marriage would send a bad message that undermines the rationality of the marriage norms. The result will be increases in divorce, adultery, broken homes, and all of the associated social ills. Some Natural Law theorists might claim that marriage itself is an objective human good and so weakening the institution would be bad, even if it did not affect the well-being of married individuals or have any other harmful effects on society. The argument is made more plausible, however, by the added claim that weakening the institution of marriage is bad for married couples, their children, and society at large. The last step is not unreasonable, given that marriage is, at least ideally, beneficial to married persons, their children, and society in general.

Personally, I find this argument highly counterintuitive. As a happily married straight man, I cannot see how allowing gay people to marry each other could in any way weaken my commitment to my wife, or her commitment to me. Nor can I imagine any way that it might diminish the quality of our shared life together. If anything, extending the institution of marriage to include gay people and their same-sex partners could only serve to strengthen the commitment that opposite-sex spouses have to their marriage. Heterosexuals are not generally inclined to envy gay people for their same-sex relations or for their homosexual activities. But, in those rare moments when the burdens of married life are weighing heavily on them, they might envy unattached singles (be they gay or straight) for their seemingly carefree lifestyles. With gay marriage as an option, there would be a significant reduction in the number of mature uncommitted adults. With fewer (seemingly) carefree singles in their peer group, married straight people might be less tempted by the illusory, but enticing, single lifestyle and less inclined to worry that they are missing out on something.

WHAT DOES IT MEAN TO SAY MARRIAGE WOULD BE "WEAKER"?

The claim that extending marriage to gay couples would "weaken the institution of marriage" strikes me as absurd on its face. But let us try to make as much sense of it as we can and try to find some way that it might be true. To make sense of the argument, we first have to understand what conservatives might mean when they say the institution of marriage would be *weakened*. I suspect that when some opponents of same-sex marriage make this argument, what they really mean by "weakening" the institution is simply that it will no longer be exclusively heterosexual. If weakening is just another way of saying that it will include same-sex couples, then of course it is true that legalizing gay marriage would "weaken" the institution of marriage. But to use that claim to argue that we should not legalize same-sex marriage would be circular reasoning. It would amount to saying that we should not allow gay marriage because it will make the institution of marriage *gayer*.

More likely, when conservatives say that same-sex marriage will weaken the institution of marriage, they mean that marriages will be less stable and less enduring. "Strength," then, would mean something like *consistency* and *endurance*. But there is no reason to think that consistency and endurance in a marriage is always or automatically a good thing. Not every marriage is a good marriage; there are bad marriages. No one can seriously deny that. And a bad marriage is a bad thing; it is bad *tout court*. By that I mean that the world would be a better place (*ceteris paribus*) if there were fewer bad marriages. "Weakening" marriage, in the sense of making marriages less consistent or less enduring, is not a bad thing if it is mostly bad marriages that will be less consistent and less likely to endure.

Many opponents of gay marriage claim that it would redefine marriage as being based on love instead of procreation and child rearing. When marriage is based on love, it will be less stable, since emotions are unreliable. But happily married couples would be unlikely to terminate a good relationship just because they don't have kids to worry about. And those couples who want to end their marriage because they no longer love each other are much more likely to have a bad marriage than a good one. Conceiving of marriage as primarily for the sake of love and companionship could thus improve the *quality* of marriages. Even if it made marriages less consistent or less enduring on average, this negative consequence would be more than compensated for by the improved quality of marriages. I think the world would be a better place if most people had happy marriages based on love than if most people had unhappy but unbreakable marriage based on kids.

Maybe there is something to be said in favor of strengthening marriage, if that is taken to mean improving the stability of *good* marriages. Married life has its challenges, and people are often tempted to take the easy route, even when they know it will not be the best option in the long run. Weaker marriage norms might result in couples splitting up in hard times, even though they would be rewarded with marital bliss in the long run if they were to stick it out. The more we think of the norms associated with marriage as being binding, the more we will preserve those good marriages that would otherwise end due to weakness or laziness. That may be true, but there are better ways to help good marriages survive—ways that do not require grounding the institution in procreation and thus excluding same-sex couples. Public policies that might help to strengthen marriage include labor laws calling for a shorter work week and longer vacation time, better family and medical leave policies, public support for marriage counseling and other mental health treatments, better laws against domestic violence and better enforcement of those laws, public support for child care, and tighter enforcement of child-support laws.[9] These alternative approaches to strengthening marriages would be more effective than "legally enshrining the conjugal conception of marriage." It would also not involve denying marriage to same-sex couples.

Furthermore, empirical evidence contradicts the claim that gay marriage and tolerance of the gay lifestyle threaten the institution of marriage by making marital duties weaker and making marriages less stable and enduring. If that claim were true, then we should expect higher divorce rates in regions of the United States where gay marriage is accepted. That is because, according to the conservatives' argument, either 1) the practice of same-sex marriage will have already started to erode the institution, or 2) people in those regions already took marriage norms lightly, and that is why they approve of same-sex marriage. In fact, the opposite is the case. States that have legalized same-sex marriages tend to have significantly lower divorce rates than those states where same-sex marriage is explicitly banned.[10] The fifteen states with the lowest divorce rates in the United States, starting with the lowest, are Jew Jersey, Massachusetts, Wisconsin, New York, Minnesota, Pennsylvania, South Carolina, Maryland, Idaho, North Dakota, Illinois, Connecticut, Hawaii, California, and Delaware. Nine of these states recognize same-sex marriage, and two of them (Wisconsin and Minnesota) offer domestic partnerships for same-sex couples. Only Pennsylvania, South Carolina, Idaho, and North Dakota ban all legally recognized rights for same-sex couples. By comparison, the states with the highest divorce rates, starting with the highest, are Alaska, Alabama, Arkansas, Kentucky, Oklahoma, Nevada, Maine, Georgia, Tennessee, Texas, Arizona, West Virginia, Missouri, Montana, and Washington. Only two of these states, Washington and Maine, allow same-sex couples to marry. (Nevada offers domestic partnerships, and Kentucky recognizes same-sex marriages from other states.) There is an even stronger correlation between lower divorce rates and gay tolerance generally. The top ten most gay-friendly states are, in order, Wisconsin (3rd lowest divorce rate), Maryland (8th lowest), Illinois (11th lowest), Pennsylvania (6th lowest), Hawaii (13th lowest), California (14th lowest), Minnesota (5th lowest), and New Jersey (the lowest of all). All of these states currently recognize same-sex marriage, except for Wisconsin. (Wisconsin grants domestic partnerships but gay marriage is banned by the state constitution.) The states with the highest divorce rates are Alaska (ranked 23rd in gay tolerance), Alabama (ranked 40th), Arkansas (49th), Kentucky (41st), Oklahoma (35th), Nevada (20th), Maine (27th), and Georgia (32nd).[11] Thus, not only does the recognition of same-sex marriage not weaken the institution, a case could be made that it would actually *strengthen* the institution of marriage.

WAYS THAT GAY RIGHTS COULD WEAKEN SOME MARRIAGES

Here is one possible way that allowing same-sex marriage could weaken or undermine *some* opposite-sex marriages. As we saw in chapter 7, many people who oppose homosexual relations are repressing their own homosexual tendencies. These latent homosexuals often lead, or try to lead, heterosexual lives. Many of them are presumably in heterosexual relationships. Recent empirical evidence indicates that the proportion of gay men is roughly the same in all parts of the United States.[12] Some places, such as the Bible Belt, seem to have fewer gay men. But that is not true. It only seems that way because a greater percentage of the gay men there are closeted or in denial. One piece of evidence is that in parts of the United States where there are fewer openly gay men (such as the Deep South), there is a significantly greater number of Google searches for the question "Is my husband gay?" than there are in more gay-tolerant parts of the country. If we as a society become more approving of homosexuality—and legal recognition of same-sex marriage would go a long way in encouraging and expressing such approval—then some of these people would lose the motivation to repress their homosexuality. They could more easily admit to themselves, and disclose to others, their own same-sex preferences. These people would also lose the motivation to maintain their sham marriages.

Thus, legalizing marriage could weaken some opposite-sex marriages, but the marriages that would be threatened are sham marriages of homosexuals pretending to be straight. If that is what is intended when people say that gay marriage could weaken opposite-sex marriages, then it is not a very good argument. For one thing, these sorts of marriages are hardly worth preserving. How many straight persons would want to remain married to a spouse who was secretly gay? Suppose you are married and you discover that your spouse was not sexually or romantically attracted to people of your sex? Do you think it would better for either of you if you were to continue the relationship? Would it be good for society?

Divorce is rarely easy, and there may be compelling reasons for an opposite-sex couple to stay married, even when one of them reveals that he or she is gay. If nothing else, they might still love each other and enjoy living together. But the fact that one married partner is the wrong sexual orientation must count as *some* reason in favor of terminating a marriage. And anyway, the inconveniences that might be caused by the dissolution of sham marriages would occur mostly in the short term. Once gay marriage loses its novelty and comes to be an accepted part of society, fewer gay people will feel the need to enter into sham marriages with members of the opposite sex, whom they are not physically or romantically attracted to. Thus, the effect of the law would be to disrupt undesirable sham marriages in the short run while preventing these undesirable unions in the long run. Given that sham marriages are typically unstable and unfulfilling, allowing same-sex couples to marry might lead to a greater proportion of strong marriages (with appropriately oriented partners) and fewer unstable sham marriages.

When opponents of same-sex marriage say that legal recognition will weaken heterosexual marriage, however, I doubt that what they have in mind is that it will weaken only the sham marriages of repressed homosexuals. Here is another possibility. Those who make this argument might be assuming that homosexuals are not as capable of remaining in committed relationships as straight couples are. There might be an assumption that gay people are inherently more promiscuous, fickle, unstable, or irresponsible. Thus, extending the institution of marriage to same-sex couples will require weakening the bonds of marriage in order to accommodate their diminished capacity to remain faithfully committed. Or maybe it will weaken the institution simply by having more unstable marriages.

There are several problems with this argument. For one, this assumes that homosexuals are significantly different psychologically from heterosexual people. But, as we saw in chapter 5, the empirical evidence goes against this. More importantly, those who advocate same-sex marriage are not demanding the privileges of marriage without the obligations. Although there may be some radicals in the gay community (and some radical straight people as well) who think that we should abolish legal recognition of marriage altogether, most gay people want the option to marry. And those who want to marry want their marriages to entail the same kind of commitment as those of opposite-sex married couples. If gay people were demanding something else—for example, legal recognition of temporary marriages or open marriages—then the weakening-of-marriage argument might have some legitimacy. But then the argument would be against those other kinds of marriage (temporary or open marriages) whether gay or straight. It would not be an argument against same-sex marriage per se.

Some opponents of gay marriage might claim that homosexuals are in fact more promiscuous and significantly less likely to enter into, or remain in, long-term committed relationships. This may be true, or it may just be a stereotype reinforced by confirmation bias. It is probably a little of both. But let us assume, for the sake of argument, that homosexuals are much more promiscuous and that they have fewer or less enduring committed relationships than heterosexuals. What would explain this pattern of behavior? One possibility is that there is something about homosexuality that makes someone promiscuous, fickle, shiftless, or irresponsible. Another possibility is that the behavior is largely caused by the fact that same-sex marriage has not traditionally been an option. If I grew up believing that I would never be allowed to marry an appropriate partner (for whatever reason), I would probably be more promiscuous and less commitment oriented than I am.

Once gay marriage has been around for a while, homosexuals will feel the same sorts of pressures as straight people—from family, from partners, and from society as a whole—to enter into long-term committed relationships. And once there are plenty of examples of happily married gay couples, more gay people will see the benefits of this sort of arrangement. Perhaps many homosexuals have seen marriage as a heterosexual institution and so have sought to avoid it. Legalizing of gay marriage might help to "rebrand" the institution in a way that makes it more desirable to those in the gay community. This would not involve changing the institution of marriage to fit the typical (or stereotypical) gay lifestyle. Rather, the benefits of marriage would motivate some gay people, in light of this new option, to reassess their values and revise their life plans to align with the institution of marriage as it already is: a lifetime exclusive commitment of love and mutual support.

Even if gay people were more promiscuous or irresponsible than heterosexuals *and* were unable or unwilling to change their lifestyles to conform to the demands of marriage (which, again, I doubt), it would still be very unlikely that allowing same-sex marriages would in fact significantly change the institution. If gay marriage were legalized, same-sex couples would not be *required* to marry each other, just as we do not require every straight couple to get married. And it is not likely that people will get married just because they can, even though they do not want to. If most gay people were commitment averse and determined to stay that way, then few of them would take advantage of the option of same-sex marriage. It seems, however, that every time a state legalizes gay marriage there is a mad rush of same-sex couples to the altar (or justice of the peace). That indicates to me that many, if not most, homosexuals want to have a lifetime commitment to a partner as much as do most straight people. Most gay people who seek legally recognized marital status for their relationships will be seriously committed and monogamous, while those who are unable or unwilling to commit seriously to one partner indefinitely will not be interested in marriage just because it is legal.

Denying all homosexuals the legal right to marry on the grounds that some, or even most, are unable or unwilling to maintain stable relationships and abide by the norms associated with marriage would clearly be unjust. Individuals differ greatly, and for any general tendency within a group there will be a wide range of variation. Some heterosexual people are very promiscuous and have great difficulty seriously committing to a monogamous long-term relationship, while others have no interest in having multiple sex partners and find serious commitment both easy and desirable. The same is certainly true of homosexuals (whether or not they differ from heterosexuals on average, as a group). Those gay people who are able and willing to commit to long-term relationships should not be denied the legal recognition of their same-sex unions just because so many others in their group are less commitment oriented. It would be very unfair to deny privileges to certain individuals just because other members of their group are less able to meet the responsibilities that these privileges entail. Suppose that empirical research were to reveal that other groups—Presbyterians, for example, or taxi drivers, or blondes—were *on average* more promiscuous and less able to remain in stable relationships than other groups. (We could almost certainly find *some* group variations like this, if we looked hard enough.) Surely it would be unjust to deny any of those groups the right to legally recognized marriage on the basis that doing so would weaken the institution.

NEW NATURAL LAW VERSION OF THE WEAKENING-OF-MARRIAGE ARGUMENT

Usually this weakening-of-the-institution objection to gay marriage is vague and not well fleshed out. But there has been a serious attempt by some professional scholars to give a more sophisticated formulation of the argument. These fancier versions of the weakening-of-marriage argument are generally tied up with the New Natural Law (NNL) theory that we examined in chapters 5 and 6. This argument starts with the claim that changing our traditional conception of marriage to include same-sex couples would send a bad message that would undermine the rationality of the marriage norms, in particular the expectations of exclusivity, fidelity, sexual intimacy, cohabitation, and sharing of resources. The explanation and grounding of these duties and expectations, according to this argument, come from seeing marriage as an institution that is primarily and essentially oriented toward the bearing and rearing of children—that is, the conjugal conception of marriage.

The result of abandoning the traditional conception of marriage in our laws, according to this argument, is that "adults . . . generally would be harmed insofar as the weakening of social expectations supporting marriage would make it harder for them to abide by marital norms."[13]

For example, allowing same-sex marriage would make it hard to justify the demand of exclusivity. We would have to redefine marriage as based on emotion rather than procreation. But our emotional attachments are not exclusive—it is possible to have romantic feelings for more than one person at a time. Thus, if the institution of marriage is seen as based primarily on love and affection, then it would be unclear why we should expect marriage to be monogamous or why we should expect sexual fidelity in marriage partners.

The first problem with this argument is the claim that the "conjugal" view of marriage (with an essential connection to procreation) is the only, or even just the best, way to explain and justify marital obligations. My wife and I, for example, have decided not to have children. (That is not as strange or uncommon as it may seem.)[14] But that does not mean that we take our wedding vows any less seriously than do those couples who have children or who are trying to have children. I suspect that we are not unusual in that way. The fact that we have decided not to have children does not make it any harder for me to take care of my wife and remain faithful to her. If anything, it makes it easier. We have more time to care for each other because we are not burdened with the duties of tending to a brood of rug rats.

There are many reasons why two people might want to take care of each other; love, honor, and cherish each other; forsaking all others, until death do they part. One very powerful reason is *love*. The NNL theorists fail to appreciate the strength of genuine love. They confuse romantic love with fondness, infatuation, or physical attraction, dismissing it as "mere emotion." The kind of love that motivates two people to join in the bonds of matrimony, with all its associated duties and expectations, is not the kind of love that comes and goes easily; and it is not the kind of love one can easily have for more than one person. This is not to say that people who have this sort of love are immune to any and all temptations to be unfaithful, but only that they will not be easily tempted and will have strong motivation to avoid succumbing to such temptations.

Many people who want marriage have, or at least think they have, this sort of love. Marriage is desirable to those people because they want to love someone in this way, and they want to be loved this way in return. Just as importantly, we want to be *worthy* of that sort of love. This form of love represents *my* marriage ideal; and I suspect that I am not alone. Furthermore, this ideal gives me good reasons to uphold the marital norms of fidelity, cohabitation, mutual support, and long-term commitment—and does so without requiring the ability to reproduce biologically (or the ability to engage in the kind of penis-in-the-vagina sex involved in reproduction). By comparison, sticking it out for the sake of the kids strikes me as a pretty sad reason to uphold one's marriage vows. If that were the main rationale for the norms and expectations of marriage, then marriage would be a rather mediocre institution.

NNL theorists claim that homosexuality and same-sex relations weaken marriage by destroying the (traditional, conjugal) *meaning* of marriage, thereby undermining the norms and expectations central to the institution. For example, John Finnis says that gay sex—or any kind of "non-marital" sex, including masturbation—is wrong because

> it treats human sexual capacities in a way which is deeply hostile to the self-understanding of those members of the community who are willing to commit themselves to real marriages in the understanding that its sexual joys are not mere instruments to, or mere compensations for, the accomplishment of marriage's responsibilities, but rather enable the spouses to *actualize and experience* their intelligent commitment to share in those responsibilities, in that genuine self-giving.[15]

It is hard to make any literal sense of the rhetoric here. What does it even mean to say that gay sex is "hostile" to the self-understanding of opposite-sex married couples? One possibility is that Finnis is claiming that gay people have sex out of spite, that they do it just to cheese off straight people. That is a rather bizarre, paranoid fantasy. Perhaps he means to say that it is not the gay people but their sexual acts that are hostile to straight married couples. But that would be a category mistake. A sexual act is not the kind of thing that can have hostility. Maybe he means "hostile" in a metaphorical sense. Gay sex is inconsistent with, or somehow undermines, the self-understanding of straight couples. Still, it is not clear how a sexual act that takes place in the privacy of someone else's home could cause any difficulty in how my wife and I understand our relationship. Maybe Finnis is assuming that these gay couples are openly gay; so even though their sexual activity takes place in the privacy of their homes, we all know there is *something* going on in there—and whatever it is, it sure ain't "conjugal." But how dumb does Finnis think these straight couples are that they cannot understand their own marriage unless everyone else is forced to have the same kind of relationship? Most importantly, I see no reasons why my wife and I should be obligated to make our relationship conform to some prudish, Victorian model that does not appeal to us, just so that the conservative couple next door can better understand their "conjugal" marriage. If the existence of nonmarital sex between two consenting adults (or one consenting adult, in the case of masturbation) in the privacy of their own bedroom causes conservative couples to be con-

fused about their own relationship, that is a problem that the conservative couples will have to figure out on their own. It is not the problem of
those who are engaging in nonmarital sex and minding their own business.

NEGATIVE CONSEQUENCES OF GAY RIGHTS II: WON'T SOMEBODY THINK OF THE CHILDREN?

Another of the alleged bad consequences of the legal recognition of gay
rights, according to gay rights opponents, is that gay rights or openly gay
people are a threat to children. This claim is often made by those who
oppose allowing same-sex couples to adopt children. For example, in
2003, the Vatican issued a statement claiming that "allowing children to
be adopted by persons living in such (homosexual) unions would actually mean doing violence to these children."[16] This bit of hyperbole is
especially ironic coming from the Catholic Church, an organization that
should know quite a bit about violence against children. The threat-to-
children argument, however, is used not just to oppose same-sex marriage and parenting; it is also used by those opposed to antidiscrimination laws protecting homosexuals. These homophobic conservatives
think that openly gay people should not be allowed to teach children,
for fear that they will be a bad influence and corrupt the youth.[17] For
example, former U.S. senator Jim DeMint has gone on record saying
that if someone is openly homosexual, he or she should not be teaching
in the classroom. He also thinks that unmarried female teachers should
be required to remain celibate as a condition of their employment.[18] (It
is not clear why he did not say that unmarried male teachers who are
sexually active are equally unfit to teach.)

Some of these worries are based on the irrational fear that homosexuals are more likely than straight people to be criminals or pedophiles.
These fears are absolutely groundless (see chapter 5). Another worry
gay rights opponents have about openly gay teachers is that they will
recruit young men and women, who would otherwise be straight, into
their gay lifestyle. This is false for several reasons. First, it assumes that
sexual orientation is a choice or that it is something that can easily be
shaped or redirected by environment. As we saw in chapter 4, that is
almost certainly false, at least for most people. Sexual orientation is
mostly biological in origin and considerably stable over a lifetime. This
concern about recruiting also naively assumes that teachers have considerable influence over their students and that children look up to
their teachers as role models. In fact, students are much more influ-

enced by their peers than by any of the adults in their lives. And as for their adult role models, they are more inclined to look to famous athletes or celebrities rather than their parents or teachers.

The idea of same-sex parents seems to elicit more worry than the idea of gay teachers.[19] Gay rights opponents claim that children raised by same-sex couples have more problems than children raised by heterosexual couples. This is an empirical claim and thus is subject to testing by observation. There have been many studies recently of children raised by same-sex parents and the empirical evidence overwhelmingly indicates that the children of same-sex couples do just as well as children raised by opposite-sex couples and much better than children raised by single parents.[20] This is the official view of the American Sociological Association (ASA). In an amicus for the U.S. Supreme Court cases over the Defense of Marriage Act and California's Proposition 8, the ASA claimed, on the basis of an exhaustive review of peer-reviewed scientific articles, that there is no evidence that children of same-sex parents differ in welfare from children with opposite-sex parents.[21] There is even some evidence that they do *better*. According to a nationwide study in Australia of five hundred children, "there was no statistical difference between children of same-sex couples and the rest of the population on indicators including self-esteem, emotional behaviour and the amount of time spent with parents. However, children of same-sex couples scored higher than the national average for overall health and family cohesion."[22]

It is, of course, very rare to find unanimity of opinion in ongoing scientific research, especially in sciences as fuzzy as sociology and psychology. So naturally there are a few dissenting studies on the competency of same-sex couples. Conservative activists and politicians who oppose gay marriage and adoption by same-sex couples cite one study, by conservative Christian sociologist Mark Regnerus, that purports to show that children suffer when raised by same-sex parents.[23] The Regnerus study, however, was funded by the National Organization for Marriage, an anti–gay rights lobbying group[24] and has been widely criticized for flawed methodology. As the ASA amicus points out, Regnerus did not study children raised by gay couples. Instead, the test group consisted of people with a parent who had at least one same-sex relationship while the children were still minors. As it turns out, most of these parents were in opposite-sex marriages that failed. The control group, on the other hand, consisted of children raised in stable households with two opposite-sex parents. Regnerus eliminated all divorced and single-parent families from the heterosexual parent (control) group, but the gay parent (test) group contained mostly unstable and divorced families. It does not take an expert in experimental design to see that the best explanation for the different outcomes is family stability, not the sexual orientation of the parent or parents.

Even if empirical studies were to show that children do not do as well when raised by same-sex couples as they do when raised by opposite-sex couples, it would be irrelevant. We cannot ban or even discourage less-than-perfect parents from having kids. If we looked hard enough, we could probably find statistical evidence that some groups do not do as well raising their children as do other groups (evidence that does not involve the sort of obvious sampling errors committed in the Regnerus study). Suppose we were to discover that children raised by parents of a certain race, or a certain religious affiliation, or a certain socioeconomic status, fared less well than other children. It would be unjust for us to discourage, let alone ban, people from these groups from getting married or having children.[25] Of course, there may be some groups that we should discourage from having children. For example, it might not be unjust to discourage homeless drug addicts or convicted child molesters from raising children. The state has a legitimate interest in preventing *unfit* parents from having kids. That is why we have social workers who sometimes remove children from abusive or neglectful households. But even conservative anti-gay activists like Regnerus would not go so far as to say that same-sex couples are *unfit* parents. That sort of claim would not be believable.

NNL theorists give more subtle, but no less flawed, arguments for why we should discourage same-sex parenting. They claim that the legal "enshrining" of "conjugal" marriages, based on procreation—by outlawing any other kind of marriage—reinforces in our society the idea that the union of a husband and wife is the most appropriate venue for bearing and raising children. They cite empirical evidence that they claim shows that children need both a mother and a father to develop into normal, healthy, well-adjusted adults. NNL theorists Sherif Girgis, Robert George, and Ryan Anderson (GG&A), like many anti–gay rights activists, go even further, claiming that children do best when raised by their own *biological* parents. Thus, they oppose adoption generally, though they are especially opposed to adoption by same-sex parents. In support of their claim that children should be raised by their biological parents, GG&A cite a report by Child Trends (which they go out of their way to characterize as a left-leaning organization) and research by the Witherspoon Institute.

The Witherspoon institute is not a research organization but a right-wing think tank dedicated to opposing gay marriage, stem-cell research, and abortion. So their "research" should be taken with a grain of salt. Child Trends, on the other hand, is a respectable organization, devoted to promoting child welfare. But GG&A blatantly misrepresent the report. They say the report claims that the children do better when raised by both of their biological parents. That is misleading at best. The study compares children being raised by both biological parents to children being raised by a stepparent.[26] They do not compare children being raised by biological parents to children raised by adopted parents. The problems that tend to arise with stepparents are quite irrelevant to the same-sex marriage issue. Children raised by gay parents are not going to be any more likely to be raised by stepparents than are children raised by straight parents. In fact, the very study that GG&A cite contains a note—right at the top of the title page, in bold letters—explicitly denying the interpretation GG&A give. It reads, "Note: This Child Trends brief summarizes research conducted in 2002, when neither same-sex parents nor adoptive parents were identified in large national surveys. Therefore, *no conclusions can be drawn from this research about the wellbeing of children raised by same-sex parents or adoptive parents*" [emphasis added]. This bears reemphasizing. GG&A, in their article, knowingly and willfully distort the evidence by citing, as support for their view, a report that *explicitly denies* lending any support to their view.

As someone who was raised by adoptive parents, I find this claim by NNL theorists, that children should be raised by their biological parents, quite offensive. It is based on false stereotypes that adopted children feel abandoned by their birth parents, lack a solid sense of personal identity, and feel that something is missing in their lives. There is no reasonable evidence to support these stereotypes. Some amateur hack psychotherapists have coined the term "adopted child syndrome," which they characterize by various psychological problems and antisocial behaviors. But there is no legitimate scientific evidence for any such "syndrome," and the condition is not recognized by any psychological, psychiatric, sociological, or medical organization. Adopted children, in fact, are not significantly different from children raised by their biological parents, and certainly not less well-adjusted.[27]

Some studies have found higher than normal developmental, behavioral, or psychological problems with adopted children. Some of these results, however, are due to the inclusion of children who were institutionalized for more than six months before being adopted. Obviously spending time in an orphanage or a foster home is going to be traumatic. But the detrimental effects of that kind of experience will be the same whether the child is later adopted or raised by its biological parents. Some of the studies included only children who were adopted at birth and yet still showed slight increases of mental health and behavioral problems. But that is not because they were raised by non–biological parents. Part of the explanation is that parents who give their (biological) children up for adoption are more likely to suffer from substance abuse or psychological problems than the general population. Some of the psychological problems might be inheritable, and some of the substance-abuse problems affect the fetus in utero (e.g., fetal alcohol syndrome). Also, there is evidence for referral bias with adopted children. Because of the stereotypes about adopted kids, they are more likely to be referred to a therapist than non–adopted children exhibiting the same behavior.[28]

NEGATIVE CONSEQUENCES OF GAY MARRIAGE III: VIOLATES FREEDOM OF RELIGIOUS PRACTICE

Finally, conservative opponents of gay rights argue (with a straight face) that legal recognition of gay rights would violate the religious freedom of those who oppose same-sex marriage on religious grounds. As GG&A write, if gay marriage were legalized, "the state would thus be forced to view conjugal-marriage supporters as bigots who make groundless and invidious distinctions." Given that supporters of the NNL argument against homosexuality and gay marriage *do in fact* make groundless and invidious distinctions, with bigoted implications, I do not see the problem here. But let's hear them out anyway. They go on to say that such public policies would "undermine religious freedom and the rights of parents to direct the education and upbringing of their children."[29] This is presumably the justification for the law recently passed by the Arizona state legislature, and (fortunately) vetoed by the governor, allowing for any business to discriminate against homosexuals on religious grounds.[30]

These gay rights opponents think, for example, that a Catholic adoption service should have the right to refuse to work with same-sex couples. A religiously affiliated hospital should be able to refuse visitation rights to a patient's same-sex partner. Businesses should be allowed to refuse to offer benefits to an employee's same-sex partner. This would be easier to do if gay people were not allowed to marry. The adoption agency could refuse to let unmarried people adopt; the hospital could limit visitation to married partners or immediate relatives; the business could extend benefits only to legally wedded partners. This kind of discrimination would be much more difficult to justify, legally, if these people could be married, because then it would be discrimination purely on the basis of sexual orientation, not on legal marital status. But that is a strange argument. If discrimination purely on the basis of sexual orientation is dubious, then discrimination against unmarried couples would be equally dubious if those people are unmarried only because marriage laws discriminate against same-sex couples.

The Arizona law was probably motivated by various lawsuits happening around the country in which gay couples are suing businesses that refused to serve them because they are gay. Why should businesses be forced to serve gay customers? The reasons is that businesses—including hospitals, family services, and landlords—are operating in the public realm, even if they are privately owned or not-for-profit organizations. When an individual or an organization provides services to the public at large—what in legal terms is referred to as a *public accommodation*—the state has the legitimate authority to regulate their operations. That includes forbidding certain kinds of discrimination.[31]

It is morally wrong, and in most instances illegal, for a business to discriminate on the basis of race. For example, a restaurant cannot refuse to serve customers because they are black. It should not matter whether this discrimination is motivated by religious beliefs. Suppose a bigoted Mormon restaurateur wants to refuse to serve black diners on the basis of certain passages in the Book of Mormon.[32] The law will not—and more importantly, *should not*—allow this. Of course, the law cannot force the restaurateur to serve black customers. That is because there is another option. If he feels strongly enough about it, he can simply close his restaurant. But if he wants to continue to do business, he must respect the rights of his employees and customers. If he wants to have a private dinner party for his friends and neighbors, it would be unjust for the law to compel him to invite his black neighbors. But that is because it is a private party, not a public business.

Religious institutions, such as churches, temples, synagogues, and other places of worship, do not count as public accommodations. (They do not, or do not have to, offer their services to the public at large.) The right to freedom of religion grants religious groups the right to discriminate in providing their spiritual services. A Catholic priest can refuse to give communion to a Protestant; a rabbi can refuse to celebrate the bar mitzvah of an uncircumscribed boy; Zoroastrians can ban nonbelievers from access to their fire temples. But hospitals and adoption agencies are a different matter. These are not *spiritual* services. Also, in order to protect the public, the state cannot allow medical treatment or adoption arrangements to be conducted in private, free from regulation. The potential for abuse would be too great.

It is no defense of racial or religious discrimination to say that potential patrons of discriminatory businesses and institutions can seek services elsewhere. For one thing, businesses and institutions sometimes have a virtual monopoly in the community. The Catholic hospital might be the only one in the neighborhood. Or if there are alternative institutions offering the same services, they might also discriminate. (It is a different matter with religious institutions. A Baptist church is no substitute for a Catholic church or a mosque or a Hindu temple.)

In defense of the right to discriminate on religious grounds, GG&A appeal to the right of parents to direct the education and upbringing of their children. Certainly parents have a right to raise and educate their children in the way that they see most fit, at least within reason. But nothing about legal recognition of gay rights would prohibit them from doing that. If you own or operate a business, and your business is required to serve same-sex couples, that would not mean that your children have to approve of homosexuality. Your business can also be required to serve Muslims or Mexican immigrants. But that does not mean you have to invite them into your home or that your children have to read the Koran or learn to speak Spanish. Deeply conservative parents might be irked at having to send their children to public schools that cannot discriminate against homosexuals in hiring. But they might be equally irked at having to send their children to public schools that cannot discriminate against Jewish or Muslim teachers or students. Obviously it would be crazy to insist that public schools should refuse to hire qualified Jewish or Muslim teachers, or to exclude Jewish or Muslim students from receiving an education, just because some conservative Christian parents disapprove of those other religions and do not want their children to think that these are acceptable ways of life.

There are even bigger problems with the claim that legalizing same-sex marriage would be unfair to religious folks who disapprove of homosexuality. For one thing, this amounts to justifying a substantially burdensome deprivation of rights to homosexuals in order to prevent a comparably minor inconvenience to conservative religious people. It is outrageous to think that one group's right to discriminate should outweigh another group's right to be protected from discrimination. It is outrageous to think that one group should not be allowed to marry because it might make another group uncomfortable.

Another problem with this argument is that that banning same-sex marriage violates the religious freedom of those religions that approve of same-sex marriage. That is why the United Church of Christ (UCC) sued the state of North Carolina over its ban on same-sex marriage on the grounds that the ban violated its members' constitutional right to religious freedom.[33] The UCC rejects the claim that homosexuality is a sin or that God intended marriage to be limited to opposite-sex couples. It is part of their religious belief that gay worshipers should be allowed to participate fully in all of the sacraments of the church, including marriage and serving as ordained clergy. The ban on same-sex marriage prohibited the church from exercising its religious practice of marrying same-sex couples. (On October 10, 2014, a federal judge sided with the UCC, striking down North Carolina's ban on gay marriage.)

CONCLUSION

Homosexuality is not harmful in any of the ways that conservatives claim, and gay-tolerant public policies would not have any of the negative consequences to society alleged by opponents of gay rights. That should be enough to show that homosexuality is not morally wrong and that a just society should recognize gay rights. But also, homosexual activities and lifestyles have good consequences for those people who choose them, and gay-tolerant public policies will be beneficial to society generally. We will look at the evidence for these good consequences in the next chapter.

10

ARGUMENTS IN FAVOR OF HOMOSEXUALITY AND GAY RIGHTS

Throughout this book we have examined many bad arguments against the morality of homosexuality and against the legal recognition of gay rights. These include claims that homosexuality is forbidden by the Bible, that it involves a misuse of the sexual organs, that only opposite-sex marriages can be "true" marriages, that allowing same-sex marriage would require allowing polygamous or bestial marriages, and that tolerance of homosexuality and gay rights would be detrimental to society. These arguments all had serious flaws and none of them were at all plausible once we examined them carefully.

But what about arguments in favor of homosexuality and gay rights? We have not considered positive arguments for why homosexuality is morally permissible or arguments in favor of legal recognition of gay rights. This is partly because my overall strategy has been to defend what I referred to as the "Simple Argument," which I presented in chapter 1.

1. For an action or practice to be morally wrong, it must have some wrong-making feature.
2. Wrong-making features include the following: the action or practice i) causes harm or ii) violates some competent person's autonomy or iii) is unfair or iv) violates someone's individual rights or v) etc.
3. Homosexual relations between two consenting adults do not have any of these features. In other words, i) it is not harmful, ii) it does not violate anyone's autonomy, iii) it is not unfair, iv) it does not violate anyone's individual rights, v) etc.

4. Therefore, homosexual relations between mutually consenting adults are not morally wrong.

This argument shows why homosexuality is not morally wrong. We can then go on to justify gay rights with the further claim that if there is nothing morally wrong with homosexuality, then there is no reasonable basis on which to deny homosexual individuals and same-sex couples the same rights and privileges enjoyed by heterosexual individuals and opposite-sex couples.

The weakness of the Simple Argument is that premises 2 and 3 need defending. The conservative who disapproves of homosexuality and opposes gay rights is going to argue either that there are other wrong-making properties, such as violating God's commands or being unnatural (contrary to premise 2) or by arguing that homosexuality does have at least one of those wrong-making features I cite, such as causing harm (contrary to premise 3). Thus, most of the book has been arguing in defense of premises 2 and 3. Obviously I cannot argue against every possible moral objection to homosexuality and gay rights, but I have considered the most popular and most plausible (or least *im*plausible) ones around. With premises 2 and 3 reasonably defended, we have good reason to accept the Simple Argument. We can, however, bolster the Simple Argument by giving separate arguments supporting the morality of homosexuality and gay rights. In this chapter, I will sketch some of these arguments.

WHY MARRIAGE IS VALUABLE

A central issue in the gay rights debate today is same-sex marriage. And many of the different arguments in favor of same-sex marriage share a premise that marriage in general is a good thing. This does not mean that all marriages are good; obviously there can be bad marriages. And it does not necessarily mean that everyone ought to get married or ought to want to get married. What I mean is that, on the whole, our society is a better place with the institution of marriage. Most of the opponents of gay marriage also think that marriage is a good thing, but they think so for different reasons than supporters of same-sex marriage do. So it will be helpful for us to discuss up front *why* marriage is good and *for whom* it is good.

Some conservatives who oppose same-sex marriage think that marriage is, or can be, good because God wants us to pair off into (male-and-female) married couples. Others praise marriage (between a man and a woman) as an objective human good. They claim that forming "two-in-one flesh" unions that aim at procreation helps us to fully realize our human purpose. We have seen that these are controversial reasons at best. There is no definitive proof that God exists or, if he does exist, that he commands that we marry only people of the opposite sex. We also have reasons to doubt that the unions of the "conjugal" sort really are part of some objective human good, independently of our particular preferences, goals, or values.

I have reasons why I value marriage and why I think our society should support and maintain the institution of marriage. My reasons are less controversial and are likely to seem more intuitively plausible to a wider audience. Even many conservative opponents of gay rights value marriage for reasons similar to mine. These reasons in support of the value of marriage as an institution apply equally to the marriages of same-sex couples and to the marriages of opposite-sex couples.

One reason marriage is good is that it is generally good for children. Although raising children out of wedlock is not the crime against humanity that many conservatives make it out to be, parents and would-be parents have at least some reason to prefer marriage over merely living together or raising children alone. A happily married couple will, on average, be able to provide a more stable environment, more adult supervision, and more affection for their little ones than will a single parent or two unmarried parents. Most people who plan to have children seek to enter into marriage with a suitable partner partly in order to share the burdens (and the joys) of parenthood. This reason in favor of marriage obviously does not apply to people who are planning not to have children or to people who have strong aversion to married commitment. And I would never criticize a single parent who provides a loving home to a child. But the potential benefit of marriage, to parents and their children, is a reason we should not abolish the institution altogether. The benefits to parents and children are reasons that support same-sex marriage as well as opposite-sex marriage. Many gay couples want to have children and raise a family. Most of them would like marriage to be part of that equation. Obviously, allowing those people to marry hurts no one and benefits both the married couple and their children.

Marriage is also good for society at large. For one thing, it reduces crime, violence, and social unrest. Marriage reduces crime mostly by getting single men off the streets and into the home and by giving them responsibilities as well as something to live for.[1] Single women by and large are able to keep themselves out of trouble, and so this reason primarily supports opposite-sex marriage and same-sex marriage between men. But of course, it would be unfair to allow gay male couples to marry but not allow lesbian couples to marry. Marriage is also good for the economy. For one thing, married people work harder and are more productive in that they make more money than their single counterparts, thus contributing more to GDP.[2] Also, the children of married couples are, on average, better reared and thus will be more prepared to become productive members of society. Married people also spend more than single or divorced people of the same age.[3] Since they are more likely to buy in bulk, married couples also spend more efficiently. Marriage is thus economically good for the couple, good for the children, and good for society.

Above all, however, marriage is good for the individuals who want to be married. This is in part because they want to have a marriage, so when they get what they want, they will be happier. Of course, marriage is not always all it is cracked up to be. Some people—especially naïve, idealistic, or inexperienced people—think they want marriage but do not fully understand what they are getting into. And virtually all married couples will have their moments of disillusionment. But I am optimistic enough to think that most people who have a preference for married life will find that married life, on the whole, is better for them than remaining single. Also, there is considerable empirical evidence that married people, statistically, are better off than unmarried people by measurable standards. Marriage significantly increases one's health and longevity. Married people have higher incomes and better mental health. They even have more satisfying sexual lives than single people (despite stereotypes to the contrary). Married people are also less likely to be victims of violence, even domestic violence.[4] Many of these benefits, however, apply only to happily married couples.[5] So the benefits of marriage are not legitimate reasons to discourage divorce.

Many couples want to be married and to have their marriage recognized publicly. But what exactly is it that people want when they want marriage? For some people, marriage is a sacred bond with a religious dimension. Religious practices and ceremonies, however, are not something that the state should regulate (with the exception of protecting potential victims from ceremonies or practices that would violate their rights).

Many people in our society—whether they see marriage as a sacred bond or as a secular, civil union—want their marriage to be legally recognized by the state. What does the legal recognition of marriage add to private religious ceremonies or unofficial vows of commitment? There are several rights and privileges that come with marriage, in the United States and in most industrial countries. These include the option of filing joint tax returns, of having joint custody of children, of inheritance, of hospital visitation, and so on. Some opponents of gay rights argue that same-sex couples could make private contracts that would establish most of these rights and privileges. For example, one partner could become the legal guardian of the other, or they could give each other power of attorney. Such arrangements, however, can be inconvenient or expensive to arrange. They could also face legal challenges from relatives who disapprove of the same-sex relationship. What is missing most from such private legal arrangements, however, are the benefits bestowed by public acknowledgment of one's relationship as having the social meaning of *marriage*.

In our society there is a core conception of marriage, shared by conservatives and liberals alike, and a corresponding set of norms, which constitute the social meaning of marriage. These norms include sexual intimacy, exclusivity, domestic and economic support, cohabitation, and—perhaps most importantly—a mutual commitment to sustaining the relationship. The institution of marriage, with this core social meaning, is a central part of our culture. Most people want that kind of relationship; and there is significant benefit to having this sort of commitment publicly recognized and protected. This public status, with its cultural meaning, is not realizable under private contract. One of the benefits of having the social meaning officially sanctioned by the state is that it helps to make the relationship, with all the associated marital norms, intelligible to others. It is in the couple's interests for others to understand and acknowledge their relationship.

As Ralph Wedgwood points out, "it will often be in the couple's interest for such important aspects of their lives to be understood by others—such as their employers, health care providers, and government officials."[6] For example, I currently work at a university in southern Mississippi, but my permanent residence is in Washington, D.C., where my wife works for the federal government. Because we are legally married, my colleagues and the chair of my department understand that I need to spend the summer in Washington and that I need to travel frequently during the school year. They also expect me to look for a position at a university in the mid-Atlantic region so that I can be closer to my wife. My colleagues might be less sympathetic and less accommodating, however, if it were only my "girlfriend" who lived in Washington.

A PRACTICAL APPROACH TO MORAL THEORY

Many of the arguments against the morality of homosexuality are based on bad moral theory, such as the divine command theory or the Natural

Law theory. Conversely, the arguments in support of homosexuality and gay rights are based on very reasonable, uncontroversial moral considerations and normative principles. They have their basis in, and receive their support from, very reasonable and intuitively plausible moral theories.

Moral theory is a search for criteria to determine right and wrong actions. When philosophers concern themselves with moral theory, they try to formulate some very general principles, or a set of principles, that explain what makes right actions right and wrong actions wrong. Moral theorists typically think that one theory is *the correct* theory and argue why their favored principle is better than the alternatives. Like most moral theorists, I have my pet theory and much of my scholarly academic work involves making arguments to show why the other theories should be rejected.

When we are concerned with a concrete issue like homosexuality, however, I think an ecumenical approach, borrowing moral principles from various different theories, is more useful. For one thing, there is too much disagreement over which moral theory is *the* correct one. Moral theory has been debated by philosophers for centuries, and it is unlikely that that debate will be resolved anytime soon. Fortunately, we do not have to settle that debate once and for all in order to give good moral arguments about some particular issue. That is in part because most plausible moral theories will yield the same conclusions, over a wide range of cases, about which actions are morally right and which actions are morally wrong. For example, any plausible theory will imply that lying, stealing, breaking promises, killing, and torturing are generally morally wrong. The different theories will give different explanations for *why* these actions are wrong, and they will disagree on certain tricky cases, such as lying to spare someone's feelings or keeping a promise made to someone who has since passed away. But if several different general principles, borrowed from different plausible moral theories, are all in agreement that a certain action is morally wrong, then it probably *is* morally wrong. It would not matter which theory is *the* correct theory. Some theorists even think that pluralism is the correct theory.[7] Whether or not pluralism is objectively correct, however, it is probably the most useful approach in practice.

Another benefit of the pluralist approach is that each of the different moral principles, borrowed from different theories, has its strengths and weaknesses. By using a pluralistic method, we can choose the principle that works best and is most natural to apply to the particular sort of case at hand. We can benefit from the strength of each principle while the avoiding the weakness of each. Furthermore, if we can apply several different moral theories and arrive at the same moral judgment, then we will have made a stronger case for that moral judgment than if we supported it with only one moral principle.

When we take a pluralist approach by borrowing different moral principles from different moral theories, we run the risk of incoherence or even contradiction. One principle says "Always do X" while another says "Always do Y." Sometimes, however, X and Y will conflict, and we cannot do both. The way to avoid this is to couch these moral principles in terms of prima facie duties.[8] When we say that a person has a prima facie duty to do some action, we are saying that there is *at least some* moral reason in favor of her doing that action (in those circumstances). But there might also be, at the same time, different moral reasons *against* that person doing that same action (in those same circumstances). Moral principles can conflict. Suppose a friend makes me dinner, but the food is not very good. I eat it anyway, out of politeness. But then she asks me how I like it. I have a prima facie duty to tell the truth, but I also have a prima facie obligation not to hurt my friend's feelings. Prima facie duties thus stand in contrast to *all-things-considered* duties. For a particular action to be prima facie wrong means that it is usually wrong or that there is some significant moral presumption against it. Prima facie right and wrong are a matter of general principles. When it comes to specific actions, such as telling a specific lie on a specific occasion, the right thing to do—all things considered—is to act on the prima facie duty that is the most important in that particular situation.

MORAL ARGUMENT I—DUTY TO PROMOTE HAPPINESS (OR PREVENT SUFFERING)

The first, uncontroversial moral principle that I will use to defend the morality of homosexuality and gay rights is the *principle of utility*. "Utility" in this context means happiness or freedom from suffering. We have at least a prima facie obligation to promote happiness and to prevent or alleviate suffering. Traditionally, this principle comes from utilitarianism, the moral theory that the right action is the one that results in the most overall happiness (or the least overall suffering) for everyone affected. According to utilitarianism, it is the consequences alone that determine the rightness or wrongness of the action—it does not matter what type of action it is or what motivations led one to do it. Since I am taking a pluralist approach, I will formulate the principle of utility as a prima facie obligation—one that can be outweighed by other prima facie duties.

Utilitarians disagree about the exact nature of happiness. Classical utilitarians of the late 1800s, like John Stuart Mill and Jeremy Bentham, claimed that happiness consists of pleasure and the absence of pain. "Pleasure" and "pain" should be thought of in a very broad sense so as to include physical, emotional, and intellectual pleasures (and physical, emotional, and intellectual pains). What all pleasures have in common is that they are all experiences that one desires to have (or to continue having) for theirs own sake. (Similarly, pain is any experience one prefers not to have, for its own sake.) Modern utilitarians tend to think of happiness as the satisfaction of desires. If you desire something, and that desire is satisfied, then that contributes to your overall happiness, in proportion to the strength of the desire. (We would probably want to qualify this by including only the satisfaction of rational or informed desires.)

The difference between the desire-satisfaction conception of happiness and happiness-as-pleasure is that we can desire things other than having or not having certain experiences. For example, I desire that my friends be honest with me. Suppose that they are not honest with me, but I do not know it. If happiness is pleasure, then this does not diminish my happiness, because their deception does not affect my experiences. With the desire-satisfaction theory of happiness, however, I would be worse off, even though I would not realize that I am worse off. Fortunately, we need not decide, for our purposes, which theory of happiness is correct. There is a significant overlap in what would make a person happy according to the pleasure account and what would make a person happy according to the desire-satisfaction account. The important thing is that happiness, according to either theory, is largely a subjective matter. What is good for a person depends on what he or she happens to prefer or enjoy. One thing might be good for me but not for you because you have different preferences. Marriage, for example, might be good for me but not good for someone who strongly prefers to live a carefree lifestyle.

Now let us apply this principle of utility to the issue of homosexuality and gay rights. If two men, or two women, who are both consenting adults, engage in sexual activity that brings them both great pleasure, while causing harm to no one, then that would be a good thing. It is prima facie morally right for them to do it. This does not mean that any two people should have sex with each other whenever they have the urge. That is because doing so would often *not* be harmless. If a married person has sex with someone other than his or her spouse, that will usually bring about suffering, at least in the long run. The cheater might feel guilty afterward, or the spouse might find out and feel betrayed, or it might result in the dissolution of an otherwise happy union. Even if the betrayed spouse never discovers the infidelity, he or she would be harmed according to the desire-satisfaction account of happiness (assuming he or she strongly prefers not to have a cheating spouse). Also, even if an illicit roll in the hay does not cause pain, there may be other prima facie duties, such as the duty to keep promises, that outweigh the prima facie duty to promote happiness in this particular case. But assuming that these two men, or these two women, will experience great pleasure, while causing no harm, then that is a consideration in favor of them having sex. Thus, homosexual activity, at least in some circumstances, is morally good. Not only would it be right for two people, under these circumstances, to engage in gay or lesbian sex, it would be morally right for us to enable and even encourage them to do so—or at least not to discourage or hinder them.

The principle of utility, as a theory of right and wrong actions, is best applied on a case-by-case basis. That is because the same type of action might promote happiness in one situation but might cause suffering in a slightly different situation. This is especially the case with something as sticky as sexual relations (no pun intended). Whether sexual activity will promote harm, in the long run, will depend a lot on who, how, when, and why. Sex with the wrong person, for the wrong reasons, or at the wrong time can lead to suffering, whether guilt, humiliation, feelings of betrayal, or feelings of exploitation. Thus we cannot say that gay sex between two people is always, or even usually, morally right. But there is nothing *inherently* wrong about it, and it will, at least in some cases, be morally right.

We can, however, also apply the principle of utility to general rules instead of just to particular actions. This allows for the principle of utility to play a role in determining the morality of general practices, institutions, and public policies. We can thus ask whether a rule or a law allowing same-sex couples to marry would, overall, promote aggregate happiness. We could ask the same question for rules preventing discrimination against homosexuals, allowing gay couples to adopt, allowing openly gay people to serve in the military, and so on. Would these rules result in more overall happiness, or less overall suffering, than alternative rules?

It should be obvious that laws allowing same-sex marriage would promote happiness more than any other law (including laws banning same-sex unions or allowing only "domestic partnerships"). For one thing, same-sex marriage would allow gay couples in love to experience all of the benefits of marriage discussed above. This includes all the legal rights and privileges of marriage as well as the benefits of public recognition of their status as married couple. Some conservatives might claim that the legal recognition of their union will cause suffering to other people or to society at large. For example, it will weaken the norms and duties of marriage, which in turn will lead to unstable marriages and the accompanying social ills. But as we saw in the previous chapter, those claims are unfounded and even ridiculous. Letting same-sex couples marry will not change my relationship with my wife. I will not love her any less just because gay people are shacking up together, even if those people do not take their vows as seriously as I do. Of course, allowing gay couples to marry will cause some pain to homophobes who will resent having to recognize same-sex couples as married partners or who will feel that their sacred institution has been sullied. But it is highly unlikely that the pain of spiteful resentment in some would be enough to outweigh the fulfillment of those same-sex couples who can enjoy all the direct and indirect benefits of married life. Also, society as a whole benefits from marriage. It improves the economy, benefits children, lowers crime, and improves the health of married individuals. Thus, expanding the institution of marriage will indirectly improve overall happiness in society.

Similar arguments can be made in favor of other gay rights. Laws against discrimination prevent suffering by protecting homosexuals from harassment, from being fired, or from being refused important services. It also has many indirect benefits to society, such as helping the economy. Allowing qualified gay people to serve in the military improves national defense. Allowing gay people to adopt helps to provide a loving, nurturing environment to orphaned children.

It is hard to deny that the consequences do not matter at all morally, or that we should not try to promote happiness and prevent pain, at least within the constraints of other prima facie duties. But there are problems with the utilitarian approach. One is that it seems counterintuitive to me that the resentment of bigots should count *at all* toward whether it is morally right to grant gay rights. Suppose we lived in a society where the majority of the population were Westboro Baptists. The consternation that legal recognition of gay rights would cause to these anti-gay fanatics might outweigh the benefits to gay people. In that situation, the principle of utility would imply that it would be right, at least prima facie, to deny gay people their rights in order to mollify these hateful bigots. That is highly counterintuitive. Fortunately this problem is alleviated by the importance of other prima facie principles.

MORAL ARGUMENT II—DUTY TO RESPECT AUTONOMY

Another prima facie duty that supports gay rights is respect for autonomy. This idea is drawn from the moral theory of the late-eighteenth-century philosopher Immanuel Kant. "Autonomy," which literally means "self-governing," is the capacity to make important choices about one's own life. Kant held that it is always wrong to act in a way that ignores, undermines, or interferes with another person's autonomy. His primary moral principle is that we should never use another moral agent merely as a means to our own ends. This does not mean that we cannot solicit cooperation from others to help us achieve our goals. It only means that their cooperation must be freely given.

Paradigm violations of respect for autonomy would include deception, coercion, or manipulation. This way of describing respect for autonomy makes it out to be a *negative* normative principle, one that tells us only what *not* to do. We can satisfy a negative duty by simply doing nothing. But there is also a positive side to the duty to respect autonomy. We should try to promote autonomy in ourselves and in others. This might include educating and informing people so that they can make better decisions, providing them with opportunities that expand their range of options, helping them to gain control over their lives by liberating them from domination or oppression, and helping them to obtain a measure of independence so that they are less reliant on others.

The principle of respect for persons is especially important in healthcare ethics. It grounds the widely recognized duty of informed consent and the right to refuse treatment. In the past it was commonplace for doctors to withhold information from their patients for fear that bad news might cause them undue anxiety (so-called "therapeutic privilege"). Doctors would routinely make many of the treatment decisions for the patient. These days, doctors are expected to provide patients with full information about their condition, a list of all treatments options, and the potential risks and benefits of each option. The patient is then allowed to make his or her own decision, without undue pressure from the physician. This duty is, of course, limited to the capacity of the patient. Young children, mentally disabled patients, or patients with dementia might not be capable of making such decisions. As long as the patient is of sound mind, however, the doctor cannot choose for the patient. This is, in part, because the doctor might not share the same beliefs and values as the patient. For example, some patients prefer pain relief over lucidity, but other are willing to endure pain in order to retain full use of their cognitive faculties. Doctors also have the positive duty to promote autonomy in their patients. One of the goals of medicine is to restore capacities whenever possible, and this includes the capacity to make important decisions. When a patient is unable to make a decision—due to denial or anxiety, for example—the doctor should try to help restore autonomy, by prescribing anti-anxiety medication or psychotherapy.

This respect for autonomy goes beyond merely rejecting paternalism (discussed in chapter 8) or the liberty principle (discussed below). For one thing, the respect for persons includes not only the negative duty of leaving people alone to make their own decisions but also the positive duty to help them acquire the ability to make decisions and the power to control their own destiny. Also, the rejection of paternalism and the liberty principle are based largely on the claim that people usually know what is in their own best interests better than others do. Thus, letting people make their own decisions about their lives will tend to promote their happiness. But the duty to respect autonomy is not derived from some other principle, such as the duty to promote happiness. The value of autonomy is based on the dignity of persons as moral agents and the inherent right to be self-determining. Thus, we should allow, enable, and encourage people to determine their own values and make their own decisions, based on their self-chosen life plan, even if we know they will make bad decisions (and even if their decisions will be bad by their own assessment). If we were to take the principle as absolute, then the only justification for interfering in the decisions of rational competent persons would be to prevent them from destroying or severely compromising their capacity for autonomy or to prevent them from violating the autonomy of others. However, I am employing this principle as a merely prima facie duty, one that could be outweighed by the duty to prevent harm. But it would have to be substantial and relatively irreversible harm for it to override the right to autonomy.

This principle of respect for autonomy applies in a rather straightforward way to homosexuality and gay rights. It would be wrong for some people (for example, religious conservatives) to try to coerce or manipulate other people (openly gay people) into living a certain lifestyle based on their (the conservatives') values. We may not agree with the values of other people in our society, and we might even have good reason to think that their decisions conflict with their own values or life plans. But we still owe them the respect to let them choose for themselves. We also have a duty to protect people from coercion. Thus, we have a duty to enact and enforce strict antidiscrimination laws in order to protect people from coercion by their employers, landlords, or others who might abuse their power. Finally, we also have a duty to provide them with opportunities to live their lives in the way they see fit, even if we disapprove of those lifestyle choices. In the case of homosexuals, this would support the legal recognition of same-sex marriage, allowing openly gay people to serve in the military, and so on. The principle of autonomy would support these rights even if they would diminish the overall happiness in society—as long as legally recognizing these rights would not involve violating the autonomy of others.

OUTING

Respect for autonomy also has implications for other moral issues involving homosexuality, such as the practice of outing. Some gay rights activists support the practice of publicly revealing the same-sex preferences of those who are trying to hide their homosexuality. They insist that people who remain in the closet are undermining the cause of gay rights by helping to keep homosexuality hidden from the public. The "closet" is a conventional practice, a kind of etiquette, with rules requiring respect for another's privacy on matters of sexual orientation. Gay people, so the pro-outing argument goes, need not play along with the rules calling for cooperation with closeted homosexuals in their efforts to keep their homosexuality secret. That is because the closet-convention is ultimately degrading to homosexuals, and playing along with the practice implicitly supports the idea that homosexuality is shameful. As one proponent of outing claims, "living by the convention of the closet—whether one is closeted oneself or not—is a commitment to viewing gayness as disgusting, horrible, unspeakably gross, in short, as abjection."[9]

According to the Kantian principle of respect for persons, outing is morally wrong because it violates the outed individual's right to control important decisions regarding his or her own life. Coming out as openly gay is, for most people in our society today, a big decision, often with serious consequences. Individuals should be allowed to make this decision for themselves. They should also be allowed, to whatever extent it is possible, to control how, when, and to whom such personal information should be disclosed. By outing people as gay, we are essentially taking this decision out of their hands, choosing for them whether they should live openly, and making that choice according to *our* goals and values. We might have legitimate objections to someone's motivations for staying in the closet, but it would be an affront to that person's dignity to disregard his reasons for living his life according to his own values. It does not matter that we are outing people in order to promote the worthy cause of tolerance and gay rights. Doing so would involve using these people merely as a means for promoting our own political agenda. Respect for person requires that we should instead try to persuade closeted homosexuals to help the cause by coming out on their own.

MORAL ARGUMENT III—THE VIRTUE APPROACH

The oldest form of moral theory in Western philosophy is *virtue ethics*, which dates back to the ancient Greek philosophers Plato and Aristotle. While other moral theories are action based, virtue ethics is character based. The primary question for virtue ethics is not "What should I *do*?" but rather "What kind of person should I *be*?" This does not mean that virtue ethics is any less concerned with right and wrong actions. But for the virtue approach, right and wrong are derivative concepts. The right action is the kind of action that a morally good person would do; the wrong action is the kind of action that a morally good person would avoid doing. Also, instead of simply labeling actions as *right* or *wrong*, virtue ethicists tend to describe actions with character terms. Actions— like people—can be described as honest or dishonest, brave or cowardly, generous or greedy.

Virtue ethics is primarily concerned with character and character traits. A large part of a person's character, of course, is a matter of how she behaves. But it is not individual actions that determine what kind of person you are. If I tell the truth on one occasion, that does not make me an honest man; and if, just once in my life, I share with those less fortunate, I am not thereby a generous person. Character involves a pattern of behavior over a long period of time. The honest person tells the truth all the time (or almost all the time), not just occasionally; the generous person shares with others regularly, not just once. Furthermore, it is not just what you do that determines your character; just as important is why you do it. Character is as much a matter of motivation as it is action. If I give to charity so that others will admire my generosity, then my gift is an act of vanity, not generosity. Character is constituted by a person's behavior and also by his or her values and priorities.

Traditionally, virtue theories assume an *objective list* theory of human well-being. There are certain character traits, activities, and experiences that make a life well lived, even if we do not want those things and they do not give us pleasure. These objective goods are things that we *should* want and *should* enjoy; and we would want them and would enjoy them, if we were virtuous. The human good is determined by a universal human nature, not by our individual subjective preferences or pleasures. These goods help us achieve our human telos and constitute "flourishing." (This idea of an objective human good is something that virtue ethics has in common with Natural Law theory.)

Different versions of virtue ethics (and Natural Law theory) give differing lists of these objective human goods. The New Natural Law theorists, for example, include "conjugal marriage" among the human goods, while claiming that any nonmarital sex is objectively bad. This is something that the ancient Greeks, who were a lot less prudish about sexual matters, would have found bizarre.[10]

The most complete and systematic account of the good life is found in the writings of Aristotle. For him, the good life consists in pleasure, friendship, philosophical contemplation (of course!), and various moral virtues, especially wisdom, courage, moderation, prudence, and justice. On a more formal level, Aristotle held that virtue consists of a disposition to act or feel the right amount for the circumstances. For any kind of action or feeling, there was the right amount, the virtue, between two extremes, which were vices. Consider the activity of working. One who works too little is lazy, one who works too much is a workaholic. The right amount is somewhere in between, though probably closer to the workaholic end of the continuum. The same thing is true for feelings, such as anger. One who gets angry too easily is an ill-tempered hothead, whereas someone who never gets angry is apathetic.

It is not just the right amount of acting or feeling that constitutes virtue for Aristotle, it also depends on the situation. There is a time and place for work and a time and place for relaxing. There are situations in which anger is appropriate, such as in response to injustice. Other times anger is inappropriate or out of proportion, such as when people succumb to road rage. Thus, Aristotle would probably agree with the conservatives that promiscuity is a vice, but, in sharp contrast to the conservatives, so is the opposite vice of prudishness, asceticism, or "conjugal" sex for procreation only. Some conservative opponents appeal to Aristotle's philosophy in opposition to same-sex marriage.[11] I think they are mistaken to claim that Aristotle, an ancient Greek pagan, would support their very medieval Catholic notion of "conjugal" marriage. Most experts on Aristotle's philosophy agree with me on that.[12] But even if Aristotle were to denounce homosexuality, so much the worse for Aristotle. His views on particular moral issues are hardly authoritative. After all, he believed that slaves and barbarians were inherently inferior to free Greeks and that women were inherently inferior to men.

Applying virtue ethics to the issue of homosexuality and gay rights is a lot trickier than applying the principle of utility or respect for persons. One problem with the virtue approach is that there is too much disagreement as to exactly which character traits are virtues and which are vices.[13] For example, devout Christians think that faith is a virtue, while many less religious folks think that belief without evidence is a vice.

The conservative Natural Law theorists claim that "conjugal marriage" is part of the good life and that engaging in sex for pleasure, or even love, is a vice. Their claims are controversial at best. Less controversial are their claims that marriage and family life are part of the good life. Of course, they have a very narrow, prudish notion of what "marriage" means. But if we interpret "marriage" in a more modern, commonsense way—not as a "two-in-one flesh" aimed at "biological unity," but as two people united by love vowing to care for one another and love each other exclusively—then the claim might be plausible. With this interpretation, the value of marriage supports recognition of same-sex marriage. Allowing same-sex couples to marry will enable them to achieve the goods associated with marriage and the virtues that can be cultivated and expressed in a marital relationship, such as responsibility, faithfulness, selflessness, and patience.

More importantly, virtue ethics is primarily a self-oriented moral approach. Although we can and should encourage virtue in others and help them cultivate morally sound character traits, we should above all cultivate moral virtue in ourselves. As Jesus said, "First cast out the beam out of thine own eye; and then shalt thou see clearly to cast out the mote out of thy brother's eye" (Matthew 7:5). Of course, parents have a special obligation to raise their children to be morally decent members of society, but that is part of being a good parent. I would be a nosy meddler if I were overly concerned in shaping the virtue of my neighbors or casual acquaintances.

For that reason, conservative heterosexuals should be less concerned about the moral character of gay people and more concerned about how their stance against gay rights reflects on their own character. Some of those who oppose gay rights are motivated by genuine concern but are simply ignorant about the facts. For example, they are concerned about the welfare of children in our society and falsely believe that homosexuals are a threat to children. Even in that case, however, their opposition to gay rights is based on a culpable, pigheaded ignorance. More often conservative opposition to gay rights is motivated by vices such as priggishness, arrogance, and intolerance. A case for gay rights can be made on the basis that many obvious virtues would support respect for homosexuals, their lifestyle choices, and their relationships. These would include the virtues of compassion, tolerance, respect, and humility. In other words, virtuous people would not be so quick to judge others and their lifestyles. They would not be so determined to deny basic rights to harmless people just because they have a different sexual orientation. And, perhaps above all, virtuous people would mind their own damn business.

POLITICAL ARGUMENT I—LIBERTY, THE HARM PRINCIPLE, AND DOMINATION

Several very plausible normative principles and approaches to moral theory—the principle of utility, respect for autonomy, and the virtue ethics approach—imply that homosexuality is morally permissible and lend support to the legal recognition of gay rights. Likewise, there are several attractive political ideals and plausible principles of political theory that also lend support to legal rights for homosexuals, including legal recognition of same-sex marriage, the right to adopt, and protection from discrimination.

Many of these political arguments have their basis in the political theory known as *liberalism*. "Liberalism" as a political theory, however, must not be confused with liberal ideology. Even most conservatives in our society today accept some form of liberalism. Liberalism has its critics, too. Some of these critics can be dismissed as extremists with wildly implausible or highly unattractive political ideals. This would include fascists, Taliban-style perfectionists, and libertarians. Other critics—such as feminists, multi-culturists, Marxists, civic republicans, and communitarians—present more reasonable alternatives to liberalism. These political theories, however, might be compatible with important elements of liberalism. Some of these alternative theories might even add their own independent principles in support of gay rights. Nevertheless, since liberalism is the dominant political theory in modern, industrialized, democracies, the political principles I will draw on come from the liberal tradition.

Liberalism is a political theory based on individual liberties and individual rights—especially the rights to free speech, freedom of religion, and property. According to liberals, a society is first and foremost a collection of individuals. The purpose of the state is primarily to serve the good of the individuals that constitute society. And those interests consist of happiness and autonomy. There may be some social goods over and above the good of the individuals, such as solidarity, tolerance, civic involvement, and harmony. But these are only *instrumental* goods; they are good only because, and only insofar as, they tend to promote individual well-being and autonomy.

Since different people have different values and goals, different things are good for different people. For that reason, liberalism is committed to some form of "state neutrality." The state should not promote any values that are not universally accepted or give preference to any particular way of life over others. Public policies are not to be justified by appeal to controversial beliefs or value systems. For example, since many people in our society do not accept the Bible as the word of God, the state should not base legislation on the Scriptures or select policies aimed to give preference to the Judeo-Christian lifestyle over other lifestyles. This is why Thomas Jefferson—who was a philosophy major in college and was deeply influenced by proto-liberal political philosopher John Locke—advocated a strict separation of church and state.

Many versions of liberalism support what has come to be known as the *Principle of Liberty*, also known as the "no-harm principle." This principle was defended at length by John Stewart Mill, which he formulated thus: "The only purpose for which power can be rightfully exercised over any member of a civilized community, against his will, is to prevent harm to others. His own good, either physical or moral, is not a sufficient warrant."[14] According to this principle, people should be free to do whatever they please as long as they are not causing harm to others (or at least not harm that those others could easily avoid). Mill used this principle to defend freedom of conscience, freedom of speech, freedom of religion, and freedom of association. Mill also used this principle to reject any form of paternalism, at least for competent adults, and to defend what we might today call "alternative lifestyles." Mill's principle may go too far in forbidding all forms of paternalism. We might want to prefer a weaker version of the principle of liberty that allows some paternalism, even for competent adults, but only if the activities to be regulated are likely to pose substantial and irreversible harm. Also, according to liberalism, what counts as a harm to an individual must be determined according to the standards of that individual. For example, if my neighbor thinks that my hobby of making graven images poses the threat of eternal damnation to my immortal soul, that would not be legitimate reason to prohibit me from pursuing this hobby. It is none of his business, especially if I could not be convinced that there is any such threat. To curtail my graven-imaging hobby would be to allow him to impose his religious views on me, violating my freedom of conscience.

Mill was especially concerned with what political theorists refer to as the *tyranny of the majority*. This form of injustice occurs in democratically governed societies when the majority imposes unjust restrictions of freedom on a hated minority or unfairly promotes the interests of the majority at the expense of the interests of the minority. For this reason, democracy needs to be supplemented with constraints that protect the rights of individuals. That is why the framers of the U.S. Constitution felt the need to add the Bill of Rights.

The principle of liberty would clearly support the right of homosexuals to live as they see fit, without interference from the state and without harassment from meddling homophobes or religious puritans. But as a purely negative principle, it might not be of much use in supporting the legal recognition of gay rights or same-sex marriage. The principle of liberty, however, could be interpreted not merely as a negative duty not to interfere with others but also as a positive duty to protect the liberty of others, especially those who are vulnerable or belong to persecuted minorities. Threats to liberty come not just from state coercion but also from domination by other people or by nongovernmental institutions, including businesses, banks, landlords, and religious organizations. If, for example, your boss could fire you on the basis of your religion, then he could use the threat of termination to coerce you into attending his church against your will. In this interpretation, the principle of liberty would support antidiscrimination laws and other gay rights.

The notion of state neutrality goes even further in supporting legal rights, liberties, and privileges for homosexuals, especially same-sex marriage. Justification of laws, especially laws allowing different people to be treated differently in certain ways, must be justified without appeal to controversial beliefs or values. Support for bans on same-sex marriage—unlike bans on polygamous, incestuous, or bestial marriage—requires appeals to controversial beliefs such as religious scripture or even more mysterious ideas like "the real essence of marriage" or "two-in-one flesh" union. Instead, we must justify laws in terms of what liberals refer to as "public reason"—considerations that all reasonable members of our pluralist society could accept. Marriage has multiple meanings in our society, but there is significant overlap in terms of certain core features and basic norms. Justification of marriage law can only appeal to this shared meaning, what John Rawls would refer to as the "overlapping consensus."[15] Given that most people, even most opponents of gay rights, are comfortable with the expression "same-sex marriage," it is not a part of this meaning that the two who are united must be of the opposite sex. Nothing in this core meaning could justify excluding committed same-sex couples.

POLITICAL ARGUMENT II—THE RIGHT TO MARRY

When we move from talking about liberty as merely noninterference by the state to talking about protection from domination, coercion, and exploitation, we are led to the notion of moral or legal rights. While the liberty principle posits a general right to be left alone, free from coercion or domination, the rights-based approach appeals to specific liberties and protections, such as the right to due process or the right to privacy. Also, unlike the principle of liberty, there are rights that entitle us to certain goods or services, such as the right to an education or the constitutionally guaranteed right to legal counsel. In terms of gay rights issues, some people have argued that mutually consenting adults have a right to marry each other and to have their marriage recognized by the state.

The U.S. Supreme Court has acknowledged that there is a legal right to marry in this country. For example, in 1967, Earl Warren wrote, in the unanimous opinion that overturned anti-miscegenation laws, "The freedom to marry has long been recognized as one of the vital personal rights essential to the orderly pursuit of happiness by free [persons]."[16] Some conservatives claim that this applies only to opposite-sex couples because "marriage" can only mean a union between a man and a woman. But obviously "marriage" need not be defined that way. To claim otherwise would be to posit a mysterious, objectively real *essence* of marriage.

Some conservatives who oppose gay marriage claim that the right to marry is absurd. For example, certain NNL theorists write that "there is no general right to marry the person you love, if this means a right to have any type of relationship that you desire recognized as marriage."[17] Of course, they are right. There is no right to marry *if you put it that way*; but no reasonable person would put it that way. For one thing, marriage requires mutual consent. A fan of the *Hunger Games* movies, for example, would not have a *right* to marry Jennifer Lawrence, no matter how much he might be in love with her. Also, the right to marry does not mean the right to have *any type of relationship* that you desire. For one thing, you do not have the right to enter into relationships that violate the rights of others, such as master/slave relationships. Secondly, although the concept of "marriage" can be revised and redefined, and marriage means different things to different people in our society, it still has a definite core social meaning. Which people have the right to marriage *is defined by that shared, core meaning*.

Some philosophers, such as Martha Nussbaum, have provided arguments to support the courts' claim that this there is a moral right to marry.[18] Marriage, she points out, is ubiquitous and central to social life in our culture. Denial of marriage thus entails exclusion from an important and defining ritual of social life. She identifies three aspects of marriage. First, there is the religious aspect, the regulation of which should be left to the church, not the state. Next, there is the cluster of civil rights, liberties, and entitlements associated with legal marriage, such as those involving taxes, inheritance, insurance, custody, and hospital visitation. These rights, however, could be granted through some lesser institution, such as "domestic partnership." Most important, according to Nussbaum, is the "expressive" aspect. Marriage is a public rite of passage in our society, one that bestows privileged civic status. In order to obtain this status, it is not necessary that we prove our virtue. Rapists and murderers can get married. We also do not need to prove that we are ready for it. The state does not require taking a test to prove we are responsible enough to meet our marital duties or committed enough to maintain the relationship. Withholding this status expresses disapproval of the couple and their relationship. This is why civil unions and other "compromise" proposals are unjust. Relegating same-sex relations to lesser institutions, even if they differ in name only, is stigmatizing. Since there is a right to marry, this right must be one that all couples have equally. This brings us to the third political principle that supports gay rights, the principle of equality.

POLITICAL ARGUMENT III—THE EQUALITY ARGUMENT AND ANTIDISCRIMINATION

Justice, according to any political theory or ideology (except fascism), requires *equality*. People of different political persuasions do not disagree on *whether* the state should recognize equality. They disagree on what *sense* of equality the state should promote.[19] Those further on the left think that the state should promote economic equality by means of redistribution of wealth. Those who are more moderate think that the state should only promote equal opportunities, not equality of outcome. Those on the right might deny even that. But even those on the far right (with the exception of fascists) believe that the state should promote some minimal form of equality in that the laws should apply equally to everyone. Every citizen should have the same rights and liberties, and they should have them simply by virtue of being citizens. If some people have the right to vote, then everyone must have the right to vote (and each person must get the same number of votes). Those who think otherwise are not concerned with justice in any familiar sense of the word.

Justice requires at least the minimum of equal rights and equal protection under the law. If the state protects the liberties or promotes the interests of one group, then it must do the same for everyone equally unless there is some important difference that warrants differential treatment. Why the qualification about important differences? Well, for one thing, we should treat convicted criminals differently from law-abiding citizens. Even then, this unequal treatment is justified on the basis of laws that apply to everyone equally. If armed robbery is a crime, then everyone who commits armed robbery should be punished—and punished to the same extent—regardless of race, gender, religion, or sexual orientation. It would be unjust, for example, to make it a crime for black people to smoke marijuana but not white people or to punish black people differently from white people or even simply to enforce the law unequally.

It is not enough that the laws apply equally to all citizens. It is also necessary that the content of those laws does not have the effect of treating different citizens differently. For example, in the United States, possession of crack cocaine was traditionally punished much more harshly than possession of cocaine in its powdered form. Crack cocaine is used mostly by poor black people while powdered cocaine is more often used by affluent whites. Establishing different punishments for each drug, even though they are essentially the same substance, has the consequences of treating white and black drug users differently. This is true even if laws and penalties regarding the two drugs are *applied* equally without regard to race. Because of this de facto unequal treatment, the federal government passed the Fair Sentencing Act in 2010, aimed at ending this form of inequality.

The equal protection doctrine implies that same-sex couples should have equal access to the civil status that marriage confers, with the same benefits and burdens. The rationale for legal recognition of marriage is that the institution supports the interests of married couples. Same-sex couples, at least those who wish to be legally married, have the same interests, and same-sex marriage would support those interests in the same way that marriage supports the interests of opposite-sex couples. Thus the state is obligated to treat same-sex couples the same way it treats opposite-sex couples.[20] The differences between same-sex couples and opposite-sex couples are irrelevant to the justification for state recognition of marriage. The equal protection principle also supports antidiscrimination laws protecting homosexuals.

A specific application of the equality principle is the constraint, generally recognized in U.S. legal system, that no law can make reference to, or distinctions on the basis of, "suspect classification." The legal criteria for suspect classification is that 1) the class of individuals has historically been the target of purposeful discrimination, 2) discrimination violates an established constitutionally protected right, and 3) there must be a set of features to identify membership in that class (i.e., membership cannot be easily changed or faked).[21] Racial minorities, especially African Americans, are a clear example of a suspect class. There is a long history in this country of discrimination against African Americans; this discrimination has been aimed at depriving them of their constitutional rights, and one cannot easily change or lie about one's race. Gender also counts as a suspect classification. This, however, requires some qualification, since there are some differences between men and women that might legitimize some distinction in the law. For example, since women can bear children and men cannot, it would not be unjust for laws to grant pregnant women certain protections or entitlements not available to men.

Sexual orientation seems to fit the criteria of suspect class. There has been a long history of discrimination against homosexuals; this discrimination has been aimed at depriving them of constitutional rights, such as the right to privacy and the right to marry; and, as we saw in chapter 4, sexual orientation is something that most people do not choose and cannot change.

U.S. courts have traditionally failed to acknowledge sexual orientation as a suspect class. Whether this refusal is legitimate does not matter because we can argue for recognition of gay rights on the basis of already acknowledged suspect classes, namely race and gender. First, consider a law that would require black voters, but not white voters, to pass an exam before registering to vote. Such a law would be unjust because it makes a distinction on the basis of suspect class. That is because if a particular citizen is black, then he or she must pass the test, but if that same citizen were white, he or she could register without passing the test.

Now compare this with laws that ban multiracial couples from marrying (which were struck down as unconstitutional in the Supreme Court case *Loving v. Virginia* in 1967). Defenders of the law argued that it applied to white and black people equally, since it banned members of each group from marrying someone from the other group. But this defense is obviously flawed. In the case of *Loving v. Virginia*, Mildred Jeter was not allowed to marry her white fiancé, Richard Loving, because she was black. Had she been white, she would have been allowed to marry him. That is clearly discrimination on the basis of race. The same argument applies to same-sex marriage and discrimination on the basis of gender. For example, Steve is not allowed to marry his boyfriend, Adam, because Steve is a man. If Steve had been a woman, he would have been allowed to marry Adam. So laws against same-sex marriage can be seen as a kind of gender discrimination.[22]

CONCLUSION

There are many arguments conservatives present for why they think homosexuality is morally wrong and why the state should not recognize gay rights. Careful examination of these arguments has shown that none of them are any good. The anti-gay conservatives would not have any stronger of a case if they tried to combine these various arguments. A bad argument is like a leaky bucket; it does not hold water. Combining several leaky buckets is no solution—doing so does not stop the leaking.

On the other side of the debate, we have several decent arguments showing that homosexuality is morally okay and that a modern democratic society like ours should recognize gay rights. These include the principle of utility, respect for persons, the principle of liberty, the principle of equality, and so on. Perhaps none of these arguments, considered in isolation, will be decisive. But just as a post lends support to a lintel, a decent argument lends support to the conclusion. One post might not, by itself, be enough to support the structure, but a series of posts will. Similarly, these good arguments combine to make a convincing case for the defense of homosexuality and the legal recognition of gay rights.

Moral judgments and public policies should be based on good reasons, solid evidence, and sound arguments—not on irrational fears, subjective emotions, wishful thinking, habit, superstition, or post hoc rationalizations. Given the appalling weakness of the arguments on the conservative anti-gay side, and the combined strength of the arguments on the gay-tolerant side, the only reasonable stance is to approve of homosexuality and support equal rights for gay people, including the legal recognition of same-sex marriage.

NOTES

I. INTRODUCTION

1. In early November of 2013, the U.S. Senate passed the Employment Non-Discrimination Act, a federal law that would prohibit discrimination on the basis of sexual orientation or gender identity. As of this writing, the bill is still awaiting a vote in the Republican-controlled House of Representatives.

2. Some would argue that entertainment has been a major factor in changing attitudes about homosexuality. See for example Andrew O'Hehir, "Did TV Change America's Mind on Gay Marriage?" Salon.com, 30 March 2013.

3. Ben Goessling, "86 Percent OK with Gay Teammate," ESPN.com, 17 February 2014.

4. "Support for Gay Marriage Growing, but U.S. Remains Divided," *New York Times*, 12 December 2012.

5. "Poll: 51% Support Gay Marriage," CBS News, 30 November 2012.

6. Richard Powell, "Social Desirability Bias in Polling on Same-Sex Marriage Ballot Measures," *American Politics Research* (2013), doi: 10.1177/1532673X13484791.

7. "Growing Support for Gay Marriage: Changed Minds and Changing Demographics," *Pew Research Center*, 20 March 2013.

8. See for example, "The Truth about Voter Fraud," a study done by the Brennan Center for Justice, New York University (2009), http://www.brennancenter.org/sites/default/files/legacy/The%20Truth%20About%20Voter%20Fraud.pdf.

9. This argument is borrowed from Scott Aikin and Robert Talisse, *Why We Argue (And How We Should): A Guide to Political Disagreement* (Routledge, 2013).

10. Jonathan Haidt, "The Emotional Dog and Its Rational Tail: A Social Intuitionist Approach to Moral Judgment," *Psychological Review* 108 (2001).

See also Haidt's *The Righteous Mind: Why Good People Are Divided by Politics and Religion* (Random House, 2004), 45–47.

11. This story is fictional, but it is based on various true stories of unwitting sibling incest. In his experiments Haidt used a more controversial (and fictional) story involving intentional incest.

2. WHAT IS MORALITY?

1. See my *Fetal Position: A Rational Approach to the Abortion Issue* (Prometheus Books, 2010).

2. There are many contemporary philosophers who defend more sophisticated versions of this kind of theory. These improved versions are usually referred to as "expressivism," to distinguish them from the crude emotivist theory. It would take us far off topic to examine this issue in more detail. For a complete introduction to emotivist and expressivist theories, see Mark Schroeder's *Non-Cognitivism in Ethics* (Routledge, 2010).

3. Laurie Goodstein, "Pope Says Church Is 'Obsessed' With Gays, Abortion and Birth Control," *New York Times*, 19 September 2013.

4. I was relieved to find that this was only how the *New York Times* described his comments and not how the Pope himself used the term "moral." For the complete interview, see Antonio Spadaro S.J., "A Big Heart Open to God," *America: The National Catholic Review*, 30 September 2013, available online at http://www.americamagazine.org/pope-interview.

5. H. L. Mencken, *A Mencken Chrestomathy* (Alfred A. Knopf, 1949).

6. For statistics on gambling in the United States, see the PBS *Frontline* website http://www.pbs.org/wgbh/pages/frontline/shows/gamble/etc/facts.html.

7. Specifically, this would be what philosophers call the fallacy of appeal to popularity (or *argumentum ad populum*). Just because most people believe something is no reason to think it is true. The majority are often mistaken.

8. "The War of the Simpsons," Season 2, Episode 2, originally aired on 2 May 1991.

9. Ruth Benedict, "Anthropology and the Abnormal," *The Journal of General Anthropology* 10 (1934).

10. I am arguing against *normative* relativism: the view that the right action is whatever is approved of by one's society. If you accept normative relativism, then you endorse the principle that people should follow whatever moral code prevails in their society. There are more sophisticated versions of relativism that make metaethical claims, not normative claims. On that sort of view, we simply cannot judge the actions of people whose moral views are radically different from ours. For an account of this sort of view, see Gilbert Harman, *The Nature of Morality* (Oxford University Press, 1977).

11. This proposed test is similar to G. E. Moore's "open question argument" (*Principia Ethica*, Cambridge University Press, 1903). The difference is that Moore hoped to show that moral concepts were not definable and that moral properties could not be identical with any non-moral properties. My use of this

device is much more modest. If it makes sense to doubt whether M is D, then that does not show that M cannot be identical with D. It only indicates that M and D are not synonymous.

12. This would not imply that if an action harms someone, then it is automatically wrong. What I mean by saying that moral norms involve harm is that they involve situations when we should not harm people and when it is okay to harm people (as for example, in punishing wrongdoers or in self-defense).

13. I borrow this expression from Richard Joyce, who gives a similar conceptual analysis of moral terms in *The Evolution of Morality* (MIT Press, 2007).

3. MORAL THEORY AND DIVINE COMMAND

1. For a good introductory survey of moral theory, I recommend Julia Driver, *Ethics: The Fundamentals* (Wiley-Blackwell, 2006).

2. To be more precise, we should say that the argument fails *if it is false that* God disapproves of homosexuality. This is because it could be false in one of two ways. It would be false if there is a God and he does not disapprove of homosexuality; it would also be false if there is no God at all.

3. For example, Dostoyevsky's character Ivan Karamazov famously argues that if God does not exist, then everything is permitted. Fyodor Dostoyevsky, *The Brothers Karamazov* (1880).

4. Abortion is nowhere mentioned in the Bible, not even implicitly. The only place where killing a fetus in the womb is mentioned is Exodus 21:22–23, where it is considered a relatively minor offense.

5. For a lengthy discussion see Daniel Helminiak's *What the Bible Really Says about Homosexuality* (Alamo Square Press, 2000). Most of the alternative interpretations of biblical passages on homosexuality I review can be found in Professor Helminiak's work.

6. See Helminiak, *What the Bible Really Says*, for more on the meaning of these terms .

7. Again, however, it is important to remember that we are assuming many things for the sake of argument—that God exists, that the Bible is true, etc.

8. There is no universal agreement on the exact numbering of the commandmentss. I went with the traditional Catholic numbering, but it does not really matter, for our purposes, how the commandments are individuated.

4. DESTINY OR CHOICE? BIOLOGY, SEXUAL ORIENTATION, AND RESPONSIBILITY

1. Lindsy Van Gelder, "The 'Born That Way' Trap," *Ms.*, May/June 1991.

2. Donald P. Haider-Markel and Mark R. Joslyn, "Beliefs about the Origins of Homosexuality and Support for Gay Rights: An Empirical Test of Attribution Theory," *Public Opinion Quarterly* 72 (2008).

3. For example, see Michel Foucault, *The History of Sexuality*. 1: *An Introduction* (Vintage Books, 1978).

4. As we will see below, this might not be so true of all women. But it certainly seems to be true for most men.

5. For example, Ritch Savin-Williams, ". . . And then I Became Gay": *Young Men's Stories* (Routledge, 1998).

6. Again, this is true particularly for men. It might be a different story for some women. See below.

7. Robert L. Spitzer, "Can Some Gay Men and Lesbians Change Their Sexual Orientation? 200 Participants Reporting a Change from Homosexual to Heterosexual Orientation," *Archives of Sexual Behavior* 32 (2003).

8. At about the same time as the Spitzer report came out, two psychologists published an article on the failure of conversion therapy. But this study was also seriously flawed. Their recruitment of test subjects targeted those who felt victimized by conversion therapists. Thus it was not a representative sample. Michael Schroeder and Ariel Shidlo, "Ethical Issues in Sexual Orientation Conversion Therapies: An Empirical Study of Consumers," in *Sexual Conversion Therapy: Ethical, Clinical, and Research Perspective*, ed. Jack Drescher et al. (CRC Press, 2002).

9. Erik Eckholm, "Gay 'Conversion Therapy' Faces Test in Courts," *New York Times*, 27 November 2012.

10. Paul Elias, "California Gay Conversion Therapy Ban Upheld by Federal Court," *Huffington Post*, 29 August 2013.

11. Ed Payne, "Group Apologizes to Gay Community, Shuts Down 'Cure' Ministry," CNN.com, 8 July 2013.

12. J. Michael Bailey, Michael P. Dunne, and Nicholas G. Martin, "Genetic and Environmental Influences on Sexual Orientation and Its Correlates in an Australian Twin Sample," *Journal of Personality and Social Psychology* 78 (2000).

13. J. Michael Bailey and Richard Pillard, "A Genetic Study of Male Sexual Orientation," *Archives of General Psychiatry* 48 (1991).

14. Dean Hamer, Stella Hu, Victoria Magnuson, Nan Hu, and Angela Pattatucci, "A Linkage Between Markers on the X Chromosome and Male Sexual Orientation," *Science* 261 (1993).

15. Andrea Camperio-Ciani, Francesca Corna, and Claudio Capiluppi, "Evidence for Maternally Inherited Factors Favouring Male Homosexuality and Promoting Female Fecundity." *Proceedings of the Royal Society B: Biological Sciences* 271 (2004).

16. Steven Goldberg, "What is Normal?" *National Review* 3, February 1992.

17. Paul Gringras and Wai Chen, "Mechanisms for Differences in Monozygotic Twins," *Early Human Development* 64 (2001).

18. Nessa Carey, *The Epigenetics Revolution* (Columbia University Press, 2012).

19. There are two major kinds of epigenetic marker: methylation and histone modification. In methylation, a tiny molecule of $CH3$ is added on the spine of the DNA in a promoter region. (Promoters tell the cell where a gene starts.) This causes a relatively permanent shutdown of that gene. Histones are sets of protein molecules that the DNA is wrapped around so that the long DNA chain can be squeezed into the nucleus of the cell. Modifications to the histones are relatively temporary and can increase or decrease expression of adjacent genes (Carey, *Epigenetics Revolution*).

20. When I say "genetic" here, I mean it in the broad sense, including epigenetic mechanisms as well as genetic mechanisms.

21. David France, "The Science of Gaydar," *Time*, 25 June 2007.

22. The endocrine system is a system of glands—including the sex glands (testes and ovaries)—that produce and respond to hormones.

23. As we will see below, the ultimate physiological source of homosexuality might have more to do with aggression in young children, not in sexual drives of adults.

24. The original study was conducted by Simon LeVay, "A Difference in Hypothalamic Structure between Heterosexual and Homosexual Men," *Science* 253 (1991).

25. Anthony Bogaert, "Biological versus Nonbiological Older Brothers and Men's Sexual Orientation," *Proceedings of the National Academy of Science* 103 (2006).

26. Note that this 33 percent increase is only a 33 percent increase over the baseline chance of being gay. In other words, for each successive male child, the chance of being gay is 1.33 times more than the previous male child. So suppose that first-born sons have a 9 percent chance of being gay; that means that second-born sons would have a 12 percent likelihood of being gay (not a 42 percent likelihood!).

27. William Rice, Urban Friberg, and Sergey Gavrilets, "Homosexuality as a Consequence of Epigenetically Canalized Sexual Development," *Quarterly Review of Biology* 87 (2012).

28. Daryl J. Bem, "Exotic Becomes Erotic: A Developmental Theory of Sexual Orientation," *Psychological Review* 103 (1996).

29. This is known as the "Westermarck" effect, after Finnish anthropologist Edvard Westermarck. Evidence supporting the phenomenon can be found in Joseph Shepher, *Incest: A Biosocial View*, Studies in Anthropology (Academic Press, 1983).

30. Or at least that is the perception. A recent report by the Johns Hopkins Medical School casts doubt on that claim: "Study Finds Women Not Under-Represented in U.S. Clinical Trials," http://www.jhsph.edu/news/news-releases/2000/women-in-trials.html. At any rate, it seems to have been true of research on sexual behavior, until very recently (Daniel Bergner, "What do Women Want?" *New York Times Magazine*, 22 January 2009).

31. For a review of the relevant findings, see Meredith L. Chivers, "A Brief Review and Discussion of Sex Differences in the Specificity of Sexual Arousal," *Sexual and Relationship Therapy* 20 (2005); and also Noam Shpancer, "What Do Women Want? New Research Challenges Old Ideas about Female Sexual Desire," *Psychology Today*, 22 August 2013.

32. Kelly Suschinsky and Martin Lalumiere, "Prepared for Anything?: An Investigation of Female Genital Arousal in Response to Rape Cues," *Psychological Science* 22 (2011).

33. This is not to say that the two are entirely disconnected. Often when a woman is psychologically aroused, she will anticipate sex, and then her body will react accordingly. But there is still that intermediate step, a step not usually needed for men to become physically aroused.

34. Carla Golden, "Diversity and Variability in Women's Sexual Identities," in *Lesbian Psychologies: Explorations and Challenges* (University of Illinois Press, 1987). See also Gelder, "The 'Born that Way' Trap."

35. There are some who might disagree with this. For example, in Matthew 5, Jesus is quoted as saying, "Anyone who looks at a woman lustfully has already committed adultery with her in his heart." But I assume that the sin is not for desires that happen against our will but only those desires that we endorse, indulge, or actively cultivate. That is how Peter Abelard interpreted this passage.

36. For an introduction to existentialism, see my "If I Only Had an Essence! Existentialism and *The Wizard of Oz*," *Midwest Quarterly* (2011).

5. HOMOSEXUALITY AND MORALITY I—THE NATURAL LAW ARGUMENT

1. Many other philosophers (as well as several nonphilosophers) have presented criticisms of the Natural Law argument and the teleological argument similar to those I present in this chapter and the next. The prevalence of these criticisms is largely a reflection on how weak these arguments are (like fish in a barrel). Here are just a few of the many sources in which one can find such criticisms: Burton M. Leister, "Homosexuality, Morals, and the Laws of Nature," in *Ethics in Practice*, ed. Hugh LaFollette (Blackwell, 1997); Richard D. Mohr, "Prejudice and Homosexuality," in *Morality in Practice*, 7th edition, ed. James Sterba (Thomson Wadsworth, 2004); James A. Gould, "The 'Natural' and Homosexuality," *International Journal of Applied Ethics* 4 (1988); John Corvino, "Why Shouldn't Tommy and Jim Have Sex?" in *Same Sex: Debating the Ethics, Science, and Culture of Homosexuality*, ed. John Corvino (Rowman & Littlefield, 1997).

2. The original text of this report can be found online at http://abcnews.go.com/images/Politics/Holsinger_on_Homosexuality.pdf.

3. Michael Levin, "Why Homosexuality Is Abnormal," *Monist* 67 (1984).

4. For example, Judith Butler's *Gender Trouble: Feminism and the Subversion of Identity* (Routledge, 1990).

5. The first use of the word "homosexual" in print appeared in a medical article in 1892, written by Richard von Krafft-Ebing, translated into English by another doctor, Charles Gilbert Chaddock (*Oxford English Dictionary*).

6. This view was first argued by Noam Chomsky. For an account of this theory that is suitable for nonexperts, see Steven Pinker's *The Language Instinct: How the Mind Creates Language* (HarperPerennial, 2007).

7. Chimps can learn words, but they seem unable to learn proper grammar or syntax. For example, they cannot tell the difference between "the dog bit the man" and "the man bit the dog." All they can understand is a string of discrete words: man/dog/bite.

8. David Crews and Kevin T. Fitzgeraldt, "'Sexual' Behavior in Parthenogenetic Lizards (Cnemidophorus)," *Proceedings of the National Academy of Sciences USA* 77 (1980).

9. "Homer's Phobia," Season 8 of *The Simpsons*, Episode 15, first aired on 16 February 1997.

10. A recent study estimates the percentage of men who are homosexual to be a little over 5 percent. Seth Stephens-Davidowitz, "How Many American Men Are Gay?" *New York Times*, 8 December 2013.

11. "Ask Marilyn," *Parade*, 11 December 2005.

12. Many studies have shown that Rorschach tests results are inconsistent and mostly register expectations of the psychiatrist analyzing the response. For a summary, see Scott O. Lilienfeld, James M. Wood, and Howard N. Garb, "What's Wrong with This Picture?" *Scientific American*, May 2001.

13. Arthur Koestler, *The Sleepwalkers: A History of Man's Changing Vision of the Universe*, Part IV "The Watershed," (Macmillan, 1955).

14. A copy of the original *DSM* can be found online at http://www.turkpsikiyatri.org/arsiv/dsm-1952.pdf.

15. Evelyn Hooker, "Reflections of a 40-Year Exploration: A Scientific View on Homosexuality," *American Psychologist* 48 (1993).

16. For a more detailed history of homosexuality and psychology, see Henry L. Minton's *Departing from Deviance: A History of Homosexual Rights and Emancipatory Science in America* (University of Chicago Press, 2002).

17. For a summary and evaluation of these arguments and more, see *The Fetal Position: A Rational Approach to the Abortion Issue*, by yours truly (Prometheus Books, 2010).

18. David Hume, *A Treatise of Human Nature*, Book III, Part I, Section ii, (1738).

19. Kristin Leutwyler, "Exploring the Musical Brain," *Scientific American*, 22 January 2001. Leutwyler reports that every human culture has music, and music probably predates the advent of agriculture.

20. Of course, it could be argued that some nonhuman animals have a capacity for music, in particular, songbirds and whales. This might depend on exactly how we define "music." But I am not claiming that humans are the only animals with innate musical ability. I am only claiming that some animals seem to lack musical ability altogether.

21. About 95 percent of Americans today have premarital sex. Lawrence B. Finer, "Trends in Premarital Sex in the United States, 1954–2003," *Public Health Reports* 122, January–February 2007.

22. American Red Cross web site, http://www.redcrossblood.org/learn-about-blood/blood-facts-and-statistics.

23. The most comprehensive account of the NNL argument can be found in Sherif Girgis, Robert P. George, and Ryan T. Anderson, "What is Marriage?" *Harvard Journal of Law and Public Policy* 34 (2010).

24. Jeremy Garrett provides a very thorough and detailed reconstruction of the NNL argument against gay marriage in his "Why the Old Sexual Morality of the New Natural Law Undermines Traditional Marriage," *Social Theory and Practice* 34 (2008). He also gives his own rather compelling argument against it, showing that the arguments are ad hoc and self-defeating.

25. See also John Finnis, "The Good of Marriage and the Morality of Sexual Relations: Some Philosophical and Historical Observations," *American Journal of Jurisprudence* 42 (1997).

26. This claim can also be found in Robert George and Gerald Bradley, "Marriage and the Liberal Imagination," *Georgetown Law Journal* 84 (1995).

27. In fact, there is some debate about whether the zebra is a genuine natural kind at all. The problem is that there are three zebra species, and each of them evolved separately from wild horses, not from a common zebra ancestor. Stephen J. Gould, "What, if Anything, Is a Zebra?" in his collection *Hen's Teeth and Horse's Toes: Further Reflections in Natural History* (W.W. Norton, 1983).

28. Ralph Wedgwood, "The Fundamental Argument for Same-Sex Marriage," *The Journal of Political Philosophy* 7 (1999).

6. HOMOSEXUALITY AND MORALITY II—THE TELEOLOGICAL ARGUMENT AND MORAL INTUITIONISTISM

1. A version of this argument in found in Michael Levin, "Why Homosexuality Is Abnormal," *Monist* 67 (1984), footnote 3. See also Levin, "Homosexuality, Abnormality, and Civil Rights," *Public Affairs Quarterly* 10 (1996).

2. As a matter of fact, Edison's friend and partner, Edward H. Johnson, invented the first Christmas tree lights.

3. Larry Wright gives a broad definition of "function of X" as those effects of X that explains X's existence. This works both for the products of natural selection, artifacts, as well as human practices and voluntary actions. "Functions," *The Philosophical Review* 82 (1973).

4. See for example Neil R. Carson, *Foundations of Behavioral Neuroscience*, 8th edition (Pearson, 2011), or any other decent biology or neuroscience textbook.

5. Nadine Striepens, Keith M. Kendrick, Wolfgang Maier, and Rene Hurlemann, "Prosocial Effects of Oxytocin and Clinical Evidence for Its Therapeutic Potential," *Frontiers in Neuroendocrinology* 32 (2011).

6. Nina G. Jablonski, *Skin: A Natural History* (University of California Press, 2006); Daniel Lieberman and Dennis Bramble, "The Evolution of Marathon Running: Capabilities in Humans," *Sports Medicine* 37 (2007).

7. W. L. Jungers, "The Foot of Homo Florensiensis," *Nature* 459 (2009).

8. About two-thirds of Americans under the age of twenty-five practice oral sex and almost 80 percent under 44. Casey E. Copen, Anjani Chandra, and Gladys Martinez, "Prevalence and Timing of Oral Sex with Opposite-Sex Partners among Females and Males Aged 15–24 Years: United States, 2007–2010," *National Health Statistics Reports*, 16 August 2012.

9. Sherif Girgis, Robert P. George, and Ryan T. Anderson, "What is Marriage?" *Harvard Journal of Law and Public Policy* 34 (2010). [Hereafter, GG& A.]

10. GG&A, 254.

11. In fact, the Catholic Church denied marriage to a paraplegic man in Brazil for exactly these reasons. For more details, see the documentary film, *Forbidden Marriage*, directed by Flavia Fontes, Means of Productions, Inc. (2001).

12. This is actually less feasible than it might seem. The problem is that epigenetic markers on the egg cell's chromosome identify the genes as coming from the mother, while epigenetic markers on the sperm cell's chromosomes identify those genes as coming from the father. Nessa Carey, *The Epigenetics Revolution* (Columbia University Press, 2012).

13. When a friend of mine gave birth to a baby girl about ten months after I got married, my wife said that she must have conceived the weekend of our wedding in New Orleans. I pointed out that she probably conceived on the airplane ride back to California.

14. GG&A.

15. Jeremy Garrett makes a similar objection, using the example of therapeutic massage. "Why the Old Sexual Morality of the New Natural Law Undermines Traditional Marriage," *Social Theory and Practice* 34 (2008).

16. For a rather thorough defense of intuitionism in ethics, see Robert Audi, "Intuition, Pluralism, and the Foundations of Ethics," in Walter Sinnott-Armstrong and Mark Timmons (eds.), *Moral Knowledge?* (Oxford University Press, 1996).

17. Robert George and Gerald Bradley, "Marriage and the Liberal Imagination," *Georgetown Law Journal* 84 (1995).

18. Nicholas Buccola also takes the NNL theorists to task for their claims to have superior intuition into the nature of marriage and the moral wrongness of non-procreative sex. "Finding Room for Same-Sex Marriage: Toward a More Inclusive Understanding of a Cultural Institution," *Journal of Social Philosophy* 36 (2005).

19. For more on disagreement and moral realism, see my article "Defending Moral Realism from Empirical Evidence of Disagreement," *Social Theory and Practice* 39 (2013).

7. DEBUNKING PSYCHOLOGICAL EXPLANATIONS FOR
DISAPPROVAL OF HOMOSEXUALITY

1. Thalia Wheatley and Jonathan Haidt, "Hypnotic Disgust Makes Moral Judgments More Severe," *Psychological Science* 16 (2005); Haidt, "The Emotional Dog and Its Rational Tail," *Psychological Review* 108 (2001).

2. Here is a partial list: Washington State Representative Richard Curtis, Florida State Representative Bob Allen, Alabama Attorney General Troy King, Puerto Rican Senator Robert Arango, New York Senator Carl Kruger, Louisiana Congressman Jim McCrery, California Senator Roy Ashburn, and Virginia Congressman Edward L. Schrock. The phenomenon is so widespread that HBO aired a documentary on secretly gay opponents of gay rights, entitled *Outrage*. (Get it? *Out*-Rage?)

3. Henry E. Adams, Lester W. Wright Jr., and Bethany A. Lohr, "Is Homophobia Associated with Homosexual Arousal?" *Journal of Abnormal Psychology* 105 (1996).

4. The results of the study would have been even stronger if they had included only *strongly* homophobic (75–100) and *strongly* gay-tolerant (0–25) test subjects, eliminating the more moderate subjects (25–75). Unfortunately, there were not enough heterosexual men who scored below 25 on the IHP. This study, however, was conducted eighteen years ago. It might be easier today to find straight men who score below 25.

5. Netta Weinstein et al., "Parental Autonomy Support and Discrepancies Between Implicit and Explicit Sexual Identities: Dynamics of Self-Acceptance and Defense," *Journal of Personality and Social Psychology* 104 (2012).

6. Ibid.

7. Yoel Inbar et al., "Disgust Sensitivity Predicts Intuitive Disapproval of Gays," *Emotion* 9 (2009). See also, Yoel Inbar, David Pizarro, and Paul Bloom, "Disgusting Smells Cause Decreased Liking of Gay Men," *Emotion* 12 (2012), doi: 10.1037/a0023984.

8. In the implicit homophobia test, subjects are shown images and words on a screen and must place them into categories as quickly as possible, using two keys of the keyboard. In some trials, one key is used for both homosexual images and negative words (such as "unpleasant" or "horrible") and the other key is used for heterosexual images and positive words (such as "pleasant" or "wonderful"). In other trials, things are switched so that homosexuality and positive words are identified with one key and heterosexuality and negative words identified with the other key. The computer measures reaction time. If a subject has significantly slower reaction time when gay images and positive words are linked by the same key than he does when gay is linked to negative words, then that is evidence of implicit homophobia.

9. For a good review of the psychology of disgust, see Paul Rozin, "Disgust," in Michael Lewis, Jeannette M. Haviland-Jones, and Lisa Feldman Barrett (eds.), *Handbook of Emotions* (Guilford Press, 2010).

10. Simone Schnall et al., "Disgust as Embodied Moral Judgment," *Personality and Social Psychology Bulletin* 34 (2008).

11. Paul Rozin et al., "The CAD Triad Hypothesis: A Mapping between Three Moral Emotions (Contempt, Anger, Disgust) and Three Moral Codes (Community, Autonomy, Divinity)," *Journal of Personality and Social Psychology* 76 (1999).

12. Richard Shweder et al., "The 'Big Three' of Morality (Autonomy, Community, Divinity) and the 'Big Three' Explanations in Suffering," in Allan Brandt and Paul Rozin (eds.) *Morality and Health*, (Routledge, 1997).

13. When I say that we have a duty to care for our parents, I do not mean to imply that we should be *motivated* by a sense of duty. One would hope that children would be motivated by love, not duty. But if, for whatever reason, the love is not there, it is still wrong to neglect one's elderly parents (assuming they were not abusive or neglectful).

14. I might agree that humans should not eat pigs, but for different reasons. The raising and slaughtering of pigs for food causes terrible suffering to the animals and significant damage to the environment. But those are autonomy judgments. These are also reasons that would apply equally to eating beef, lamb, chicken, and most other meats. The disagreement is over whether pigs have some sort of "stain" that cows, lambs, and chickens do not.

15. Angela Burr, "Pigs in Noah's Ark: A Muslim Origin Myth from Southern Thailand," *Folklore* 90 (1979).

16. Charmaine Borg and Peter deJong, "Feelings of Disgust and Disgust-Induced Avoidance Weaken Following Induced Sexual Arousal in Women," *PloS ONE* (September 2012), doi: 10.1371/journal.pone.0044111.

17. Eric Koukounas and Marita McCabe, "Sexual and Emotional Variables Influencing Sexual Response to Erotica," *Behavior Research and Therapy* 35 (1997).

18. This is nicely illustrated by the King Missile song, "Miracle of Childbirth." The lyrics go like this: "Your father fucked your mother. At least once, your father and your mother were in bed and your father got a hard-on and he stuck it inside your mother and they fucked." It goes on like that, though I have never been able to listen to the entire song all the way through.

19. Kass writes, "Worst of all from this point of view are those more uncivilized forms of eating, like licking an ice cream cone—a catlike activity that has been made acceptable in informal America but that still offends those who know eating in public is offensive." *The Hungry Soul* (University of Chicago Press, 1994).

20. Paul Rozin, Linda Millman, and Carol Nemeroff, "Operation of the Laws of Sympathetic Magic in Disgust and Other Domains," *Journal of Personality and Social Psychology* 50 (1986); Paul Rozin and April E. Fallen, "A Perspective on Disgust," *Psychological Review* 94 (1987).

21. *From Disgust to Humanity* (Oxford University Press, 2010).

22. Terrence DesPres, *The Survivor* (Oxford University Press, 1976).

23. Lasana Harris and Susan Fiske, "Dehumanized Perception: A Psychological Means to Facilitate Atrocities, Torture, and Genocide?" *Journal of Psychology* 219 (2011), 175.

24. Lasana Harris and Susan Fiske, "Dehumanizing the Lowest of the Low: Neuroimaging Responses to Extreme Out-Groups," *Psychological Science* 17 (2006).

25. Carlos Navarrete and Daniel Fessler, "Disease Avoidance and Ethnocentrism: The Effects of Disease Vulnerability and Disgust Sensitivity on Intergroup Attitudes," *Evolution and Human Behavior* 27 (2006).

26. Nussbaum is no naïve idealist. She is well aware that the actual practices in the new United States often fell far short of the explicit ideas, particularly in the brutal injustice of chattel slavery. She is a progressive who appeals to the explicit ideals and principles of the founders, not a conservative who wants to return to the practices and customs of the ordinary folk of that time, or even to a romanticized vision of those customs and practices.

8. HOMOSEXUALITY, CONSEQUENCES, AND JUSTICE I—SLIPPERY SLOPE ARGUMENTS

1. John Finnis, "Is Natural Law Theory Compatible with Limited Government?" in *Natural Law, Liberalism, and Morality: Contemporary Essays*, ed. Robert George. (Clarendon Press, 1996).

2. For example, John Rawls, *Political Liberalism* (Columbia University Press, 1993); and Ronald Dworkin, "Liberalism," in *Public and Private Morality*, ed. Stuart Hampshire. (Cambridge University Press, 1978).

3. For example, Joseph Raz, *The Morality of Freedom* (Clarendon Press, 1986).

4. Brian J. McCabe, "Public Opinion on 'Don't Ask, Don't Tell,'" *New York Times: FiveThirtyEight*, 30 November 2010. This is up from a mere 44 percent in 1993.

5. Jeffery M. Jones, "Record-High 86% Approve of Black-White Marriages," Gallup.com., 12 September 2011.

6. Sherif Girgis, Robert George, and Ryan Anderson, "What Is Marriage?" *Harvard Journal of Law and Public Policy* 34 (2010). [Hereafter, GG&A.]

7. John Corvino, "Homosexuality and the PIB Argument," *Ethics* 115 (2005).

8. Oddly, Abraham stops once he talks God down to saving the town if there are ten good men living there. But he could have continued. If God would save the town for ten good men, then why not for nine? Etc.

9. Maia Szalavitz, "Marijuana as a Gateway Drug: The Myth That Will Not Die," *Time*, 29 October 2010.

10. "Marriage is distinguished from every other form of friendship inasmuch as it is comprehensive. It involves a sharing of lives and resources, and a union of minds and wills—hence, among other things, the requirement of consent for forming a marriage." GG&A.

11. For a positive (though perhaps naïvely optimistic) depiction of arranged marriages, I recommend the film *Arranged*, Cicala Filmworks (2009).

12. John Locke, *Second Treaties of Government*, chapter 5 "Of Property," sections 27, 31, and 35 (1689).

13. This problem was the subject of a feature documentary film, *Sons of Perdition* (Left Turn Films, 2010).

14. Irwin Altman and Joseph Ginat, *Polygamous Families in Contemporary Society* (University of Cambridge Press, 1996).

15. Varghese I. Cherian, "Academic Achievement of Children from Monogamous and Polygynous Families," *The Journal of Social Psychology* 130 (1989). A good summary of the numerous evils of polygamy can be found in "Polygyny and Canada's Obligations under International Human Rights Law," Chapter II ("Harms of Polygyny"), by the Canadian Department of Justice, http://canada.justice.gc.ca/eng/dept-min/pub/poly/chap2.html (September 2006).

16. M. M. Tabi, C. Doster, and T. Cheney, "A Qualitative Study of Women in Polygymous Marriages," *International Nursing Review* 57 (2010).

17. Douglas R. White and Cynthia Veit, *White–Veit EthnoAtlas* (1999): http://eclectic.ss.uci.edu/~drwhite/ethnoatlas/nindex.html.

18. Douglas R. White et al., "Rethinking Polygyny: Co-Wives, Codes, and Cultural Systems," *Current Anthropology* 29 (1988).

19. Michael Wiederman, "Extramarital Sex: Prevalence and Correlates in a National Survey," *Journal of Sex Research* 34 (1997).

20. GG&A.

21. GG&A.

22. GG&A.

23. Four of the six "scholars" they reference are journalists/activists/bloggers. And Stacey is a sociologist. Brake is the only philosopher in the group.

24. Scott F. Aiken and John Casey, "Straw Men, Weak Men, and Hollow Men," *Argumentation* 25 (2011).

25. In his defense, Farrow and Allen lived in separate houses and Allen was never officially Soon-Yi's father or stepfather. But public criticism was based on the *perception* that the relationship was between father and adopted daughter.

26. This argument is made by William Saletan, "Incest Is Cancer: The David Epstein Incest Case: If Homosexuality Is OK, Why Is Incest Wrong?" Slate.com: *Human Nature*, 14 December 2010.

27. Kathryn Harrison, *The Kiss* (Harper Perennial, 1998).

9. HOMOSEXUALITY, CONSEQUENCES, AND JUSTICE II: ALLEGED BAD CONSEQUENCES OF GAY-TOLERANT PUBLIC POLICIES

1. For an excellent discussion on the arguments for and against paternalism, see Gerald Dworkin, "Paternalism," *The Monist* 56 (1972).

2. John Stuart Mill, *On Liberty* (1859).

3. As described by Reverend Lovejoy, *The Simpsons*, "Bart Sells His Soul," Season 7, Episode 4, originally aired on October 8, 1995.

4. Jeffrey Satinover, *Homosexuality and the Politics of Truth* (Baker Books, 1996). Baker Publishing is an evangelical Christian publishing house.

5. L. T. Puig, *What Nature Intended* (PublishAmerica). This book is an obscure vanity-press product with no publication date. But quotes from it can be found on many conservative Christian websites, including *The Catholic Education Resource Center* (CERC), www.catholiceducation.org.

6. This statistic is from the Centers for Disease Control website: http:// www.cdc.gov/tobacco/data_statistics/fact_sheets/health_effects/tobacco_ related_mortality/index.htm#cigs.

7. Michael Levin makes claims like this. He says that "homosexuals are bound to be less happy than heterosexuals," and: "Thus, when evaluating the empirical evidence that bears on this account, it will be pointless to cite cases of well-adjusted homosexuals. I do not say they are non-existent; my claim is that, of biological necessity, they are rare." "Why Homosexuality is Abnormal," *The Monist* 67 (1984). He thinks that this is not so much that homosexuals are harmed by their gay lifestyle but that they miss out on the benefits of the heterosexual lifestyle.

8. I am not claiming that the discriminatory treatment that homosexuals face is worse than the treatment other groups confront. That would be a pointless debate. I just want to point out how they are *different* and that this will probably mean different challenges and problems.

9. Martha Nussbaum, "A Right to Marry? Same-Sex Marriage and Constitutional Law," *Dissent*, summer 2009.

10. "Divorce Rates by State: How Does Your State Stack Up," *Huffington Post*, 5 September 2013.

11. "20 Most Tolerant States," *The Daily Beast*, 16 January 2011.

12. Seth Stephens-Davidowitz, "How Many American Men Are Gay?" *New York Times*, 7 December 2013. This is demonstrated by examining online pornography viewership. The proportion of gay to straight pornography viewing online is virtually the same in all regions of the United States.

13. Sherif Girgis, Robert George, and Ryan Anderson, "What Is Marriage?" *Harvard Journal of Law and Public Policy* 34 (2010). [Henceforth, GG&A.]

14. About 20 percent of women 40–44 years old in the United States today are childless, and about half of them by choice. Lauren Sandler, "The Child-free Life," *Time*, 12 August 2013.

15. John Finnis, "Law, Morality, and 'Sexual Orientation,'" in *Same Sex*, ed. John Corvino (Rowman & Littlefield, 1997).

16. "Vatican Fights Gay Marriage," CNN.com, 31 July 2003.

17. Melanie Smollin, "'Don't Ask, Don't Tell' Is Alive and Well for Gay Educators," *Take Part*, 25 February 2011.

18. "Sen. Jim DeMint: Gays and Unmarried, Pregnant Women Should not Teach Public School," *Huffington Post*, 25 May 2011.

19. Public approval of openly gay elementary teachers was over 60 percent in 2004 and is probably much higher today. "Gay Soldiers and Teachers," *New York Times*, 2 April 2004. Somewhat surprisingly, approval of adoption by gay couples is actually slightly higher than approval of same-sex marriage—about

52 percent versus 48 percent in 2012. "Section 2: Long-Term Views of Homosexuality, Gay Marriage and Adoption," *Pew Research*, online at Pewforum.org, 31 July 2012.

20. This is not to say that the children of same-sex parents do not differ *in any way* from those of opposite-sex parents. For example, children of same-sex couples are more approving of same-sex relations and have less stereotyped notions of male and female social roles. But they do not differ in terms of psychological heath, school performance, or delinquency. (Also, they are not any more likely to be gay.) Erica Goode, "A Rainbow of Differences in Gays' Children," *New York Times Health*, 17 July 2001.

21. The text is available online through a link on the ASA website, Asanet.org: http://www.asanet.org/documents/ASA/pdfs/12-144_307_Amicus_%20%28C_%20Gottlieb%29_ASA_Same-Sex_Marriage.pdf.

22. Vince Chadwick, "Tick for Same-Sex Families," *The Age*, 5 June 2013.

23. Mark Regnerus, "How Different Are the Adult Children of Parents Who Have Same-Sex Relationships? Findings from the New Family Structures Survey," *Social Science Research* 752 (2012).

24. John Becker, "In Supreme Court Brief, American Sociological Association Obliterates Claim That Same-Sex Couples Are Inferior Parents," *Huffington Post*, 28 February 2013.

25. A similar argument is made by Ilana Yurkiewicz, "Why Mark Regnerus' Study Shouldn't Matter, Even if It Were the Most Scientifically Robust Study in the World," *Unofficial Prognosis—Scientific American Blogs*, 16 June 2012.

26. "Marriage from a Child's Perspective: How Does Family Structure Affect Children, and What Can We Do about It?" http://www.childtrends.org/wp-content/uploads/2002/06/MarriageRB602.pdf.

27. U.S. Department of Health and Human Services, "Impact of Adoption on Adopted Persons," *Child Welfare Information Gateway*, https://www.childwelfare.gov/pubs/f_adimpact.cfm.

28. Steven L. Nickman et al., "Children in Adoptive Families: Overview and Update," *Journal of the American Academy of Child & Adolescent Psychiatry* 44 (2005).

29. GG&A.

30. Michael Paulson and Fernando Santos, "Religious Right in Arizona Cheers Bill Allowing Businesses to Refuse to Serve Gays," *New York Times*, 21 February 2014.

31. A similar argument is made by Linda Greenhouse, "After the Veto," *New York Times*, 5 March 2014. See also, Michael Kent Curtis, "A Unique Religious Exemption from Antidiscrimination Laws in the Case of Gays? Putting the Call for Exemptions for Those Who Discriminate Against Married or Marrying Gays in Context," *The Wake Forest Law Review* (April 2012).

32. "And he had caused the cursing to come upon [the Lamanites], yea, even a sore cursing, because of their iniquity. For behold, they had hardened their hearts against him, and they had become like unto a flint; wherefore, as they were white, and exceedingly fair and delightsome, that they might not be

enticing unto my people the Lord God did cause a skin of blackness to come upon them." 2 Nephi 5:21

33. "United Church Of Christ Files Lawsuit Against Gay Marriage Ban In North Carolina, Citing Threat To Religious Freedom," Yonat Shimron, *Huffington Post*, 28 April 2014.

10. ARGUMENTS IN FAVOR OF HOMOSEXUALITY AND GAY RIGHTS

1. Robert Sampson, John Laub, and Christopher Wimer, "Does Marriage Reduce Crime? A Counterfactual Approach to Within-Individual Causal Effects," *Criminology* 44 (2006).

2. W. Bradford Wilcox, "Strong Marriages and Economies," *New York Times*, 19 January 2012.

3. Frank Newport and Joy Wilke, "Economy Would Benefit if Marriage Rate Increases in U.S.," *Gallup Economy*, 28 October 2013.

4. Linda J. Waite and Maggie Gallagher, *The Case for Marriage: Why Married People Are Happier, Healthier and Better Off Financially* (Broadway Books, 2001).

5. Tara Parker-Pope, "Is Marriage Good for Your Health?" *New York Times*, 14 April 2010.

6. Ralph Wedgwood, "The Fundamental Argument for Same Sex Marriage," *The Journal of Political Philosophy* 7 (1999).

7. For an argument that pluralism is, or least might be, the correct moral theory, see my "Defending Moral Realism from Empirical Evidence of Disagreement," *Social Theory and Practice* 39 (2013).

8. The concept of prima facie moral obligation comes from W. D. Ross, *The Right and the Good* (Oxford University Press, 1930).

9. Richard Mohr, "The Case for Outing," in *Same Sex*, ed. John Corvino. (Rowman & Littlefield, 1997). Mohr does not defend the practice of *vindictive* outing, aimed at punishing enemies. Vindictive outing relies on, and thus implicitly supports, homophobia.

10. Plato had a rather dim view of pleasures of the flesh generally, but he was not particularly uncomfortable with same-sex relations.

11. John Finnis says, "At the very heart of the reflections of Plato, Xenophon, Aristotle, Musonius, Rufus, and Plutarch on the homoerotic culture around them is the very deliberate and careful judgment that homosexual conduct (and indeed all extramarital sexual gratification) is radically incapable of participating in, or actualizing, the common good of friendship." "Is Homosexual Conduct Wrong? A Philosophical Exchange—Disintegrity," in *Homosexuality*, ed. Robert M. Baird and M. Katherine Baird. (Prometheus Books, 1995).

12. For example, Martha Nussbaum, "Is Homosexual Conduct Wrong? A Philosophical Exchange—Integrity," in *Homosexuality*, ed. Baird and Baird.

13. For a thorough, if rather facile, criticism of virtue ethics, see Robert Louden, "On Some Vices of Virtue Ethics," *American Philosophical Quarterly* 21 (1984).

14. John Stuart Mill, *On Liberty* (1859).

15. John Rawls, *A Theory of Justice* (Harvard University Press, 1971).

16. *Loving v. Virginia*, majority opinion, written by Chief Justice Earl Warren, available online at Findlaw.com.

17. Sherif Girgis, Robert George, and Ryan Anderson, "What Is Marriage?" *Harvard Journal of Law and Public Policy* 34 (2010). [Hereafter, GG&A.]

18. Martha Nussbaum, "A Right to Marry?"

19. Adam Swift, *Political Philosophy: A Beginner's Guide for Students and Politicians* (Polity, 2007). Swift argues that this is true not only of equality, but also justice, liberty, community, and democracy.

20. Adrian Alex Wellington, "Why Liberals Should Support Same-Sex Marriage," *Journal of Social Philosophy* 26 (1995).

21. Kory Schaff argues for same-sex marriage on the basis of equality and that homosexuals constitute a suspect, or quasi-suspect, class. "Equal Protection and Same-Sex Marriage," *Journal of Social Philosophy* 35 (2004).

22. Andrew Koppelman, "Why Discrimination Against Lesbians and Gay Men Is Sex Discrimination," *New York University Law Review* 197 (1994).

BIBLIOGRAPHY

Adams, Henry E., Lester W. Wright Jr., and Bethany A. Lohr, "Is Homophobia Associated with Homosexual Arousal?" *Journal of Abnormal Psychology* 105 (1996): 440–45.

Aikin, Scott, and Robert Talisse. *Why We Argue (And How We Should): A Guide to Political Disagreement.* New York: Routledge, 2013.

Altman, Irwin, and Joseph Ginat. *Polygamous Families in Contemporary Society.* Cambridge University Press, 1996.

Audi, Robert. "Intuition, Pluralism, and the Foundations of Ethics." In *Moral Knowldege?* edited by Walter Sinnott-Armstrong and Mark Timmons, 101–36. Oxford University Press, 1996.

Bailey, J. Michael, and Richard Pillard. "A Genetic Study of Male Sexual Orientation." *Archives of General Psychiatry* 48 (1991): 1089–96.

Bailey, J. Michael, Michael P. Dunne, and Nicholas G. Martin. "Genetic and Environmental Influences on Sexual Orientation and Its Correlates in an Australian Twin Sample." *Journal of Personality and Social Psychology* 78 (2000): 524–36.

Bem, Daryl J. "Exotic Becomes Erotic: A Developmental Theory of Sexual Orientation." *Psychological Review* 103 (1996): 320–35.

Benedict, Ruth. "Anthropology and the Abnormal." *The Journal of General Anthropology* 10 (1934): 59–80.

Bogaert, Anthony. "Biological versus Nonbiological Older Brothers and Men's Sexual Orientation." *Proceedings of the National Academy of Science* 103 (2006): 10771–4.

Borg, Charmaine, and Peter de Jong. "Feelings of Disgust and Disgust-Induced Avoidance Weaken Following Induced Sexual Arousal in Women." *PloS ONE* (September 2012): doi: 10.1371/journal.pone.0044111.

Buccola, Nicholas. "Finding Room for Same-Sex Marriage: Toward a More Inclusive Understanding of a Cultural Institution." *Journal of Social Philosophy* 36 (2005): 331–43.

Burr, Angela. "Pigs in Noah's Ark: A Muslim Origin Myth from Southern Thailand." *Folklore* 90 (1979): 178–85.

Butler, Judith. *Gender Trouble: Feminism and the Subversion of Identity.* New York: Routledge, 1990.

Camperio-Ciani, Andrea, Francesca Corna, and Claudio Capiluppi. "Evidence for Maternally Inherited Factors Favouring Male Homosexuality and Promoting Female Fecundity." *Proceedings of the Royal Society B: Biological Sciences* 271 (2004): 2217–21.

Carey, Nessa. *The Epigenetics Revolution.* New York: Columbia University Press, 2012.

Carson, Neil R. *Foundations of Behavioral Neuroscience,* 8th edition. Upper Saddle River, NJ: Pearson, 2011.

Cherian, Varghese I. "Academic Achievement of Children from Monogamous and Polygynous Families." *The Journal of Social Psychology* 130 (1989): 117–19.

Chivers, Meredith L. "A Brief Review and Discussion of Sex Differences in the Specificity of Sexual Arousal." *Sexual and Relationship Therapy* 20 (2005): 377–90.

Corvino, John. "Why Shouldn't Tommy and Jim Have Sex?" In *Same Sex: Debating the Ethics, Science, and Culture of Homosexuality,* edited by John Corvino. Lanham, MD: Rowman & Littlefield, 1997.

———. "Homosexuality and the PIB Argument." *Ethics* 115 (2005): 501–34.

Crews, David, and Kevin T. Fitzgeraldt. "'Sexual' Behavior in Parthenogenetic Lizards (Cnemidophorus)." *Proceedings of the National Academy of Sciences USA* 77 (1980): 499–502.

Curtis, Michael Kent. "A Unique Religious Exemption from Antidiscrimination Laws in the Case of Gays? Putting the Call for Exemptions for Those Who Discriminate against Married or Marrying Gays in Context." *The Wake Forest Law Review* (April 2012).

Des Pres, Terrence. *The Survivor*. Oxford: Oxford University Press, 1976.

Driver, Julia. *Ethics: The Fundamentals*. Malden, MA: Wiley-Blackwell, 2006.

Dworkin, Gerald. "Paternalism." *The Monist* 56 (1972): 64–84.

Dworkin, Ronald. "Liberalism." In *Public and Private Morality*, edited by Stuart Hampshire, 113–45. Cambridge: Cambridge University Press, 1978.

Finnis, John. "Is Homosexual Conduct Wrong? A Philosophical Exchange—Disintegrity." In *Homosexuality*, edited by Robert M. Baird and M. Katherine Baird, 44–46. Amherst, New York: Prometheus Books, 1995. [Excerpted from legal depositions for trial of Colorado's Amendment 2.]

———. "Is Natural Law Theory Compatible with Limited Government?" In *Natural Law, Liberalism, and Morality: Contemporary Essays*, edited by Robert George. Oxford: Clarendon Press, 1996.

———. "The Good of Marriage and the Morality of Sexual Relations: Some Philosophical and Historical Observations." *American Journal of Jurisprudence* 42 (1997): 97–134.

———. "Law, Morality, and 'Sexual Orientation.'" In *Same Sex*, edited by John Corvino, 31–43. Lanham MD: Rowman & Littlefield, 1997.

Foucault, Michel. *The History of Sexuality 1: An Introduction*. New York: Vintage Books, 1978.

France, David. "The Science of Gaydar." *Time*, 25 June 2007.

Garrett, Jeremy. "Why the Old Sexual Morality of the New Natural Law Undermines Traditional Marriage." *Social Theory and Practice* 34 (2008): 591–622.

George, Robert, and Gerald Bradley. "Marriage and the Liberal Imagination." *Georgetown Law Journal* 84 (1995).

Girgis, Sherif, Robert George, and Ryan Anderson. "What Is Marriage?" *Harvard Journal of Law and Public Policy* 34 (2010): 248–87.

Goldberg, Steven. "What Is Normal?" *National Review* 3, February 1992.

Golden, Carla. "Diversity and Variability in Women's Sexual Identities." In *Lesbian Psychologies: Explorations and Challenges*. Edited by Boston Lesbian Psychologies Collective, Lee Sahli, and Zevy Cavallaro. Urbana: University of Illinois Press, 1987.

Gould, James A. "The 'Natural' and Homosexuality." *International Journal of Applied Ethics* 4 (1988): 51–54.

Gould, Stephen J. *Hen's Teeth and Horse's Toes: Further Reflections in Natural History*. New York: W.W. Norton, 1983.

Gringras, Paul, and Wai Chen. "Mechanisms for Differences in Monozygotic Twins." *Early Human Development* 64 (2001): 105–17.

Haider-Markel, Donald P., and Mark R. Joslyn. "Beliefs about the Origins of Homosexuality and Support for Gay Rights: An Empirical Test of Attribution Theory." *Public Opinion Quarterly* 72 (2008): 291–310.

Haidt, Jonathan. "The Emotional Dog and its Rational Tail: A Social Intuitionist Approach to Moral Judgment." *Psychological Review* 108 (2001): 814–34.

———. *The Righteous Mind: Why Good People Are Divided by Politics and Religion*. New York: Random House, 2004.

Hamer, Dean, Stella Hu, Victoria Magnuson, Nan Hu, and Angela Pattatucci. "A Linkage Between Markers on the X Chromosome and Male Sexual Orientation." *Science* 261 (1993): 321–27.

Harmon, Gilbert. *The Nature of Morality*. Oxford: Oxford University Press, 1977.

Harris, Lasana, and Susan Fiske. "Dehumanizing the Lowest of the Low: Neuroimaging Responses to Extreme Out-groups." *Psychological Science* 17 (2006): 847–53

———. "Dehumanized Perception: A Psychological Means to Facilitate Atrocities, Torture, and Genocide?" *Journal of Psychology* 219 (2011): 175–81.

Helminiak, Daniel. *What the Bible Really Says about Homosexuality*. Estancia, NM: Alamo Square Press, 2000.

Hooker, Evelyn. "Reflections of a 40-Year Exploration: A Scientific View on Homosexuality." *American Psychologist* 48 (1993): 450–53.

Hume, David. *A Treatise of Human Nature*. 1738.

Inbar, Yoel, David Pizarro, and Paul Bloom. "Disgusting Smells Cause Decreased Liking of Gay Men." *Emotion* 12 (2012), doi: 10.1037/a0023984.

Inbar, Yoel, David Pizarro, Joshua Knobe, and Paul Bloom. "Disgust Sensitivity Predicts Intuitive Disapproval of Gays." *Emotion* 9 (2009): 435–39.

Jablonski, Nina G. *Skin: A Natural History*. Berkeley: University of California Press, 2006.

Joyce, Richard. *The Evolution of Morality*. Cambridge, MA: MIT Press, 2007.

Jungers, W. L. "The Foot of Homo Florensiensis." *Nature* 459 (2009): 81–84.
Kass, Leon. *The Hungry Soul.* Chicago: University of Chicago Press, 1994.
Koestler, Arthur. *The Sleepwalkers: A History of Man's Changing Vision of the Universe.* London: Macmillan, 1955.
Koppelman, Andrew. "Why Discrimination against Lesbians and Gay Men Is Sex Discrimination." *New York University Law Review* 197 (1994): 197–287.
Koukounas, Eric, and Marita McCabe. "Sexual and Emotional Variables Influencing Sexual Response to Erotica." *Behavior Research and Therapy* 35 (1997): 221–30.
Leister, Burton M. "Homosexuality, Morals, and the Laws of Nature." In *Ethics in Practice*, edited by Hugh LaFollette. Oxford: Blackwell, 1997.
Leutwyler, Kristin. "Exploring the Musical Brain." *Scientific American*, 22 January 2001.
LeVay, Simon. "A Difference in Hypothalamic Structure between Heterosexual and Homosexual Men." *Science* 253 (1991): 1034–37.
Levin, Michael. "Why Homosexuality Is Abnormal." *Monist* 67 (1984): 251–83.
———. "Homosexuality, Abnormality, and Civil Rights." *Public Affairs Quarterly* 10 (1996): 31–48.
Lieberman, Daniel, and Dennis Bramble. "The Evolution of Marathon Running: Capabilities in Humans." *Sports Medicine* 37 (2007): 288–90.
Lilienfeld, Scott O., James M. Wood, and Howard N. Garb. "What's Wrong with This Picture?" *Scientific American*, May 2001.
Meyers, C. D. *The Fetal Position: A Rational Approach to the Abortion Issue.* Amherst, New York: Prometheus Books, 2010.
———. "If I Only Had an Essence! Existentialism and *The Wizard of Oz*," *Midwest Quarterly* (2011): 95–110.
———. "Defending Moral Realism from Empirical Evidence of Disagreement," *Social Theory and Practice* 39 (2013): 373–96.
Mill, John Stuart. *On Liberty.* 1859.
Minton, Henry L. *Departing from Deviance: A History of Homosexual Rights and Emancipatory Science in America.* Chicago: University of Chicago Press, 2002.
Mohr, Richard D. "The Case for Outing." In *Same Sex: Debating the Ethics, Science, and Culture of Homosexuality*, edited by John Corvino, 284–288. Lanham, MD: Rowman & Littlefield, 1997.
———. "Prejudice and Homosexuality." In *Morality in Practice*, 7th edition, edited by James Sterba. Belmont, CA: Thomson Wadsworth, 2004.
Moore, G. E. *Principia Ethica.* Cambridge: Cambridge University Press, 1903.
Navarrete, Carlos, and Daniel Fessler. "Disease Avoidance and Ethnocentrism: The Effects of Disease Vulnerability and Disgust Sensitivity on Intergroup Attitudes." *Evolution and Human Behavior* 27 (2006): 270–82.
Nickman, Steven L., Alvin A. Rosenfeld, Paul Fine, James C. Macintyre, Daniel J Pilowsky, Ruth-Arlene Howe, Andre Derdeyn, Mayu Bonoan Gonzales, Linda Forsythe, and Sally A. Sveda. "Children in Adoptive Families: Overview and Update," *Journal of the American Academy of Child & Adolescent Psychiatry* 44 (2005): 987–95.
Nussbaum, Martha. "Is Homosexual Conduct Wrong? A Philosophical Exchange—Integrity." In *Homosexuality*, edited by Robert M. Baird and M. Katherine Baird, 47–48. Amherst, NY: Prometheus Books, 1995. [Excerpted from legal depositions for trial of Colorado's Amendment 2.]
———. "A Right to Marry? Same-Sex Marriage and Constitutional Law." *Dissent*, summer 2009.
———. *From Disgust to Humanity.* Oxford: Oxford University Press, 2010.
O'Hehir, Andrew. "Did TV Change America's Mind on Gay Marriage?" Salon.com, 30 March 2013.
Pinker, Steven. *The Language Instinct: How the Mind Creates Language.* New York: Harper Perennial, 2007.
Powell, Richard. "Social Desirability Bias in Polling on Same-Sex Marriage Ballot Measures." *American Politics Research* (2013). Doi: 10.1177/1532673X13484791.
Rawls, John. *Political Liberalism.* New York: Columbia University Press, 1993.
Raz, Joseph. *The Morality of Freedom.* Oxford: Clarendon Press, 1986.
Regnerus, Mark. "How Different Are the Adult Children of Parents Who Have Same-Sex Relationships? Findings from the New Family Structures Survey." *Social Science Research* 41 (2012): 752–70.
Rice, William, Urban Friberg, and Sergey Gavrilets. "Homosexuality as a Consequence of Epigenetically Canalized Sexual Development." *Quarterly Review of Biology* 87 (2012): 343–68.
Ross, W. D. *The Right and the Good.* Oxford: Oxford University Press, 1930.
Rozin, Paul. "Disgust." In *Handbook of Emotions*, edited by Michael Lewis, Jeannette M. Haviland-Jones, and Lisa Feldman Barrett, 757–76. New York: Guilford Press, 2010.

Rozin, Paul, and April E. Fallen. "A Perspective on Disgust." *Psychological Review* 94 (1987): 23–41.

Rozin, Paul, Laura Lowery, Sumio Imada, and Jonathan Haidt. "The CAD Triad Hypothesis: A Mapping between Three Moral Emotions (Contempt, Anger, Disgust) and Three Moral Codes (Community, Autonomy, Divinity)." *Journal of Personality and Social Psychology* 76 (1999): 574–86.

Rozin, Paul, Linda Millman, and Carol Nemeroff. "Operation of the Laws of Sympathetic Magic in Disgust and Other Domains." *Journal of Personality and Social Psychology* 50 (1986): 703–12.

Sampson, Robert, John Laub, and Christopher Wimer. "Does Marriage Reduce Crime? A Counterfactual Approach to Within-Individual Causal Effects." *Criminology* 44 (2006): 465–508.

Satinover, Jeffrey. *Homosexuality and the Politics of Truth*. Grand Rapids, MI: Baker Books, 1996.

Savin-Williams, Ritch. ". . . And Then I Became Gay": Young Men's Stories. New York: Routledge, 1998.

Schaff, Kory. "Equal Protection and Same-Sex Marriage." *Journal of Social Philosophy* 35 (2004): 133–47.

Schnall, Simone, Jonathan Haidt, Gerald Clore, and Alexander Jordan. "Disgust as Embodied Moral Judgment." *Personality and Social Psychology Bulletin* 34 (2008): 1096–109.

Schroeder, Mark. *Non-Cognitivism in Ethics*. New York: Routledge, 2010.

Schroeder, Michael, and Ariel Shidlo. "Ethical Issues in Sexual Orientation Conversion Therapies: An Empirical Study of Consumers." In *Sexual Conversion Therapy: Ethical, Clinical, and Research Perspective*, edited by Jack Drescher, Ariel Shidlo, and Michael Schroeder. Boca Raton, FL: CRC Press, 2002.

Shepher, Joseph. *Incest: A Biosocial View, Studies in Anthropology*. New York: Academic Press, 1983.

Shpancer, Noam. "What Do Women Want? New Research Challenges Old Ideas about Female Sexual Desire." *Psychology Today*, 22 August 2013.

Shweder, Richard, Nancy Much, Manamohan Mahaparta, and Lawrence Park. "The 'Big Three' of Morality (Autonomy, Community, Divinity) and the 'Big Three' Explanations in Suffering." In *Morality and Health*, edited by Allan Brandt and Paul Rozin, 119–69. New York: Routledge, 1997.

Spitzer, Robert L. "Can Some Gay Men and Lesbians Change Their Sexual Orientation? 200 Participants Reporting a Change from Homosexual to Heterosexual Orientation." *Archives of Sexual Behavior* 32 (2003): 403–17.

Stephens-Davidowitz, Seth. "How Many American Men Are Gay?" *New York Times*, 8 December 2013.

Striepens, Nadine, Keith M. Kendrick, Wolfgang Maier, and Rene Hurlemann. "Prosocial Effects of Oxytocin and Clinical Evidence for Its Therapeutic Potential." *Frontiers in Neuroendocrinology* 32 (2011): 426–50.

Suschinsky, Kelly, and Martin Lalumiere, M. "Prepared for Anything?: An Investigation of Female Genital Arousal in Response to Rape Cues." *Psychological Science* 22 (2011): 159–65.

Swift, Adam. *Political Philosophy: A Beginner's Guide for Students and Politicians*. Cambridge, UK: Polity, 2007.

van Gelder, Lindsy. "The 'Born That Way' Trap." *Ms.*, May/June 1991.

Waite, Linda J., and Maggie Gallagher. *The Case for Marriage: Why Married People Are Happier, Healthier and Better Off Financially*. New York: Broadway Books, 2001.

Wedgwood, Ralph. "The Fundamental Argument for Same-Sex Marriage." *The Journal of Political Philosophy* 7 (1999): 225–42.

Weinstein, Netta, William Ryan, Cody DeHaan, Andrew Przybylski, Nicole Legate, and Richard Ryan. "Parental Autonomy Support and Discrepancies Between Implicit and Explicit Sexual Identities: Dynamics of Self-Acceptance and Defense." *Journal of Personality and Social Psychology* 102 (2012): 815–32.

Wellington, Adrian Alex. "Why Liberals Should Support Same-Sex Marriage." *Journal of Social Philosophy* 26 (1995): 5–32.

Wheatley, Thalia, and Jonathan Haidt. "Hypnotic Disgust Makes Moral Judgments More Severe." *Psychological Science* 16 (2005): 780–84.

Wright, Larry. "Functions." *The Philosophical Review* 82 (1973): 139–68.

INDEX

ABOUT THE AUTHOR

Chris Meyers is associate professor in the philosophy and religion department at the University of Southern Mississippi. He teaches applied ethics and ethical theory. Meyers has published numerous articles in peer-reviewed professional philosophy journals. His first book, *The Fetal Position*, analyzed the most prominent arguments on both sides of the abortion debate.